NEV GOODBYE

A Love Story of Life After Death

by

MARY M. FERN

PUBLISHED
BY
BRIGHTON PUBLISHING LLC
501 W. RAY ROAD
SUITE 4
CHANDLER, AZ 85225
WWW.BRIGHTONPUBLISHING.COM

NEVER SAY
GOODBYE

A Love Story of Life After Death

by

MARY M. FERN

PUBLISHED
BY
BRIGHTON PUBLISHING LLC
501 W. RAY ROAD
SUITE 4
CHANDLER, AZ 85225
WWW.BRIGHTONPUBLISHING.COM

COPYRIGHT © 2013

ISBN 13: 978-1-62183-081-8
ISBN 10:1-621-83081-0

PRINTED IN THE UNITED STATES OF AMERICA

First Edition

COVER DESIGN: TOM RODRIGUEZ

Table of Contents

Author's Note

The title *Never Say GOODBYE* came as a direct result of those kind—but misguided—folks who, following the death of my son, almost immediately advised that I get over him and get on with me. The exact words I usually heard were, "You've got to let him go, Mary. Let him go and say goodbye."

I began healing the day I realized that I didn't ever have to say goodbye. This child of ours whom we could never again hold in our arms was enclosed in our memories, in our dreams, in our hearts. He is a part of our souls forever. There could be no goodbye. There should be no goodbye.

Daniel Mark Hammericksen (D'Mark)
April 1960-May 1980

Dedication

This journey is dedicated to you the reader.
It comes from Danny, through me, to you.
From despair to healing to peace.
The Spirit goes on and on.

"It isn't the mountain we conquer,
but ourselves."

~ Sir Edmund Hillary

Reader Reviews

"I would recommend Mary Fern's book to anyone suffering the loss of a loved one. *Never Say GOODBYE* is a heart wrenching read. It is too compelling to put this book down. A person drowning in sorrow could benefit by following Mary's grieving journey. There comes a time when a person can enjoy a rainbow or a moonbow; it is bittersweet!"

~ DwynAnne Lean
Library Assistant at King Co. Library System

"*Never Say GOODBYE* is a poignant narrative of the worst loss possible for a parent. Perceptively sub-titled, "A Love Story", this book offers not only a well-written living tribute to her son, Daniel, lost in a fire, it also offers praise to her family whose challenges strained each of them to the last sinew of their strength. For those who have lost a family member (as I have) or know those who have, don't walk by *Never Say GOODBYE*. Insight and support will be in your hands."

~Winfred G. Allen, Ph. D.
Professor (ret.) Pepperdine University, author

"A stunning job of conveying how surreal loss is. The question reverberates through this piece as to whether we can survive loss. I wonder if the part of us that survives is the part that does not say good-bye and is willing to go on in the face of it. Mary Fern conveys the value of community and humanity that helps us get our bearings when we are spinning in sorrow."

~ Chris Adams, M.D.

"This book is genuine and moving. It would be a powerful companion to other parents who have endured the loss of a child or people supporting those who have experienced this type of loss. It was very powerful and educational for me to read as a therapist who works in the field of grief and loss."

~ Tanya Ranchigoda, LICSW
Mental Health Therapist, Faculty at UW School of Social Work

"In my more than thirty years of experience helping others light the candle of hope, I believe that Mary Fern's *Never Say GOODBYE* proves the 'candle of hope continues to burn as brightly as ever'."

~Darcie D. Sims, Ph.D., CHT, CT, GMS
 Director, The American Grief Academy®
Author of: *If I Could Just See Hope.*

"Wow...A MUST read! — 5 Stars"

"More about life than death, more about love than sadness, this beautifully told story is a mother's daily journal about how she and her family triumph over tragedy. Neither morbid nor campy, the writing is so well-executed you feel as if you yourself are a character in the story, experiencing each day's high or low. Along the way we are introduced to strangers and acquaintances alike, who react so differently when learning about Dan's death. Sometimes shockingly rude, but more often than not, embrace the family with support and friendship. This book is a page-turner to the end and you will love every minute of it!"

~ Amazon Reader Review

"Unflinching honesty — 5 Stars"

If you have experienced grief, and even if you haven't, this book is for you. With deep insight and unflinching honesty, Mary Fern has fearlessly mined the depths of her soul to speak of that which is never spoken of. Gut wrenching and glorious, this book will stay with you always."

~ Amazon Reader Review

"So very well-written — 5 Stars"

"You will find yourself immersed in this story. So well-written you will smell the coffee brewing and feel the fresh ocean air on your skin. I truly couldn't put it down. Filled with life lessons and great reminders of what truly matters. Anyone can relate in some way. So glad this book made its way into my life."

~ Amazon Reader Review

"Beautiful Story — 5 Stars"

"This is a beautifully written story about a family losing their son and brother and what they went through. Well-written and a loving tribute to a loved one. I think anyone who has lost a loved one would benefit from reading this book. It tells the tale of the first year after her son died."

~ Amazon Reader Review

"Mary M. Fern draws back the shroud of loss and grief as she presents a singular and altogether different meaning to the oft misunderstood term...closure. She presents an unflinching love story that is both beautifully written and finely crafted into a memorial to life."

~ Publisher Review

Acknowledgements

Opening my private journals to public eyes was not a decision I took lightly. *Never Say GOODBYE* was not an easy birth. I found myself quitting time and time again, stopping because it was too hard, because I was too tired or sad, too busy or frustrated. I was often discouraged by those in the publishing world who said my story was too melodramatic, so painful to read that it was unrealistic to expect that it would be published. I stopped because of life's interruptions, publishers' rejections, and my own procrastination. I stopped when I didn't believe enough in myself.

And then I would begin again.

I would start because this story needed to be told. I would start because even when my resolve faltered, my loved ones believed in me. I would start because I could hear in my inner ear, the heartbreak in the tones of the many grieving people in my bereavement groups as they asked the same questions I had asked—questions for which I now had a few answers.

I would begin once again because Danny was in my heart, saying, *"You can do it Mom."*

"It takes a village" has become such a cliché that it seems to have lost its significance, but *Never Say GOODBYE* is testimony to the truth of that statement. So it is with the greatest pleasure, heartfelt appreciation, and luminescent gratitude, I introduce you to my village:

To Margaret Fern, my mom: There are no words…just thankful love.

To my siblings, John and Bob, who teased, pushed and believed.

To Betsy Sullivan, Patty Hallgarth, Jackie Hollett, and my sister Ellen, all who championed me and were my earliest readers and toughest but best critics.

And to Sandy, who struggled, helped, and struggles still. Peace to you my friend.

To the encouraging women of The International Women's Writing

Guild, with special gratitude to founder Hannelore Hahn.

And to Ernest, my cheerful go-to guy at Kinko's.

To my daughter in law Jayna, friend Nancy Goodfellow, and George, typists extraordinaire who volunteered for this duty.

To Lisa Smith, who caught all my dangling participles and saved me from my many mixed tenses.

To Marcia DePew, Cheri Grimm, Sam Horn, and Mary Kooistra, who rode in at the last minute with great information and words of encouragement.

To Krista Goldstine-Cole and Andrea Ripki, new friends and fellow writers whose insights were so helpful. Thank you all.

To the courageous friends who wrapped me in their love and would not let me go: Bobbie Vchulek, Rosalyn Williams, Darlene Schickling, Joe Martin, and Jeff Lane. I will never forget you.

To Jack Hutt, Dave Stroh and Loren Donahue, the young men who wrapped my precious son in their caring and lifted him. And to Paige Vchulek, Suzanne Williams, and Shenan Compton who did that same thing for my precious daughter.

To my granddaughter Annde Danielle, whose middle name remembers the uncle she never met and who upon hearing me say I was writing about her daddy's brother went into my library and shyly returned to my office with Dan's last photo in her hands and whispered, "This needs to be in here, Grandma." She was so right. Thanks Magic.

To Ashley Brilliant, creator of, "Pot Shots," whose little picture stories often said it all.

To Richard Bach, author of *Jonathan Livingston Seagull*, and numerous other beautiful stories of hope. My heart is grateful for your words of encouragement and your generosity in sharing.

To Alisa, my "Chosen Child" since she was seven years old, and to her husband, Trevor Johnson. For your hard work, computer skills, and attention to every detail—for our shared laughter, tears, and love. Flutterbye you are one of my life's treasures, and you have truly "passed it on."

And my heartfelt halleluiah to the nameless ragamuffin little boy who rescued my life with a wink. Thank you kiddo, I get it now, and I am winking back.

To Kathie and Don McGuire at Brighton Publishing for loving

Dan's story and believing in me.

Finally, I introduce you to my David and Melisa who lived this story. Kids, it was your presence that helped your dad and me survive. I trust our presence has helped you thrive. Thank you for loving me enough to allow me to expose our family's sorrow and share the finding of our joy. You are the love within. I love you.

And last, meet my heart. George, what a wonderful dad and husband you have grown to be. I gave you my heart long ago and you carry it still as I carry yours, carefully, as if it were life's greatest treasure. I love you.

This world is growing old and has seen many changes in its long turning history. Seas have risen and fallen, continents have shifted. From Lucy leaving her footprints in the dust of Africa to Neil Armstrong leaving his footprints on the moon, from togas and chariots to jeans and jets it has all changed. But some things do not change. Throughout history the human heart in love and in grief has not changed.

"There is no friendship, no love, like that of the parent for the child."

> *~ Henry Ward Beecher 1813-1887*

"What greater grief can there be for mortals than to see their children dead."

> *~ Euripides ca. 480-406 BC*

"God give me strength to face a fact though it slay me."

> *~ Thomas Huxley 1825-1895*

"In this sad world of ours, sorrow comes to all. It comes in bitterest agony. Perfect relief is not possible, except with time. You cannot now realize that you will ever feel better and yet this is a mistake. You are sure to be happy again. To know this, which is certainly true, will make you somewhat less miserable now."

> *~ Abraham Lincoln 1809-1865*

"We are healed of suffering only be experiencing it to the full."

> *~ Marcel Proust 1871-1922*

"To live in hearts we leave behind is not to die."

> *~ Thomas Campbell 1777-1844*

The End

If you, the reader, are wondering why this is not titled *Prologue*, it is because my story starts with the end. The end of my son's life.

Danny is dead. There, I can say it now.

My son Danny is dead. He died in a house fire.

The house was very nice. It was almost new, a split-level home in an average neighborhood just outside of Seattle. It was part brown painted cedar and part natural honey-colored cedar, a favorite tree in the Northwest. The yard where the house stood was lovely, landscaped with azaleas and rhododendrons and big, old evergreen trees.

The yard is still beautiful.

Dan was the first of our children to leave home. It was May when he left, an achingly lovely month in our corner of the country. Sixteen days later, he was gone. At twenty years, plus one month, and twelve days...Danny is dead.

There. I can say it now.

But it wasn't always that way.

Chapter One

THE BEGINNING

"Grief fills the room of my absent child."

~ William Shakespeare, King John

My new husband, fresh out of the Marine Corp is twenty-one and I am barely seventeen when the doctor turned to us and grinning said, "Congratulations, it's a boy!" It's a boy who quickly grew through a normal childhood and into an often turbulent adolescence. Time really does fly, you know. Twenty years rushing by in a blink. But because this is a true life story and not a fairy tale, sometimes people don't live happily ever after. There is a tiny pause that comes for each of us between adolescence and adulthood. A click of time when you catch your breath from the rush of learning and growing, before you step into the world, hopefully as a responsible adult. In that place, for us, tragedy struck. That healthy, handsome young man died. He left behind a brother, a sister, and a father, almost broken by their sorrow. And he left me, his mother, who wished to join him.

Danny's death was called an accident. The expert we hired told us it might have been wiring that caused the fire which took our son's life and spared his two roommates, but the evidence was inconclusive. He had been out of the family home for sixteen days and he was dead. For me, that was conclusion enough.

Our family felt, each in their own way, such a terrible grief that it became, for the most part, truly unspeakable. But I am a journalist, a story-teller, a keeper of family history, and what I could not speak, I could write.

Now I am finally ready to put into words what it is to walk through Hell. Why, you might ask, would I want to expose our family so starkly? Why would I risk diving back into such pain? Why not allow the private thoughts in my journals to remain private?

Those are fair questions and I have asked them of myself many times. Each time, the answers were the same. As the world moves perpetually forward, it can move with pretense and lies into more darkness, or it can move into the light. The human race grows closer to its potential each time any of us sees the world's truths and speaks out. To the best of my ability, that is what I have tried to do.

Most of us live a life of polite social facades. The truth is very hard to come by. And what was true for me need not be the same for you—still there are universal truths that must be held as sacred. "Know the truth and the truth shall make you free. (John 8:32)". This is my truth.

In the United States, grief and mourning are taboo. We must hide and hush. Crying in public will clear a room fast. Speaking of grief, showing flag-draped coffins—though not forbidden or illegal—is certainly discouraged. From the very first instant of hearing of a death, we are encouraged to find closure. We are urged to celebrate the life rather than mourn the death. But we are human. We laugh *and* we cry. We birth and love, we live and die, and we mourn—as we should. Who can imagine living a life with only one or two emotions? Who would want to? Not I. That would be like having only vanilla ice cream—very good, but very limited. I want all the flavors, and I guess, I want all the emotions, too. Even the hard ones.

Underneath my mask and pretense that all was well, there was tumultuous agony and self-destructive thought. I was often made to feel selfish in my desire to speak of Danny, to weep, and to wish he was here. One religious tract, sent to me by a friend who, I believe, never could have imagined the crushing guilt it threw over me like a shroud, warned that I must rejoice that my son was going to heaven and that my grief was a detriment to his getting there. But how could I possibly rejoice!? I wasn't brave or heroic—I was angry and sad and beaten down. He was dead and I didn't want his death to be true. I was told that God had called him home but I was fighting God. This was his home, and here, with our family, was where he belonged.

I was angry at people who told me, "The good die young." And after just few weeks, "You should be getting over it by now," and, "Isn't it time to let go, say goodbye and move on?" I wasn't ready then and I am still not ready to forget, and although I have most assuredly moved on, I will never say goodbye.

Those mothers we hear about who lose a child and seem to rise above, turning their grief into heroic deeds, are an anomaly. I would love to look back and see that I had handled myself with grace, dignity, and

2

elegance. Close friends, honest friends, say I did. They shake their heads with sad amazement and tell me how in awe they were of how we triumphed through a parent's worst loss. But my own words speak of a different truth—the truth inside of me. I believe my family's experience is more common among those who lose a child. And I believe a part of me is every mother, and this is how it was for me.

Chapter Two

THE JOURNEY

Humpty Dumpty sat on a wall
Humpty Dumpty had a great fall
All the King's horses
And all the King's men
Couldn't put Humpty Dumpty
Together again.

May 17

Until eleven this morning, I thought I was a rational, intelligent human being. I thought I was in control. I thought I knew who I was and where I was going in my life. Now the only thing in the world is this nightmare and I can't wake up. I can't wake up!

Ineluctable From the Latin:

"Not to be resisted by struggling—not to be avoided or escaped—certain—inevitable—as ineluctable fate."

Joe, our neighbor, is over having coffee and sharing his pain at having to put his beautiful old Siamese cat Rebel to sleep. Joe is a proud son of The Lone Star state, so of course his cat's name is Rebel. I hear a car door slam and look up from the table to see George, my husband, standing in the warm May sunshine. Before I can voice my surprise at his being home in the middle of the day, I get a good look at his face. A sick premonition socks me in my belly.

"Something is wrong, terribly wrong," I say. "I wonder if his mom is sick or…"

I stand, braced stiffly, in front of the door. But I don't open it. I wait. It's as if I know he's bringing something horrible with him, something I don't want. Then he is standing in front of me. Still, I don't speak. I wait. And his disjointed words etch on my heart—they will brand me forever, though at this moment, they make no sense.

"Honey, Honey, our son perished in a fire. He perished. Oh, Honey."

I feel my face pull into a frown. What on earth is he talking about? Son? I don't understand. And where did he ever get that word, "perish?" Nobody uses a dumb word like that anymore. Why is he standing here in this child scuffed room looking so dreadful and mouthing archaic words in a tongue I can't comprehend? Why is he looking at me so oddly? As if he is waiting for…what?

"Don't you hear me? A fire, Honey, a fire."

He reaches out to pull me into his arms but I avoid his grasp, retreating from him until my back is tight against the wall. He is a mad man. I can't let him touch me. God, he's profaned this room. He doesn't have a right to be here. I want him out. I want him gone.

Suddenly I flash deep into the center of my being. I feel myself split into three parts—there are three of me. One is disembodied, beside me, watching from the sidelines to see what will happen next. I see a second me crushed against the wall, being pelted with unbearable words like knives thrown during a circus act. And the soul of me, the real me, is shrinking down into the core, to a place I've so rarely been before, and plaintively this me whispers, *Danny*? But there is only emptiness and the word ricochets and echoes in the gathering darkness.

My thoughts are like drops of water on a searing skillet. *A fire? Where? At Dan's store? But the building is all cement, isn't it? No, that's impossible. George has gone crazy.*

At last I begin to make sense of his words. In a rage I hiss, "Who told you? Who told you that? God, George! God! What a terrible thing to say."

"It's true," he says, and his voice is flat and blank. "The house Dan moved into burned down this morning. Danny didn't get out. The boss called me into the office and told me." Again he reaches for me, but I fuse myself to the wall and his arms drop to his sides. "Do you remember Jeff's mom?" he queries.

I nod. Jeff is Dan's best friend. Dan and Jeff have just moved in together.

5

Anyway, George is still looking at me with such a strange expression, almost as if he's afraid of me. "Jeff's mom is a friend of my boss. Jeff came to his mom's house this morning. He had been with Dan. The fire broke out while they were sleeping. Jeff got out of his bedroom. It was on the ground floor. And their other roommate, he got out too. But Dan was upstairs. Honey. He's gone."

I think my head is exploding. "That's disgusting," I rage. "You heard it from someone who heard it from someone else and now you want me to believe you? No! People don't find out these things this way. Why haven't the police been here? Why hasn't some official told us? If Dan were in trouble, I would know. I would feel it. You know he could never get away with anything that I didn't know, didn't feel. The kids and I…we're wrapped so tight …he's part of my soul. "I would know, George. I would know, I'm his mom!"

I grab the phone to call the police to find out for myself, but my voice is too shrill and I can't make my shaking fingers work as I try to dial. George takes it and speaks as I listen on the extension. All I can hear is a swishing sound like water rushing through a far off pipe as the police transfer him to the coroner. And the coroner won't answer our question. He hems and haws and asks question after question until I break in and hear myself shout. "STOP! STOP! I can't stand this! Just TELL ME! Is my son dead?"

"Yyeessssss."

When your child dies you die also.
because in the deepest and most profound way
your child is you.
Your broken heart has ceased to beat in your breast and
your task now is to stand your empty shell of a self
by the grave
for as long as it takes
until the still beating pieces of your heart,
that you have buried with your child,
can be disinterred.

~ Mary M. Fern

6

George and I are holding each other now, and Joe is gone. I had forgotten he was here and I don't know when he left. We are at the top of the stairs when Dave, who worked until 2:00 this morning, wakes and comes out of his room. I watch his face as the words are dragged from his mouth with a reluctance I can feel.

"Mom? Mom, what is it?"

I call him to us and he comes in slow motion up the stairs into our arms. The detached part of myself watches me hugging him, but I cannot feel his body against mine.

I can see that George is crying and my mind doesn't know what to do with that information, though the watcher inside me, looking on, nods approval. Maybe George's tears, never seen before, will show Dave that it's okay to cry as I tell him that his brother, older by a scant nine months, eleven and a half hours, is dead.

Our very premature Dave has never drawn a breath without Danny somewhere within his world. They shared a room and toys, friends, secrets, laughter, schools, treats and punishments for nineteen years. The day we finally got to bring Dave home from the hospital, the first thing we did was place him in his big brother's very small arms, and Dan said one of his first words, trying to say Davey he chirped "Dabe."

Dave listens to what I say but he can't stop shaking his head. He is silent. Disbelieving he asks no questions. He rejects our information and retreats to his room. He shuts his door so softly, so very softly. Why is it I imagine I heard it slam?

And so it begins.

George and I plunge into a whirlwind that buffets us topsy-turvy, without control through the rest of the day.

I call a new friend, Bobbie, the mother of one of Melisa's classmates. "Will you pick her up and take her to your house after school?"

"Of course," she answers, and I can hear her shock, sharp as broken glass. She too has teenaged sons.

"Please don't tell Melisa about her brother," I say, "that is something I must do. We'll come as soon as possible."

7

First we have to go to the grandmothers' houses and break the news before they get it from some other source. My mom first. Mom is one of my heroes, so gentle but the strongest person I know. Now we have to break her heart. But Mom will have family and friends who will rally to try to share her pain.

I don't remember the ride out there but…do I really say those awful B movie words when she comes to the door all smiles at seeing us? "Mom, maybe you better sit down."

The muscle in her lip weakens, her face changes, ages in front of my eyes. For the first time I say to that core of me deep inside, *I do not think I will be able to stand this.*

My brother comes into the room and goes pale at our news. We leave them in the silence of their disbelief.

Back to town and parked in front of George's mom's apartment, the car door is too heavy for me to push open. I can't do it. George comes around, opens it and holds out his hand. I try to lift my arm to take his hand but it weighs a million pounds.

We can't avoid this—we have to go in. And we dread it. I know she will fall apart, she will scream, she might faint. Oh, god.

I have already called her doctor, our family doctor for many years, as her health is not good. He was shocked at the news and gave me permission to give her a tranquilizer. I thought, as a doctor, he would be somewhat accustomed to death, certainly more than we are, but all he has to offer is a tranquilizer. The word clangs in my head. *Tranquil, tranquil.* I don't know what I feel, but it is not tranquil. He has suggested we take them too, but I'm afraid it might weaken and relax our muscles and we need those muscles if we are to stay on our feet.

It is so horrible. Hysterics in George's arms—he can barely contain her. Still, I stand back. I ache for her, but she would not want what comfort I might share. George is her only child and I am still an interloper after all these years. I am so sorry for her and this pain we have brought through her door, into her lonely apartment. I am panting as if after a hard run. I cannot breathe in here, I cannot breathe. We place a call to her sister for support, and then head for home to whatever comes next.

Once again at home, I call Dan's job to explain why he won't be in. He has been skating on thin ice there as he is often late and I don't want them to think he's going to be late again. I don't want them to think badly of him.

I hear myself speaking and I'm wonderful—calm, polite, controlled, so socially conditioned, and so brainwashed that I have become a complete phony. I don't have enough guts to be honest. I should be throwing things. I should be screaming and fainting on the floor. But I hear myself say, "I'm sorry he won't be in, blah, blah, blah... Thank you for your sympathy... No, thank you, nothing you can do. We appreciate the words, offers, thoughts..." and I think to myself, *You slug! What is the matter with you? Why aren't you prostrate? Why aren't you tearing your clothes, your hair, your body? Why are you still alive?*

Melisa comes in with George. "How come I got to go home with Paige? Why is dad home? Why didn't you pick me up? Have you been crying?" Her nine year old exuberance falls without echo into the cotton ball atmosphere of the house. What do I say to her? Are we to be treated to the sight of her, our baby, also aging before our eyes? How much of this can a person bear?

I throw a prayer to wherever prayers go. *Please let me find the right words—let me say these awful things in a way that causes as little harm as possible. Help me to help her.* I take her to the couch and sit her next to me. I hug her and speak into her soft hair. Her moan of denial cuts like a dull scythe as she buckles against me.

"Noooo."

"Nor ear can hear nor tongue can tell
the tortures of that inward hell."
~ Lord Byron, the Giaour

Now it is evening and Jeff and Mark have come. With all of us weeping, Jeff has told their tale of terror. He still smells of smoke. His eyes and his face still reflect the flames. His voice, hoarse with shouts and smoke, makes us feel the heat and the fear. The room shimmers before me as if I am seeing through super-heated air.

He woke to find an inferno. The house was engulfed. He screamed at Dan's window but got no answer. He ran to the neighbors for a ladder and raced back to put it up to the window. Power lines connected to the house a few inches to the left of Dan's window were singing with blue electricity and as Jeff began climbing, the windows of Dan's room exploded with an impenetrable gush of fire.

"I thought I saw him at the window, but I'm not sure. We kept screaming for him to jump—maybe he said something, I think he did, but I don't know what it was. Then there was nothing in the window but flames." Jeff finishes in a rush, his eyes wide, tears washing his face, voice cracking with pain. Then, "The coroner didn't get hold of you because Mark and I begged him not to. We wanted to tell you ourselves because we thought it would be easier for you. But we couldn't. I'm so sorry…we just couldn't. We went home and told my mom and asked her to call George's boss."

Now I understand why the police didn't contact us, and we don't blame anyone. No one wants to deliver news like this, and these guys, well, they're not much more than kids. We hug them and pat them and ask, "Were you hurt?"

Their injuries are painful but small. Glass cuts on their feet and hands, some minor burns, sore throats and sore lungs. We hurt for their fear and pain and are so thankful that they are safe and that they had the courage to come and face us, not knowing what they might find when they knocked on our door.

Dave and Melisa, Jeff and Mark, George and I, we have been swirled and spun into a cocoon, wrapped and trapped and alone in the world together. Have I ever felt closer to another human being than I do right now to Jeff and Mark as I listen to them explain how they tried to save my Danny? We are entwined and smothered in this helpless, hopeless web.

A knock on the door startles us to our feet and dazed, we seem unable to think of what to do. How long do we just stand and stare at one another? I don't know. At, last Dave crosses the few feet of living room to open the door.

Another of Dan's special friends, Riley, stands on the porch with tears flowing down his face and a Boston fern cradled in his arms. Tiny hairs rise on the back of my neck. Danny is one of those kids with dozens of friendly acquaintances. He hangs out with a large group, but only Jeff and Riley, besides us, are part of his heart.

I gesture at the cascading fronds of the plant. "How did you know?" I whisper. And the core of me registers an infinitesimal question mark that seems to glow with light.

Riley doesn't know he is fulfilling Danny's last promise to his little sister and he is puzzled by my question.

Just two weeks ago, Dan brought me a beautiful fern for Mother's Day that is still thriving, which seems to me a miracle in itself, since I'm not the most knowledgeable about plants. Melisa has begged to have it in her room, but her room doesn't get a great deal of light, so I just let her borrow it a day at a time, but mostly leave it in the living room so all of us can enjoy it.

Danny overheard her pleading with me one day and promised to get her a fern of her own. And here it is.

Riley explains that Dan had ordered it through the store and it arrived this morning. The co-workers decided to chip in and send it to us in lieu of flowers. Of course they know nothing of a big brother's promise to his little sister.

The night drags by at jet speed, swift seconds lasting forever. Time is so strange. Everything is so strange.

The house is full of people, full of tears. My brother and his wife, sister and husband, my mother, neighbors as well as friends, all tiptoe in as if a baby is sleeping, or stumble across the threshold, disoriented and bewildered. No one seems to know what they are doing here, but still they come. All weeping, disbelieving, trying to say the things you try to say. And we are comforting, hugging, holding on, saying, "It's okay— It's alright. We know you loved him. Thank you for coming, thank you for caring."

Darlene is a neighbor and good friend. I ask her how her teenagers are reacting to the news. I feel so terribly sorry for the kids. For all the young friends who over the years, have made our house a chaotic second home. This will be, for most of them, the first time death has come close, the first time they must peek at their own mortality. Is there any kid who doesn't think he or she is invincible? That omnipotence is one of the frightening, endearing, foolish glories of the young. What a cruel plunge into reality.

Darlene answers that the kids are okay, except for Alisa who is so broken up that they've insisted she stay home. Alisa is thirteen.

"Is it okay if I go to her?" I ask. "She is one of my own, you know. I can't let her cry alone." My heart tells me she needs to be with us and oh, how we need to be with her, with her health and youth and life.

I walk next door and discover what *dissolved into tears* means as she sags, damp and boneless in my arms.

Arms around her, I bring her back to the house. Other kids come in, so frightened to enter, but so brave to do so. We hold them and do what we can to comfort them. We tell them how infinitely important each of them is.

"Go on downstairs if you want to," I tell them. Dave and Melisa and some of the gang are down there." I pray a silent prayer that being together will do some good. Maybe without adults around they can open up and begin to...what? Accept? Understand? I don't know. Maybe talk like they won't in the presence of this many adults. I wish I knew what to say, to them and to myself.

All night I stand outside myself, watching as George and I carry on a lifetime of host and hostess habits, comforting, reassuring. And I wonder, is George outside himself too? Present in the flesh, but with soul far, far away?

My older sister and her husband leave, but in a moment she is back alone. She pulls me onto the front porch and she, normally so undemonstrative, yanks me into her arms, puts her face to mine and whispers so intensely, "I need to do something! Tell me what I can do."

Her vehemence rocks me and I say, "Let me get through tonight. Just let me get through tonight. There will be something, I promise."

Grief is the proper rational response to loss.
Huge grief is the proper rational response to huge loss.

~ Mary M. Fern

The house is finally quiet. We have held and hugged Melisa and Dave and at last forced ourselves to release them to their own rooms for the night. George's knees seem to go weak and as he staggers I reach to lend him some strength as he has done for me more than once today. As we head dry-eyed toward our room, I realize that we will never know what has kept us upright and sane through these last twelve—impossible—has it only been twelve?—hours.

On my dresser I find an envelope with our names, written in my mother's hand. I search for something to slit the fold, but cannot think what could do the job and end up tearing it in jagged pieces with my fingers to find money and a note.

I know you will not want to accept this. I know you'll protest that I can't afford to do this, but PLEASE take it and use it in whatever way you wish. Please let me do this for my firstborn grandson in memory of all the joy he always gave dad and me. I love you. I share your pain.

Love, Mama.

I pass the note to George and the tears I have hidden all this long evening begin. This day is over. And my life. I reach for my journal and write, *I don't know how to say it. A statement of fact, dry and dusty. A question? A whisper of disbelief or a scream of ultimate agony. He's dead...He's dead?...HE'S DEAD!*

May 28, 4:00 a.m.

I can't sleep. I keep thinking I am going to be sick. Bile burns through my stomach, swirls high in my throat.

Detached, I listen to George's soft snore. I feel no resentment, only vague wonder.

After a while I get up and get some paper and start writing. Compulsion is pushing my pen. I write to my two brothers and my sister. I write to my brother John's four children who are our godchildren. John's two eldest and our two boys were all born within two years of each other. Dan was born in April, and Dave the following January. Johnny was born three days after Dave and Colleen almost exactly a year later. Scott and Gary, John's younger two, followed a couple of years later, and our Melisa, only nine and a half, is the youngest of the cousins. I can't count the holidays, vacations, and birthdays we have celebrated together.

Now I worry, how will this affect those kids? What can I say to them? The words flow with memories of happy times and with reassurances of our love. Most importantly to me, I need to give them permission to come to the memorial or not, as they wish. I tailor my words to the various ages—Colleen and John are eighteen and nineteen, Scott is sixteen and Gary is fourteen.

To Scott I write:

It is so hard to know what to say to you. Like our Dave, you pull emotion inside yourself and feel your pain privately. I know the idea of a gathering after the memorial will seem to you a horror. I know because I used to feel that way too and still do a little. Maybe you think the whole world's crazy to gather as if at a party and maybe it is. But after the sad ceremony is over, people seem to have to act funny, as if they're waking from a dream. It's like saying, "Hey, I'm still alive and the world is still here."

I just want you to know that it's okay for each of us act in our own way by the dictates of our personality. Dan loved to party. He got noisy to cope. You get quiet. I know Saturday is going to be a little bit of Hell for all of us. If you want to stay home or be with your buddies, you do it. Uncle George and I really do understand. Just know we love you and are proud of you. I know, and you know, that we cannot shirk our responsibilities, but you have our permission, this time, to hang in there and do the best you can, however you choose to do it.

I love you Honey,

Aunt Mary

I'll never forget the first funeral I went to as a young adult. I was shocked at the gathering at my aunt's house after the service—everyone eating, talking, telling jokes and laughing. It still gives me the shivers.

We have to be there on Saturday. If we didn't, I would be gone.

As I seal this envelope I become aware of the sound of a calliope tinkling in my head. It is playing the theme from an old movie cartoon of *Popeye the Sailorman*, and it is repeating over and over again, "I yam what I yam because that's what I yam, I'm Popeye the Sailorman." With each repeated note, a rainbow of colors begins to bumble through the turbulent blackness of my brain and I wonder if I am actually seeing a rainbow or if my head has exploded.

Dan loved crowds, noise, and his music. The louder the better, but he knew others, like me, ached to be alone and he understood that too—it was okay either way. If we must go through this and are really doing it with Danny in mind, I am taking a page from his book and we'll do it his

14

way. Everybody will be accepted exactly as they are. That is one of his great gifts. And everyone will get the benefit of all the understanding we can muster. I'm not saying society be damned, I don't think I am anyway—what I am saying is it is society's turn to be understanding. And there will be no criticism of those kids, all of the stunned, shocked, young people, on Saturday if I can help it.

And our Dave and our Melisa. What do I say to my precious children whose value I truly realize for the first time? I always assured them that Mom and Dad would take care of them. I lied. We can't take care of anything. Whatever made us think we could? We are as helpless in the face of the fates and heavens as the weakest infant. Where did I get the notion that we were the ultimate masters of ourselves? Who foisted that absurdity onto us and why didn't I know it for the foolishness it is?

What do I say to my kids about their brother? Just, he loved you. And he knew that you loved him.

We love you too. Much more than even we could have ever guessed.

Chapter Three

A WALK IN HELL

"And it ever has been that love knows not its own depth
until the hour of separation."

~ Kahlil Gibran, The Prophet

Afternoon, May 28

The assistant funeral director brings an oversized manila envelope into the room and upends it in the center of the octagonal polished table. He says "I haven't had a chance to look at it myself yet, we only just got the body in. Oh, it's only a chain."

He's so casually matter-of-fact.

I hear, and will hear to my dying day, the sound of metal slithering against the envelope. I hear and I stare, but the black chord that sullies the gleaming table surface is unrecognizable.

Everything is magnified and vivid, much more so than real life. I am so focused, so intent.

Can this possibly be the chain we just gave him last Christmas? That ugly object is all that is left? Are those little pieces of flesh stuck there? Oh, no no. No. And my mind begins another stupid litany that I recognize as a protective device. Over and over it repeats a line from Tolkien, "All that is gold does not glitter, all that glitters is not gold." Again and again until I am able to handle this horror and move onto the next one. I convince myself I did not see what I know I saw.

Voices from a long way off are coming closer. He and George are still talking. How weird to be sitting right next to them and I just died and they didn't even notice. Maybe they didn't notice because it didn't really happen. Maybe none of this is happening. Maybe I better test it. *Oh, please, is it a dream?* Let it be a dream. I move to the next pain. Testing, testing. In anger, I rivet George with my stare and breaking into their chatter say, "I want to see him."

16

It is real. It really is happening. Two shocked faces gape at me, and then George's crumples and I barely hear the funeral director as he protests swiftly and firmly tells me, "Oh, no, we don't recommend that."

I seal my lips tight against my curses and repeat, "I want to see my son."

My peripheral vision catches the sight of the director shaking his head toward George and mouthing, "No." and it strikes me as comical in this place, with its artificially contrived façade of glazed dignity.

"Honey, please," my husband pleads. "It's better if we don't see him."

Again I am aware of my three separate selves: Physical Me, sitting on the edge of the deep blue, fabric-covered chair, reacting to the current situation—Observer Me, overseeing the entire room where Dan's small, blackened chain still dominates—and finally, Real Me, the memory keeper and clear thinker, the me who is disdainful at these cowardly men who are afraid to see my boy. I know if I insist, George won't let me go alone, but he looks as if he might die if he makes himself go in with me.

I listen to the anguish in his voice and ungraciously, give in. Yet I am annoyed as I think, I held this boy and loved him while the doctor cut the cord, little knowing that at the instant of severance, the fleshy cord became an invisible cord that could never be broken. I held this boy and loved him after a dirt bike accident when I could not see his features for the blood and gore. I've held him and loved him covered in baby spit up and big boy vomit, through joyous moments and crushing ones. I want to hold him now.

But I do not… No, I do not.

I wonder too, why this funeral director is going behind my back to consult with George. Is he trying to protect me? Does he think that I, as the woman, as the mom, am the weaker one here? Is he afraid he can't handle it if I make a scene? Fool! Can't he see that this man in front of him, this young man's dad, is being crushed by grief just as much as I am?

Suddenly my mind floods with everything I have ever seen or heard or experienced about burns. I shudder and my soul shrinks as I am blessed with mindlessness. I am fully aware. Just blank.

I feel my soul tear with the sound of an awful moaning cry that came from somewhere deep inside me. It hangs in the stillness of that damned room. If Hell had opened before us and allowed one sound to escape, it would have been that awful moaning cry.

Today was so very different from what we had planned. I thought I would spend the morning making lasagna and Dan's favorite pineapple dessert to take to his new home.

The last time I saw him, he invited us over and I offered to make enough dinner for everyone. We knew Jeff, but hadn't met the other roommate, so all of us were to get together, and we were all pretty excited to see the new place. Danny was enthusiastic and that pleased me. We hadn't parted on the happiest of terms when he moved out. But I got an extra hug and a kiss on that last visit six days ago, just six days. The thought of those dishes now makes me ill.

Our house is overflowing with friends. Some stay for a while, some drop off food or flowers or kind words and quickly leave. The phone has not stopped ringing and I jump each time, expecting to hear his voice. All our visitors come in tears and we try to comfort them.

"Call if you need anything."

"Can I do anything?"

We tell each one the same thing, the only important thing in the world, "Go home and hug your children. Look into their beautiful eyes and say I love you. Hold them tight."

One after another they say to us, "That is exactly what I did. I hugged them and…they let me."

Imagine it's a beautiful Saturday morning
and you are absolutely craving
peanut butter and blackberry jam on your toast.
The toaster is plugged in and the cupboard yields
bread and peanut butter but no jam.
You run next door to your good neighbor who
hustles to her cupboard so pleased that she can do something
for you, her friend.

18

"Here, I have honey, I have strawberry. Here."
But all you want is blackberry jam.
You knock at the next neighbor's door.
Good friends, they would do anything for you.
Alas, only grape, boysenberry and more sticky honey,
and they so wanted to help.
You head to the grocery store,
the craving stronger than ever, but even the store's shelves are bare.
Everyone you call, every door on which you knock,
all the people who love you, all the friends who care,
none can give you what you want so terribly.
It breaks their hearts being unable to help.
They offer everything they have.
It is not enough.
They cannot give what they do not have.
And you cannot be satisfied with anything else.
So it is in your grief.
They give what you do not want. You want what they cannot give.
Do take what they have to offer.
You all know it will not satisfy, but it will sustain.
It will not complete, but it will comfort.
Do take what they offer.

~ Mary M. Fern

May 28, Evening

I seem to be able to see into people, deep into their being. I embrace someone and instantly, as if they were made of glass, I seem to read their most private feelings.

George's boss comes by to personally bring flowers and words of sympathy. It was up to him to call George into the office and give him the terrible news. He is so broken tonight. He and George grew up together in this neighborhood—they've been friends for more than thirty years. We've watched each other's families grow. He has a son and a daughter about the same age as our boys. He is a very tall man, six feet, six inches, but seems shrunken as he melts into the chair. "I would rather it be me than a young person like Dan. At least I've lived some."

I know he doesn't mean precisely that, but his sincerity is so moving. I can feel his heart beating with anguish for us. The words trite, but his pain so real, both as a friend of ours and as a father of his own young children. I love him for those words.

Through his tears, he says, "Anything, anything. Whatever you need, whatever I can do. Anything, anything."

But no one can give us what we need.

Yet another woman says all the right words, but they flow from a void, an emptiness inside her. I know she doesn't understand the meaning of her own mouthing. The things she says are only words. But instead of being angry at her, I'm surprised to find I feel only pity and compassion. We have known each other for twenty years and yet, among other things she says to us, there is this: "You're so lucky to have had two sons. Just think how sad it would be if it were me who only has one boy. At least David can help fill Dan's place."

It is in moments like this that I become aware of myself splitting and going deep inside where I ask myself, *Did she really say that? Did I hear her correctly? Did she hear herself?*

And then she goes on with more words to affirm what I heard.

"As long as you and George are on your way out to see the house, maybe we'll come along. I've never been through a burned down house before."

George and I gape speechlessly as her embarrassed, stammering husband hustles her out. His apologies hang in the air as they leave. There must not be a brain in her blonde head.

I think she must be so depthless, such a young soul, that she has no idea why we are so astonished at her suggestion, at her wanting to invade our privacy. How could she ask to walk this holy ground with us when she has no claim to it at all?

It is strange and truly awesome to see so clearly into people, but I'm glad I can. This gift, this little miracle, has made it possible for me to be aware of the warmth and truth in our friends' hearts, even if their words feel clumsy to them. Everyone tells us their words are inadequate, but I know the sincerity of them and that is enough.

I am beyond tired. My body has been rolled over by the world. Atlas slipped and he has dropped his crushing weight and it has landed on me and my family. Time, demandable time, is going so fast...like...like his life. Everything is rushing.

Stop, stop! I need it to stop, I need my son.

George got directions to the house. The road is tree-lined and huge old rhododendrons are holding back the banks. We turn into the driveway and park behind another car. A rope guardrail is strung between two big branches of drooping cedar trees. The yellow sign hanging on the rope reads, "NO TRESSPASSING BY ORDER OF SNOHOMISH COUNTY." We clamber over the rope and I wonder out loud if we can be arrested—we are usually such a law abiding couple. Then the ridiculousness of my question slaps into my ears and I think, *arrest me, jail me, shoot me. Please.*

At first glance, the house doesn't seem to be in bad shape. There is a big azalea next to the door covered in blooms that should be eye pleasing. It doesn't look as if it has even been warmed by the fire, but the tall pine next to it is badly scorched.

I find myself kneeling, clutching a hunk of blue plaid fabric in my fists. It's a piece of his bathrobe and I am remembering making it for him. He was so tall that store-bought robes looked silly on him—they hit him at the knee, and though I am not wild about sewing, I did it once in a while on special request.

George is asking me to stand up and says something about glass. My eyes focus then, and the area where I'm kneeling is covered with shards of the windows that blew out of the house.

We stumble inside. George holds my arm and tests where we will step, but I'm not worried. Somehow I know nothing is going to happen to us. I would welcome physical pain. Inside I am bleeding to death. A killing fall would be such a relief.

The stench is horrid. The house is destroyed to the point that the separate rooms are not recognizable. It is unbelievable that Jeff and Mark got out of here alive. How did they live through this? How could anyone live through this? We go down what we guess to be the hall leading to the bedrooms. My ears actually deafen with the strain I am putting on them to hear echoes, if there are any, of his cries. I go out of my body again and watch myself walk on the reeking, slimy soot.

Did he call me? Did he know it was happening and need me with him? Is his Spirit here? I have heard it speculated that in sudden death the Spirit can be caught unaware that the body has died. I ask and ask and listen and listen, *Are you here*? I hear only the sound of George's fast breath.

George turns into one room, and I turn into another. Tatters of blackened shirts hang in the open closet. Junk to anyone but to me and his dad. There is the blue silky one that he especially liked for what it did to bring out the morning-sky blue of his eyes. Oh, how they sparkled. And that red one, his Valentine present just three months ago—a lifetime ago. He looked so good in red.

I suck in a shuddering breath of putrid air and say, "George? In here, Honey." Instantly I am being supported from behind by my husband's arms and body. I can hear his breath, ragged and a-stutter. We fuse, supporting each other, as we stare into his room.

The waterbed where it heaps on the floor is an undistinguishable lump to any but us. Our family picture rests on the blackened remains of the dresser. It was the last thing I tucked into one of the boxes he had packed the day he left home. Only seventeen days ago. I pick it up and clutch it to me. It is only later, at home, that each of us in turn remark that in the picture every face except for Danny's is clear, untouched by soot or fire. One smear of blackness has almost obliterated that one precious image.

"Why did I insist he move?" I wail. "Why?"

George puts a firm hand on my arm and I realize I am moaning. We fall against each other again and cling to one another.

Wet, slick ashes cover all. Slippery and smelly. The reek of unthinkable burned things hangs in the air and indelibly tattoos my soul. The end of this dream is a nightmare.

At the end of the hall, a record is leaning against a wall, part of his collection. Something is wrong with it, but what? Oh. It isn't in a cover. Dan would never leave a record out like that. We look closer and understand. The cover has been destroyed by the fire. Only fragments of paper stick to the grooved surface here and there, but the record itself is in perfect condition, not even warped. I wrap it in my arms and clutch it, along with the portrait, to my breast when I see the title of the first song on the album, "Never Coming Home."

Somehow, I find myself outside.

George is talking to me, trying to figure out how something like this could have happened. I must be answering him, though I don't see how I could. He doesn't seem to be speaking English. Besides, I don't care how it happened only that it did, but he persists, "Did you see how black and scorched that electrical panel was? How the scorch shot right up the wall? And the wiring, the wiring!"

But I don't care.

A group of people come up the driveway. An older man and woman, a young man, and a young woman carrying a baby about a year old. We watch as they go around the back of the house. After a time, they reappear and approach us. The older woman says her brother owns the house. "It burned very early this morning. A young man died in it."

George reels. "We know. He…um…um…was our son."

There is the smallest of pauses before she speaks again. "Oh…Well. My brother is devastated. All his savings has gone into building this house. And now it's destroyed." She goes on, "Do you happen to know the other young men who were renting it?"

I am frozen in time but George nods and she continues, "If you see them, would you tell them they need to come and get their stuff out of the shed where my brother let them store it? He is upset and anxious to bulldoze the place before anyone else gets hurt."

I shut out the sound of her voice before it makes me vomit. I reach out a trembling hand to the baby boy being hugged so tightly in the young woman's arms. The only thing that makes any sense to me is the life in this little one. The precious, precious life. The baby blinks one slow blink at me, this stranger reaching out to him, and he lets me stroke his cheek, soft as a kitten's ear.

His mom's eyes meet mine and hold them. They are filled with such compassion it is tangible. Without speech her message reaches out to me, "Please forgive her, she's in shock too. I'm so sorry for you. If it were my son, I too would die." I see her arm tighten around her son.

I touch that beautiful baby's cheek once more, then turning to George say, "Our car is blocking theirs in the driveway. Will you please move it so they can leave?"

Later, I am so disgusted with myself. I should have shaken that woman. I should have screamed, "Your brother is upset because he lost his house? His house?" But, no. Even on this day I remember my manners.

Half-a-mile down the road as we drive away we come upon a young man in a wheelchair. Obviously severely compromised, he waits at the edge of the rarely disturbed country road to wave at each passing car. His grin grows wide as I lift my hand, fluttering my fingers and forcing a smile. There are many kinds of pain in this life.

On the way home our anxiety level is higher than ever. We talk about how soon it might be before the owner can tear the house down. We don't even know who to ask, what to ask, where to begin. And it feels as if we better figure it out quickly.

I know I'm not done in there. Can we get in any trouble for trespassing? I neither know nor care. How dare they? How could they even dream of destroying it?

I try to focus as I hear George calling me, over and over, "Honey, Honey, Honey?"

I must make some sound because he starts speaking.

"You know that little white building on Aurora across from the store?"

"A white building?"

"It looks like a little old-fashioned house."

"Oh. Yes?"

"Well, it's a lawyer's office. I had to go in there once and he's pretty easy to talk to. Should I see if he can answer some of our questions?"

"Absolutely. That would be great. Tomorrow?"

"Tomorrow."

Much later I call my sister and tell her I have something only she can do. "You wanted something to do for us? There is a woman," I say, "She has bleached-platinum hair. I don't know if she will come to the house after the memorial or not, but if she does, will you please keep her away from me?"

Being Ellen, she asks no questions, simply says, "With pleasure.

Even if I have to take out a contract on her. Don't worry."

I don't.

Love is falling on us like leaves in autumn. It takes away the sting of those people who, hearing of our tragedy, stare furtively at us with expressions that imply that we appear to them hunchback- like. I suppose we do. In the same fashion that many drivers, passing the scene of an accident cannot help gawking, we feel stares and I imagine they might be thinking, *That's what a family that just lost a child looks like.*

Neighbors have brought so much food I don't have to think about meals. I am very grateful. If it wasn't here I don't know what I would do. Nothing I guess. The simple thought of eating makes me ill. The sound of chewing is intrusive. When George and the kids eat, I have to leave the room. There is too much life associated with food.

George was leaning against the wall in the hall when Melisa opened her door. She searches me out and hugs me hard. She looks up at me in wonder and fear. "Daddy's crying," she says. "I didn't know daddy's cried. Do something, Mom!" I hold her and hold her.

Then I find my tormented husband and hold him and hold him.

Talking, talking, and talking. We are throat-pained, word weary and still cannot say enough. We stop only when our voices do. Then the phone rings or the doorbell chimes and we start again. The feelings are so huge and so heavy—we can't carry them anymore but there is no place to put them down and maybe the noise of our words helps cover the sound of our hearts breaking.

I look in the medicine cabinet for something and am caught by the sight of a bottle of prescription pain pills. I find myself laughing and crying, my nose and eyes running, tears running off my chin. Pain pills! How stupid are we? What a joke. We are so pain-filled that all the pills in the world couldn't alleviate this agony, but here's this little bottle.

"There was the Door to which I found no key—
There was the Veil through which I might not see. "

~ Omar Khayyam The Rubaiyat of Omar Khayyam

May 29

Melisa and Dave went to school today. We left the decision up to them. It was dreadful to let them out of our sight. Melisa is in a very small school with supportive teachers who are kind, so I thought she would be okay. Dave, on the other hand, doesn't have many options. It's the week before finals and he is in his freshman year at college. I don't know how he will manage. Both the kids are acting like a cross between a zombie and Frankenstein—pale and withdrawn, with motions either jerky or numbed.

What will Dave do? He and Dan are...were...so close. Closer, I think, than either realized, even though they were as different as the Artic from the Amazon. Dave, the younger, is far-seeing, life-planning and steady. He loves to dance but his work and studies always come before his fun. Dan has had a hard time seeing past the party next weekend, but he's—he was—so bright. Still, he wouldn't even consider college—he was done with studying and on to working, making enough money to support his music and drag races, ever eager to try anything new, different, and exciting.

I can't seem to get the present tense separated from the past tense as I write.

George and I talk about the service off and on all day. I have to keep correcting him when he uses the word "funeral." It is to be a "memorial," not a funeral. I get the heebie jeebies just hearing the word.

The memorial has to be perfect for Dan, something that he would love, something that speaks to the world of our boy so everyone will know he is there. I don't care about tradition or correctness. What is correct about planning a memorial for a twenty-year-old kid who was exuberantly healthy just forty-eight hours ago? Ideas present themselves and with instant surety, decisions are made. This feels right, that doesn't feel right. The answers come as if I had been doing this sort of thing forever, something that I've never done before.

The questions are like the ringing of the phone, and they just won't stop. What do we want to say in the newspaper? Who do we need to notify? What day...what time...how many...did he suffer...will we open the house to everyone...who will speak...did he suffer...do we even know a minister...what will we do about dishes, chairs, food...what do we do with the ashes? I bolt from the room to vomit.

George reaches to hold me when I return. Pressed against him, though I still hyperventilate, I can cling to him so as to not drop away from this world.

I inhale and when I can speak, I ask, "When we pick Melisa up from school, should we take her with us to the florist. We need to order flowers. I wonder if that would be too hard or if she'd like to help choose the family's spray?"

George is frowning but nodding thoughtfully as he says, "How would you feel about letting her choose? Would that be good for her or bad for her?"

I don't know. I don't know. I don't know. I shake my head and my shrug mirrors his.

"Let's ask her."

In the car after school Melisa is surprised and pleased with George's suggestion. "Can I pick anything I want?"

"Yes, but it's pretty important and we'd like to keep it simple, Honey."

"Dad," she says in a tone of weary patience, "Don't you even think I know what Danny would like?"

At the florist, she is just tall enough to see over the counter. She flips through the books quickly, scanning page after page, seeming to know exactly what she is looking for. Within minutes she has gone through two books as George and I look with her and say nothing. The clerk, wearing a slightly put-upon expression, sighs as she lifts a third big book to the counter. I don't think Melisa even noticed the sigh as she flipped another page. A couple of pages in, she stabs at an illustration. "That one."

Yes, it's perfect. It's what Dan might have picked for himself— white gladiolas scattered here and there, with a few white carnations, lots of ferns, and deep green fronds. No ribbons, no bows, just simple and fresh, green and white—perfect for us and perfect for him. We are pleased with her choice and are reminded once again that young as she is, she has a pretty good understanding and we need to give her more credit, be more trusting. Letting her handle this chore was a good idea after all.

We treat Melisa to lunch out, then drop her at home with Dave and drag ourselves back to the funeral home.

The director asks about music and suggests, "We have an organist on call that will play whatever hymns you choose. She is very good."

"Hymns? We don't want hymns."

The music is, for me, the most important part of the service.

"Dan is a music fanatic," I tell him. "It has to be just right. Not hymns."

He clears his throat. "It will be expected, you know. The old hymns are such a comfort. Do you expect any elderly people to attend?"

I think I hate this man.

George puts a quiet hand on my arm and I take a deep breath. "This is a kid," I enunciate carefully through gritted teeth, "a non-church-going kid. He loves contemporary music. Guitars and drums were his thing, not organs. What is there to understand? This, this...service is about him, not anyone else. We are going to do what we think is right for our son. No hymns, no organs."

We acquiesce when he asks about a Bible reading because I know just the right one. Dan had recently heard a remake of, what he didn't know was, a really old song. And, as he usually did, he invited me to his room to preview it. He was so surprised when I could mouth the familiar words the first time I heard the tune.

"How did you know the words?" he had asked. My Dan didn't have what they call a *poker face* and his expression was incredulous.

"Just call me psycho, oops, I mean psychic." My standard reply when I'm teasing him. "No, really, it's easy. That group took the lyrics straight out of the Bible."

"You're kidding."

"Nope, shall we try to find it?"

To my surprise, we found both the Bible and the passage and read, "To everything there is a season and a time to every purpose under heaven."

Here, in this terrible room, I tell the director that this will be the reading, and we're going to play the song version, the song Dan introduced to me in his room.

The questions continue and somehow the decisions are made. I am divorced from myself and looking on as we discuss cremation or burial, caskets and urns, in-ground or above.

He will be cremated. We all kind of believe that the land should be left for the living, though in the twenty-second century, cemeteries may be the only green spot left. His ashes will be laid to rest in the niche we bought for ourselves long ago.

"How many people will attend?" he asks.

What kind of question is that? How can we possibly know? Maybe just family, maybe his whole school. He just graduated from high school two years ago and the ties to the old school are still strong.

It will be on Saturday. We will invite everyone back to the house afterward. I have visions of his friends leaving the service, jumping in their cars and heading to The Gardens, where they usually hang out. I don't think that is a good idea when they're feeling so vulnerable and fragmented—lost with no maps. I hate the idea of everyone coming to the house, but worse, I hate the idea of his friends going off half-cocked, feeling that life is short and they better live fast. Maybe if they come home with us they can gather some strength from each other in a place that is safe for a little while.

May 30

Strange compulsions are driving me. I must go to Jeff's parent's house. I have only met his mom a couple of times, and still it feels essential. I must let her know how much I love her son, how glad I am that he is alive. That I would gladly give my life to have had all of the boys get out, but if that was not to be, I'm glad at least her son did. I can't bear the thought of any other death, any more death, any thing's death. I want everything to live forever.

Their yard is spread with charred, soaked possessions. It's hard to avoid eye contact with them, but I try. I catch a glimpse of the skis that he had saved for so long to buy and a sob catches in my throat. I picture

29

the big savings bank he had that was shaped and colored like a beer can where he tossed his change for months in anticipation of this purchase and of flying down the slopes on those new skis.

Jeff's mom comes to the door and is visibly shaken to see us. I tell her we won't stay, that we only want to let her know how much we appreciate her son. We all sit on the edges of our chairs, until her discomfort finally penetrates my fog and I realize what a mistake this was for us to come here. I nudge George and we clamor to our feet and skirt the edge of the wet, ruined parts of the three boy's life as we leave the yard.

Jeff comes by again. He looks better this afternoon. His face is still terrified and stunned—is it possible to be both terrified and stunned at the same time? He is. He says he can't sleep for the nightmares that come. We hug and I feel so grateful for his safety, for the friendship he and Dan had, for the comfort he is trying to bring us. And I know, how terribly difficult is his position.

Mark also comes by to lend what strength he can and pour it all out one more time. We are all obsessed—it is an eerie bond, this need we have for each other. I tell them that we spent the day planning the memorial. George is silent and I can't read his thoughts so it seems to be up to me to explain to the boys what we are thinking. I feel I am made of finely-honed steel, sharp and determined. Maybe George sees that in me today and doesn't want to interfere. Maybe he doesn't have enough energy. Maybe he's in too much pain. Maybe I am too overbearing. I don't know or care right now. And I wonder if he is furious that these kids are here in our living room and one of his sons is not.

"Can't we do something?" they plead. "Can we put together the music that you pick? We could do that for you, easy."

They help us pick the last songs that we will have time for. It is impossible to think of Danny without music so that is the most important part. Dave, Jeff, and Mark seem to get a smile out of the idea of a rock and roll, rhythm and blues memorial—we all know it is so appropriate, just right.

Jeff says everyone he has talked to at The Gardens and around the school is going to be there and they will appreciate the choice of "Sail Away." None of them have any idea what to expect and hearing their graduation song will be a nice touch. So the songs will be "Turn, Turn, Turn," "Bridge over Troubled Waters," and "Sail Away."

Dave has been sitting quiet, kind of in the background as the rest of us talked. Now he says, "Aren't you forgetting one song?" And I know what is coming next. "Aren't you going to have his favorite?"

As my shoulders slump I feel myself fall into that deep place inside where I can be safer from the reality of all of this. I see myself turn to my tortured son and I hear myself answer in a whisper, "I don't know if I can get through this if I hear that song. You're right of course, we have to play it but..."

Danny's personal talisman is Lynyrd Skynyrd's "Free Bird." Strains of it have been playing in my heart for days now and the words with new meaning are talons clawing at my brain.

"I'll listen again," I sigh, "then I'll decide."

"We can do this, Mom, can't we?" my boy begs softly, his voice cracking. I reach to touch him and can only nod.

Jeff makes a choking sound. We look over to see him wordlessly shaking his head. Danny's lifetime collection of music went with him when he moved and it too...was gone. For all of us the tears start again.

I go back to see the chapel once again. It is lovely with grains of beautiful wood and one wall of glass opening into a private garden, full at this season, with rich blossoms of rhododendrons, sword ferns and cypress bushes. It suits Dan's taste and this must be as close as I can make it to what he would have thought of as perfect, and as youth-oriented as is humanly possible.

George and I go from store to store buying big pots of green plants and I am thankful for my mom's gift of money as we are able to buy something specific for each of his special friends to take home if they wish. We need enough greenery to soften the front of the chapel, anything to soften Saturday.

He was cremated at one o'clock today.

Chapter Four

THE MEMORIAL

It's raining, it's pouring,
The old man is snoring.
He went to bed and covered his head,
And didn't get up 'til morning.
How I wish we could.

May 31

I drink my coffee and read the paper pretending it's a typical Saturday morning. A couple who write a weekly column lost their son recently and have been writing about him. Today they are printing letters they've received from readers and some of them are so angry, complaining that this couple goes on and on as if they were the only people in the world to have lost someone. I am sickened by the harshness of some of the letters.

I pick up my ever present pen and write to them.

Dear_____and_____,

Today, this very day, our family will attend the memorial for our twenty-year-old son who died just this week. We thank you and bless you for what you have been writing. Maybe there is hope for us. If you are surviving, perhaps we too can survive.

My writing and reverie is broken by Melisa. "Mama, what should I wear? Can Shanny come with us?"

I don't care. I don't care...but I do. She can't go to the memorial in her play clothes, yet, it's such an absurd topic.

She returns to her room, searches her closet and comes back for my approval in a dress that I don't think is quite appropriate, but when she insists, "Dan thought I looked pretty in this dress," what can I say? Only, "Dan was right, you do."

At first I don't think Shenan should come along, but I remind myself that it might be easier on Melisa to be with one of her friends—except that Shenan is a cute, eight-year-old chatterbox who swings her long braids with every turn of her head and my nerves are pretty strung out right now. Finally I decide she may come and later I am glad. Her presence helps Melisa, though I hear her whisper to Melisa at one point, as she is looking at Dave, "Why is your brother crying?"

What we wouldn't do to be that innocent.

We are a jeans and sweatshirt family. George works in slacks and ties but the rest of the family only owns very casual stuff. I resent having to use my energy to think about clothes. Then, I, too, put on something Dan had complimented. A powder blue blouse and medium blue slacks. He didn't like me in black. If he liked me in red and green stripes, that is what I'd wear today.

At the funeral home they pulled the shades part way down to block out the sun. I open them. I want all that outside in, the life of it, the greening spring of it.

The chapel gets more and more full, to the point that the side of the chapel where the family usually sits in seclusion, is opened to guests. We sit in the front pew, choosing inclusion over seclusion. Another idea the funeral director thought odd. I felt if our friends could come to show their support, the least we could do was to sit in the main chapel with them and share our love.

Melisa and Shenan have to go to the lavatory shortly before the service begins, so I walk with them into astonishment. I have never seen so many people sardined into one small area, although I only seem to recognize three faces—a cousin I barely know, a man George works with, and one of Dan's teachers. Most of his senior class is there. They stand like a living curtain of tears lining the back and side walls. The lobby is overflowing, and I am overwhelmed.

Back in the pew, we sit clutching hands and emotions as contemporary rock music evokes Danny's presence. Something, I don't know what, helps to hold me up. Maybe his love. I know I've heard the word surreal but it isn't quite that. It really feels as if Dan is here with us, his arm around me.

The preacher, at our insistence, doesn't get sentimental. Every note he strikes is just right. Admitting he's never met Dan, he ad-libs about how all the greenery attests to Dan's love of nature, and the crowd attests to his love of people. He doesn't do that horrible ash-to-ash thing that is often a part of this ritual. Ashes to ashes and dust to dust. Sickening.

And another coincidence? The pastor's name is Dan.

And then, too soon it's over. Out in the sun that feels so cold, we stop to greet the tens of dozens. Now I recognize most of them, though they look peculiar. Their faces have been sculpted by a mad artist. The expressions on familiar faces are molded slightly askew, barely this side of crumbling. Yet, now I can only remember the three.

Why those particular faces? I will never know.

Melisa begs to ride home with her grandma and Uncle Bob. Dave says he needs to be alone for a moment, so is it okay if he jogs the two miles home?

Without any of our children, George and I walk to the car.

Back at our over-filled house, we slip into the basement rec-room area. I know once I get upstairs with the adults, it will be hard to get away and my desire is to be downstairs with the kids. I should stop calling them kids, I guess. They are young adults, but my mind hasn't made that adjustment yet. Noisy, angry, questioning, and even in their sorrow, raging at unfair death. They are so full of life and so sweet, trying hard to say and do the right thing when none of us know what that is. So, we pat them and hug them, making our way upstairs. I notice two ex-football lettermen in the corner. They lean against each other sobbing uncontrollably. I try to dry their tears with my love. If my heart had not already broken it would now, for them.

Seeing all these friends of Dan's are a reminder to me, so when Jeff and I meet and come into each other's embrace, I tell him I need a favor. "I need you to ask around and find out if Dan owed anybody anything."

"What do you mean?"

"I just want to know if he owes anybody any money. We would want to honor any outstanding debt he might have to you or one of the other kids."

Our Dan was always broke. I think Dave has his first dollar he had ever earned—but for Dan, money was earned to be spent. He is the original *Hole in the Pocket* guy.

Ever since he graduated, he has been paying room and board, just a token amount, but it's a standing joke with us that he pays on Friday and by Wednesday is borrowing back ten dollars. The next Friday he repays the ten and board money only to borrow again as the week moves on.

Jeff is frowning at me as he says, "Why would Dan owe anybody? I bet half the guys here owe him."

"Really? Oh...Oh, okay. Listen Jeff...if that's so, just forget I said anything okay? We don't care. He wouldn't care. All of us would let it go. Promise you won't say anything. Please"

He shakes his head at me but says, "I promise."

Upstairs everything is running smoothly. My brother and sister-in-law and a couple of their friends have taken over the kitchen that is overcrowded with gifted food and everything is flowing like warm syrup. It is disconcerting to act as guests in our own home, but we know our priceless extended family has it all under control. We have already told them when we couldn't take it anymore we were going to quietly get up and simply leave. They instantly offered to stay, clean up and lock up. Bless them, and everyone who tried to make things easier, who didn't say "Call me if you need anything," but actually offered specific help, who told us exactly what they were willing to do at a time when our brains had shut down.

One offered to transport the flowers from the chapel to our house, another to bring extra chairs or food, and still another offered to discreetly take some pictures and leave them for our later viewing. Anything and everything to help. And thanks especially to Mom who is heartbroken for herself as well as for us. She is holding up and helping keep Melisa under her care. I trust her to answer with a patience that is lacking in me today all the heartrending questions our little girl might ask.

I make my way across the living room from hug to hug. George has been separated from me by the crowd but I can see him looking for me as I am for him. I feel like Gretel in the dark forest without Hansel. I am nude without his hand in mine. I find myself facing a woman who introduces herself as a distant cousin of George's. I strain for the proper response but lose that portion of my mind as I hear her ask loudly, "What have you found out? All the relatives are real curious. Did your son die of smoke inhalation or was he burned to death?"

I turn my back and search madly for George but can't find him. My eyes come to rest on a young neighbor couple who look so uncomfortable that their need overcomes my horror. It is Pat and his new wife, Nancy, who live across the street. I make my way over to sink down with them on the couch. I start chattering about whatever comes to mind, my words rush as if a vocal dam had burst. I go on till my tongue sticks dryly to my lips. Pat offers me coffee but it seems too difficult to hold the cup and if I concentrate on not spilling I might lose what little self-control I still have. Nancy offers me a Lifesaver and it saves me for the moment. Saliva floods my mouth and I can move my lips once more.

Melisa is shy and finds it an agony to meet people. She has spent the afternoon in her room with her friend. When I check on her, she and Shanny are prattling contentedly with Mom. Shanny has gotten each of them a plate, and they are comparing the merits of my potato salad with other people's. Naturally, it is my salad that is winning and I can't help but smile.

Mom is going to take Melisa to her house to spend the night and Dave has been invited to his friend's cabin to spend a couple of nights.

George and I are going to find a motel somewhere on a silent beach, escape the phone and collapse.

At last we feel we can abandon our house and we get in the car but find ourselves at a total loss. Each second of the past days has been spent on actions and choices necessary but outside ourselves, programmed to the last detail. Now there is nothing.

We stop at the top of the hill and park. We stare at each other with dry burning eyes, as witless as blowing dandelion fluff.

At last George puts the car in gear and, not surprisingly, it takes us down to Shilshole Marina. The boats and the salt water act as aloe on us. Usually. Now we stare at the bay, the Olympics, each other. Tearless. Helpless. Hopeless. Still parents…but not. And sad is the blackest word ever heard.

In the motel, George tries to hold me. To love me. Unbearable. I wept.

Chapter Five

DEEPEST ABYSS

"You must do the thing you think you cannot do."

~ Eleanor Roosevelt

June 1

I am so tired. So very, very tired. The world is exhaustion and tears. I rock back and forth, my arms wrapped tightly around my middle where I can feel the pieces of my broken heart. They grind together, pieces of razor-sharp glass, and I moan with the pain. Normally, a heart is located in the chest, but when it breaks it falls to the solar plexus as if the muscles that hold in place have no strength to go on either.

George says, "Can't you stop rocking, please?"

What? Rocking? Me? I wonder silently. I am numb, unaware.

My left hand is black and blue in a circular pattern between the thumb and the pointer finger. The palm is covered with tiny black moons. Melisa takes my hand and cautions me against making such an angry fist. I become conscious of the fact that the half-moons are the bruises of my fingernails dug hard into my flesh. The bruised circle? I catch myself biting the soft skin of my hand. I must be doing it a lot. Funny, I don't remember. There is no pain connected to it, even when I poke at it trying to make it hurt, I feel nothing.

If you have a bad tooth ache
you live in that tooth.
If you have a migraine
you live in that head ache.
If you have a grief ache
you live in that grief.

~ Mary M. Fern

I go to the mall for thank-you cards. Imagine...thank-you cards. The parking lot is full of cars. The mall is full of people. They are laughing, talking, walking. They don't seem real. It's as if they are projected on a screen and I am watching the movie—I look for subtitles and find none. It's kind of scary.

In the card store, the first cards I see are perfect. Simple and as fresh as sinlessness—a small, silver gull sails across a newly risen sun. The symbolism is wrenching—the coincidence, too much.

I touch the pendent at my throat and feel the wings of the seagull enclosed in the circle of the sun. I hear my Danny's voice when he first saw my new necklace, "Where did you get that, Mom? That's me you know, Freebird. Let me buy it for you. I'll make it your Christmas present. I want it to be from me so that I'll be close to you always."

But I said no and laughed, "We know it's your symbol, besides," I say, giving him a little thump on the arm, "you better not ever get too far away."

It was a nice moment, a warm moment, so how could I now be so cold? I become mindful of the clerk offering to assist me. Behind her in a glass case is a crystal iceberg. It must be the Spirit at work again. Etched artistically into the crystal—as if flying through a diamond—is a gull. I ask to see it and she unlocks the case. Once in my hands, I can't let it go. "Can you find three more?" I plead. I am compelled to explain our loss to her. In fact, I find myself spewing our story to almost everyone with whom I come into contact. It's as if the story of Dan is the only important thing in the world. And it is.

The woman is so kind. She searches the backroom but can find only one more, so she volunteers to call other stores until she traces down two others and has them put away for me. Thank you so much, kind lady. Perhaps someday someone will treat you as gently as you've treated me and you will know the depth of my appreciation. Now I can give one to his brother, one to each of his two best friends, and still have one for myself. What a perfect love gift and memento. I was at a loss for something extra special to give to those friends who did so much to prove their friendship. We'll engrave the icebergs with the date and the word, "Freebird."

June 2, Afternoon

There really is such a thing as a broken heart. It is called "broken heart syndrome" or stress cardiomyopathy. When stress causes adrenaline and other hormones to soar and stay at high levels for days the heart may be unable to pump enough blood. The hormones may cause small blood vessels in the heart to contract. This can produce chest pain, shortness of breath, even fluid in the lungs

Grief really hurts because grief really hurts.

~ Mary M. Fern

George and I meet at the funeral home. We pick out the stone and decide what to put on it. We choose a skier, airborne as if coming off a jump. Dan would like it, he loved the mountains. The words we choose are "Done Too Soon" from an old Neil Diamond song and "I shall lift my eyes onto the hills from whence cometh my help," a Bible verse.

We are introduced to another funeral director. He is younger and not quite as detached as the first one, but the impression he gives is one of untouchable aloofness as he explains how small the stone is that will mark the place where...where, Danny's ashes will lay. "You don't want to overcrowd it," he says as he fiddles with his black and silver pen, sliding it back and forth through his fingers. "I know what a temptation it must be to put a bit of everything that reflects your son's personality." He shudders and heaves a deep sigh and suddenly says, "I'm sorry." Tears form in his eyes. "I've got teenagers at home that I worry about all the time and it's unprofessional, but I hurt so much for folks like you.

We are supposed to stay detached in order to be strong and helpful, but sometimes that's impossible."

Oh god, here I am again, judging someone by their outer shell. How many mistakes will it take for me to learn that what we show on the outside and who we are on the inside are rarely the same?

None of us can think of the number and verse of the Bible phrase I want. I should know it, Mom used to say it all the time as she worked around the kitchen in the house where I grew up. She would look out the window over the sink toward the mighty Olympics and exalt. But my mind is gone—I can't think. I borrow the phone and I, who never forgets, ask George, who never remembers, for Mom's number, and he knows it.

"It's a Psalm," she says. "Let me check the number." She comes back to the phone almost instantly and when she speaks my name, her voice carries awe. "Mary, that's the second time this week that you have asked me for a particular passage and it is the second time my book has opened to the correct page when I picked it up. What you want is Psalm 121. Shall I read it to you?"

"I will lift mine eyes unto the hills from whence cometh my help. My help cometh from the Lord who made heaven and earth. He will not suffer thy foot to be removed: he that keepeth thee will not slumber. Behold, he that keepeth Israel shall neither slumber nor sleep. The Lord is thy keeper: the Lord is thy shade upon thy right hand. The sun shall not smite thee by day nor the moon by night. The Lord shall preserve thee from all evil: he shall preserve thy soul. The Lord shall preserve thy goings out and thy coming in from this time forth, and even evermore."

George and the funeral director are watching me and look startled when I start to chuckle. I don't even try to explain what is funny, but I think I was the one who always waited up for his coming in. I was the one who always watched his going out. Now God is going to do it, huh? Well, I hope He's up for it. He's going to be kept pretty busy.

I shake off the reverie and another thought strikes me. Does this verse answer a question that has really been bothering me? Maybe. I've worried because none of us are into formal religion and Dan, being only twenty, was full of questions and doubts.

My own thoughts on this subject are a medley gathered from many sources. I have come to believe there is a Force, a Supreme Something that I call God, for lack of other words, but it took me years of

40

questioning to begin to find my answers. Danny didn't have enough time. So what happens to his soul? Each church answers in a different way and the different beliefs are confusing. Is this Psalm my answer? It doesn't ask for anything, but simply says the Lord will preserve your soul. For now, this is what I need to believe. Raggedly, I exhale.

June 3

All day I write letters to acknowledge the kindness, food, flowers and thoughts of friends and folks we hardly know. The words flow. Apparently, it is only when speaking that my mind ceases to exist. I forget in mid-sentence what I was talking about. Even names I know well escape me.

I felt so foolish this morning at school when I ran into a woman whose daughter is a friend of Melisa's. I couldn't think of the girl's name, I couldn't think of my own daughter's name. I could only stand facing the woman and wishing something would happen to interrupt this ridiculous scene. Going blank like that is the most inhibiting phenomenon and I never know when it will strike. And I keep asking *whywhywhywhywhywhy??????* And silence answers.

George made an appointment with an attorney. We will see him tomorrow.

June 4

We meet at the lawyer's office. I had a difficult time finding it, though it is less than two miles from our house and George gave me directions. Still I got lost.

After talking to the lawyer, I feel a little better. He says the trespassing sign does apply to us, but he can't conceive of any officer penalizing us if they saw us at the house. Not under these circumstances.

There is so little we know about the fire at this time. I know more than I ever, ever wanted to know, but George is obsessed with needing to understand the cause. The county fire chief and his volunteer troops have laid the blame on the kids—probably smoking or candles, they say. But *probably* isn't good enough—George needs to know.

I hate the ease with which most adults automatically blame kids or expect the worst from them. I agree to allow the attorney (of course, his name is Dan) to hire an investigator. He warns us to be very sure because, "Once started, I know of only one way to make a report and that is in total honesty. If I find that the fire was started by cigarettes, I will have to tell you that."

"Go ahead," George says.

I nod, "We haven't been afraid of the truth yet."

We need that truth, regardless of what might be found.

I'm still writing thank-you notes when Riley stops by to present me with one yellow rosebud. It is another of the many tiny moments when a shaft of light and beauty pierce through darkness. Yellow roses were in my wedding bouquet and have been my favorite for years. How did Riley know?

Dan often brought me roses. The first time, he was about seven and he had picked a bouquet of wilted red ones from the discard pile outside the cemetery near our house. I thought he had taken them off a grave, and I was upset until he took me down and showed me. I apologized right away but I could see that spark of the joy of giving leave him for a while. The guilt I feel now for the scolding is hellacious. I seem to remember every harsh word I ever said and I can't seem to recall any kind ones.

The next time I got a flower from him, he was about ten. I know he purchased it with his first paycheck from the little paper route he and Dave had taken on as a summer project. After that, they came more often, sometimes one, sometimes a bunch, but always roses, and always red. And always him saying the same thing, "I know you like yellow best, but I like red. So this way you get the roses and I get the red and we both get to enjoy them. But someday Mom, I'll bring you a yellow rose. Just for you."

Is this it? My knees grow weak with wondering. And I'm so grateful to this tearful friend for caring so much and being so kind.

"Where did you get this beautiful idea?" I ask, and "why a single rose?" but Riley cannot explain.

Dave comes home from work and I tell him about Riley's visit. He takes one look at the perfect flower and says it all when he says, "Magic, Mom? Or a little miracle?"

June 5

There is an end-of-the-year parents meeting at school tonight. We've always been actively involved with all the kids' schooling. Should we go? Yes? No? We finally decided to go, thinking it would be better to get it over with. My motive is to let school acquaintances know we are still here so they won't forget Melisa over the summer. She is going to need all the friends and invitations she can get to help her through this trauma.

It is as hard as we expected though we hear just one whisper of shock, one tone of shame at our behavior, a woman's voice, "How could they? If it was me I would be too devastated to get out of bed."

Most of our acquaintances support us with a quick hand-squeeze or a comforting glance. Then, blessedly, don't call any more attention to us, as they go about the business meeting.

By the time we get home we are weak with exhaustion.

June 6

It is the last day of school. A whole summer stretches ahead. Melisa comes home early and brings a friend. As I am serving them lunch, Melisa tells us her tooth is out. This is one of those teeth that drive parents crazy. For some reason, it simply wouldn't let go. One tiny tug would do it, but every time we've suggested it, she hollers, so we've left it alone. Now I'm surprised because her tone is so blasé and I'm even more startled with her explanation. It seems she was talking to Dan last night—"No Mommy, not dreaming, no, not praying. Talking."

She told him how scared she was about the tooth hurting when it comes out. "I told him the big space it left behind would feel as cold as ice cubes." Dan understood and laughed but, "He said it would hurt for a bit, but only for a bit.

"I could stand it because I'm very strong, and the space isn't truly empty. He asked if I would remember the tooth and I said yes." She pauses, takes a bite and chews while my breathing is still suspended. She says, "And he said I would always remember that old tooth and a new tooth will come along to help fill any empty space." Her voice gives me shivers.

I'm having a tough time keeping my mouth closed as I nod in agreement and stare at her transformed face.

"Don't you want to know what happened then?" she demands. "He told me I could pull it out if I wanted to because he knew I was really full of courage. So he held my hand and I did."

She is speaking as if it's no big deal. As if she is discussing what to watch on TV. I am speechless, wondering if her sanity has been affected. But she seems perfectly fine, finishing her lunch and prattling with her friend about how to spend the afternoon.

What happened in her room last night? I don't know but I'm filled with wonder as I rush to my room to write every word before it drifts away.

Chapter Six

Too Much Death

*"You become all you can become
when you bear what you cannot bear."*

~ A Proverb

June 7

The funeral director calls. The stone is in place.

I meet George at the cemetery. We walk up the slope to the crest of the hill. The damp grass seems covered in glue and I must pull my feet through it. My eyes raise past one level of stone facings and another, until they reach the name that burns my sight until I wish I could not see. So real in its unreality that our only salvation is to be numb. We hold each other, transfixed. The skier soars in flight. In freedom and beauty. He has lost all earthly ties while we are pressed crushingly into the dirt.

We don't touch as we walk back to the car. I am shrouded in heavy veils of sorrow and cannot be reached. I suppose he is the same.

June 8

A little neighbor girl calls out, "Hey, it's Children's Day today." I smile and wish her a happy day while my insides grind. My child is dead.

June 9

I know I should be thankful for what I have, but I'm too sad missing what is gone. For the first time I think I understand part of the story of the prodigal son who leaves his home and family to go off and seek his fortune while his brother stays. It always seemed so cruel to me that rather than appreciate the child who stayed home everyone took him for granted, and when the selfish one returned they treated him like a king. Now I know why. What's that old folk saying? Another cliché: "You never miss the water till the well runs dry."

Is there comedy in grief? No and no and no and no. What we are feeling is probably some mild form of hysteria. Still, we can smile a little at some of the puzzling manifestations of sorrow, the weird games our minds are playing.

Melisa and I laugh, actually laugh when we find a box of cereal in the refrigerator. I think, *Gee, that's strange*, and then I walk away, leaving it there. Halfway across the kitchen I remember, but Melisa has already grabbed it to put in the cupboard and lo-and-behold, that's where she finds the missing hairbrush, fuzzy with torn strands of hair.

I just bought George new underwear—and for three days in a row, I pull it out of the garbage can. Then, on the fourth day, I witness him throwing it there instead of in the dirty clothes basket.

I have been making coffee the same way at least twice a day for the last twenty years. But now I forget to add the grounds. When I pour nothing but steaming water into my cup, I think, *How stupid*, and then remake it exactly the same way.

I peel potatoes and leaving the peels in the sink I throw the spud away. I walk around with dirty dishes in my hands, I have lost the dishwasher. Making sandwiches for lunch can take up to half an hour. Every step of the preparation must be thought and rethought. Every step is through quicksand.

I am afraid to drive. My powers of concentration are so bad I fear for others on the highway. More than once I have had to pull over to the side of the road and just let the tears come. In doing things by rote, I am probably driving adequately, but is adequate good enough? Am I going to turn in front of someone or scoot through a red light unaware? How are George and Dave managing to cope? They drive all over town every day. Is it fair to expect that level of concentration from those who are shell-shocked with grief?

It is necessary to clean my glasses constantly. They are salt sprinkled from blinking tears that have seeped from my eyes without my even being aware.

Melisa sits on the bed with me, hip touching hip. Her schoolmates have written sympathy notes and she follows my example and writes back saying thanks for the love. Notes to her read, "You are my bestest friend," "You are the prettiest girl in the whole school," and "I'm sorry your brother died. I wish he didn't have to be dead." The kids are really trying. I wonder if sitting here writing is good for her or bad? Therapy maybe? Again I don't know.

June 10

A business acquaintance of George's attended Dan's memorial ten days ago. Three days later, his son was involved in a terrible accident on his dirt bike. He is dead. And in one of those ironies of life that seem impossibly contrived, here we are at his funeral, seeing many of the same people who had been at ours. I mean, Dan's. Proving, I guess, there is some truth to the trite cliché everyone uses with such solemn wisdom, *You never know.*

We approach where they sit in the pew and they rise when they see us. We stare at each other silently, just stare, wordless, stupefied, sharing hell, and then we hug...and hold and hold.

I keep trying to pray. I need to find some comfort, but I am angry with God. Last night I lay dry-eyed and tried again to say "Your will be done," but damn it, I don't want His will to be done if this is His will. What is all this I learned as a child about God being a loving father who will always take care of His children? I think we've both done a lousy job.

I try with the mythical third eye to see my boy and all I get for the strain is pain.

Finally, hopeless and exhausted I talk to Mary. I feel like a fool. I don't know what to believe anymore, but trying anything is better than just laying here dying of pain. Mary was mortal, she was a mother, she lost a son. Even if the Bible is just a story, most stories have some truth. Did she witness her son die? Did she actually stand by the cross unable to lift a finger to help? I'll bet she was mad at God. At least she had the comfort of knowing what she believed in—I don't. But I lay still and begin to talk to her in my mind. *Please, oh Mary if you can hear me, if you really are there, please kiss him goodnight for me. Please hold him ever so tenderly.* The tears are coursing now, my throat is so tight I am strangling. *Tell him. Please Mary, oh, I love him.* I bite my pillow trying to smother sounds, trying not to wake George. Suddenly, soft, warm love covers me. I sink into sleep. For the first time in two weeks I sleep. The whole night through.

June 11

Dave went out again. He's been out every night. Each time he leaves he says the same thing, "I'll be out and about," and that is Dan's line.

It's out of character for Dave to be on the go all the time. He gets up early every morning and goes to work, and then out each night. He doesn't get in late, but he is looking so tired and drawn. I don't know how to help him. He seems to be trying in so many ways to take over Dan's habits. It doesn't take much insight to see that he is trying to keep Dan here by becoming as like him as possible. And then what? A half a Dave and a pseudo Dan? No, no, never!

The phone rings. It's eleven o'clock and Dave is still out. We're afraid to answer. I finally grab the receiver and a voice identifies himself as the police. After confirming our name, the officer asks for George and then asks him to hold. In the seconds while we wait for him to come back on the line we discover that not all of our feelings are numb. We can still feel terror. Our screams are brailed on our faces.

It is only the burglar alarm at George's company, set off by something. Because we live the closest, George is the on-call person. The police need him to come down and let them in to check it out.

Oh god, we are so sick. What if it had been Dave? What if...? No! We are so incredibly insecure and paranoid. And now so terrified.

June 12

A telephone pole is my weapon of choice. After this, I'll always remember which pole. I am driving to the store, as senseless and numb as ever, when from a block away that pole reaches out to me. I feel my foot stomp down on the gas pedal and I am locked in, ready to pull the steering wheel to the right, in such a rage it makes a shark's feeding frenzy look placid. But I can't make the wheel turn. It will not turn. As fast as the madness came upon me, it is gone. In familiar numbness, with no residue of shock or shaking, I continue on my way. Only later does it seem strange that the whole episode didn't seem strange.

June 14

Today is our goddaughter's high school graduation party. We feel we must go, but our presence tends to cast a dark shadow. It's her special day and we don't want to spoil it.

People react to us in two distinct ways—either they avoid us or they gather courage and mention him by name. When someone can manage to speak his name, it is hard for us and I know it has to be hard for them. And though they will never know this, I bless them. The four of us cling to each other like Velcro at the party and depart quickly. We're exhausted by the time we return home.

Later, we go to pick up Dan's car and tow it home. We don't have a key, and at first, we don't even know where to find the car. He'd only had the car three weeks and was so proud of it.

If it weren't for one of George's co-workers, we might never have known where it was. This man ran into George at work and offered condolences and added a story to our meager treasure trove. He had been driving home from Mercer Island, across the floating bridge from Seattle, when he saw a kid he thought he recognized as Dan, hitchhiking in the pouring rain. Of course it was Dan. His car had stalled in a parking lot so he was heading home to get some help. The man told George what a pleasure it was to chat with him for half an hour while they drove along. "He's one of those kids who knows how to shake your hand, look you in the eye, and say thanks. I enjoyed being with him."

I fold the words like fine lace and tuck them in for safekeeping. And Dan's new pride and joy, in cobalt and cream, sits dormant and desolate in the side yard.

Later, George needs my intimacy for reassurance of life and love. Why is it that on the hardest days when I want him least he wants me most? I wonder if he might lose all patience and leave, but I don't want reassurance of life. I don't want it at all.

June 15

I'm empty-headed and feel as if I'm wading through porridge. Everything looks like a solid bank of clouds. They are just gray and gray and gray.

June 16

George says, "Nothing can hurt him again. He is fine, whether he is in limbo or heaven or nothingness, he is beyond pain. What did we ever do to deserve such agony? How could we have done anything bad enough to be punished so hard? Torture like this should be saved for the Hitlers of the world." I'm glad he's not really asking because I can't really answer.

June 17

I take Pepé to the vet today and hold him while his kind, compassionate doctor gives him a shot that takes him out of his pain-filled existence. I am surprised and grateful that the doctor agrees to my request to hold our old black poodle. We've had Pepé for more than fifteen years and he has always stuck by us. There is no way I could let him down at this point.

Pepé seems to know what is happening—he seems complicit, willing. He actually leads me into the office. The doctor explains the physical things that might happen so I won't be shocked, but Pepé lies still in my arms. As my tears wet his neck he slips away peacefully, as if trying, even in his last act, to make it easier on and take care of *his people*.

Every place in the house holds his ghost. I remember the hours of companionship he gave me. And how confused he was when we brought Melisa home. He had never seen a baby before but as soon as he saw how preciously we treated her, he became her protector, giving up his bed in our room to sleep outside her door.

When she learned to stand up she did so by pulling herself erect on his fur. His expression was one of gritting his teeth but he didn't waver as he tolerated her efforts.

He had a trick, unique, perhaps, to him. When one of our kids was in trouble with George or me or we began to raise our voices, he would instantly leave the room, returning as fast as he could with something, anything that he knew he shouldn't have—one of my shoes from the closet or the newspaper. He would come dragging it right up to us and proceed to make a terrible scene, growling and shaking it, whatever it took to distract us and take the attention from the kids to him. Dogs. Such a great, happy gift to people.

Now he too, is gone. I picture him, puppy like, running around Heaven, his eyesight and hearing keen once more. Able to eat and digest what he wants. If dogs aren't allowed in Heaven, who would ever want to go? I get the absurd, but happy thought of him and Dan together.

But I'm afraid. Who am I going to lose next?

June 18

I lay in the tub staring sightlessly at a book I think I'm absorbing when into my mind pops the thought: *Day 21.* I stare at it and think how silly it looks hanging there in bold-faced type like the words in a bubble over a comic strip character. Puzzling on it, I watch it expand and lower until it fills my head, my body, and my world.

Comprehension begins and I can't turn away though I writhe in agony. It is day twenty-one. Twenty-one days since we buried our eldest son, and for the rest of our days a world of darkness in our souls. Never to see him again.

For the first time, the word *never* has a meaning and its five little letters stretch down a corridor of days and nights unmarked by any calendar. They stretch on and on, out of sight, never to stop. Never.

Hours disintegrate. The next time consciousness intrudes it finds me in the bedroom, dry-bodied, dry-eyed and dressed, the phone is ringing by my side and I can hear Dave and Melisa talking below me in the rec room with the TV on. Startled, I stare at the phone as if I've never seen such a thing. From downstairs I hear Dave's voice, "I'll get it." Then, "It's for you, Mom."

Lifting the receiver, I hear a voice more familiar than my own, but I can't put a name to it and I don't know what to do now. My mind has left me.

"Mary? Mary, are you alright? I couldn't get you out of my mind."

I must make some sound, for the next thing I hear is, "Baby? Oh, my poor Mary."

It's my mother who could always make everything okay. And I, at thirty-eight, am a child again. I need everything to be alright and nothing will be. I want it fixed and it can't be. I'm sobbing.

When I speak, I hear a child, myself, wail, "How can I live through this? Oh, Mom, Mama. What will I do?"

Then in a blink, I have myself under control. I stuff all the feelings down. I have been a helpless bystander in my own children's lives more than once in their times of agony, so I know how miserable she must feel.

"Oh Honey. It's so soon," she answers. "Give yourself some time. Please just try to give yourself some time."

I know her advice is right, but I cannot hear it.

At 1:20 a.m. I am awake. I think I know why I sit up, wide-eyed in bed each morning at this time, but it is too awful to face straight on. Only the deepest portions of my mind register that this precise moment when I wake must be the moment when he breathed his last breath. I get out of bed and stumble to the table. I pick up a piece of paper and with pen in hand, totally exhausted in Spirit and body, lay my head on the smooth surface.

Into my mind flows a vivid image of a bilious, bubbling pool of liquid grief. The picture is so clear in contrast to my thoughts. Part of me knows that in order to begin to heal I must first understand. But before I can understand I must first acknowledge that Dan is gone. I must dip into my mind as if it were this boiling pool. Knowledge is printed on the pebbles that are scattered on the bottom and I must grasp and examine them one by one until each becomes cool in my palm. Somewhere in these, obscured by steam, is the first pebble of thought with an answer written on it. My hands flex, and fingers tense for the scalding. I reach.

The pebble burns. Hard, encrusted, the words sharp as barnacles, ripping—I don't know where I get the courage to hang on, but I do. I think the thought, every mother's living nightmare: Your son is dead.

It crashes in my mind.

So, this is madness.

Eons pass.

Breathing begins again. I am still here. Again I see the steaming pool. Is this a vision? An illusion? A mirage? It is all so very clear. There are signposts scattered randomly around the pool. They have been blown free of mist by my voiceless scream. And this is what I see:

The first sign is marked OBLIVION; it ends in the pool. The one marked INSANITY spirals round and round and round, going nowhere. One is marked DIVORCE, one ESCAPE WITH DRUG AND DRINK, and one reads NUMBNESS FOR ALWAYS. The last one points up the steepest, rockiest, boulder-strewn, switchback trail filled with potholes and ditches and drop-offs at almost every step of the way. That signpost reads plain as plain, TO PEACE.

I don't understand. How can the most dangerous path lead to peace?

Somewhere in the far away past, the first parents lost a child. And even if the harsh environment of prehistoric life made sudden death more common than hunger, those first parents might have been stunned by the overwhelming and bewildering feeling they encountered. I know they would have needed ritual, would have sought a god, would have asked why. Through the ages, countless parents have felt what we are feeling, thought what we are thinking. We are not alone, but there is no consolation in that knowledge. We are unique because he was unique. We've never lost a child. No one was ever, ever in all time, Dan. Only he was our Danny. Consequently, only we have lost this son, felt this pain.

Helplessly, I follow where my mind leads me—back to the beginning. It's September, and the weather is beautiful. My new husband and I have been married two days. He is fresh out of the Marine Corp and I am not yet seventeen, and he teases me, "How many couples bring someone with them on their honeymoon?" he asks.

Though I am wild with love for this man, I am still shy enough to color at the reference of my *condition*. He laughs and puts his arms warm around me and says, "Lucky me."

I remember lying in bed relaxed and drowsy. It is late November and I feel our baby move. I am filled with awestruck wonder, unspeakable joy. I try to wake George by whispering as loudly as possible while attempting not to disturb the miracle that is happening within me.

Months later we laughingly watch the great balloon of my belly and I say, "See, that's his foot, he's going to be some punter."

But George disagrees. "Nope, that's his hand, the kid's going to pitch like a pro." And he did.

Our little Danny, what indescribable happiness he brought that hot April evening when he drew his first breath. First child. First grandchild. Oh Lord, the hopes he came with. The dreams we dreamed. Gone. All dust in our hearts.

I see him with clear blue eyes, fairly shooting sparks of excitement on the day we registered him for kindergarten—so eager to get going, to take his place in a world larger than his own front yard.

Already I'm telling him to slow down. "You've got lots of time," I would say. But he never did see it my way—he wouldn't slow down. In later years, I'd say, "Where are you going now, Hon?" and get a vague, "Out and about."

"Dan, why don't you stick around once in a while? What is there to do out there night after night anyway?"

I'd get a grin and the answer, "That's just it Mom, you never know. See you, love you. Oh, Mom, is there anything I can do for you before I go?"

And now I think, yes. There is one thing, Love, don't go, not yet, please. Stay. Stay with us just a little while longer.

Now with twenty-twenty hindsight, I know he was putting seventy years of living into the twenty he had. He never wanted to grasp and hold life tenaciously, but rather to fleetingly taste, touch, rush to and through one experience after another. Like a bee sucking just the sweetness from the flower.

A typical report card would read, *He is so bright and could do much better work if only he would buckle down and apply himself.* But he didn't want to use all of his energy. And he especially didn't want to use all his time to become proficient at any one thing—he wanted to try it all.

When he and his brother were very small, I wrote a little poem. It was one of those diamond days when you can no longer contain all the good feelings inside—you have to do something with them so you don't burst. My something was to write a simple, silly love song for my babies:

THE BESTEST DAY

Mommie, Mommie watch me play,
running lightly through the day.
Doing things others have done,
but to my eyes he's the only one.
Simple things done joyfully,
jumping a puddle, climbing a tree.
Mommie, Mommie look and see,
I saw a cat, it purred for me.
The milkman waved, the mailman smiled,
what a wonderful thing to be a child.
The world seems made just for you
hate unheard of, heartache too.
Mommie, Mommie with arms flung wide,
to give me a hug,
my heart swells with pride.
His daddy's eyes look up at me,
soul shining through for the world to see.
Lord grant me the wisdom to raise this boy
he is my life, my love, my joy.
Mommie, Mommie hear me pray.
The last soft words at the end of day.
Now he lays him down to sleep,
please Lord watch closely him to keep
because his smile to my heart brings
a song like a choir of angels sings.

Sophomoric, but that's how I felt. I have lots of interests, but everything else takes a backseat to my family.

Now I find it impossible to go forward. I need some quiet time, but life won't stop. And I'm a little afraid of examining my memories too closely for fear of them fading like a negative exposed to the sun.

But memories are more like engravings, aren't they? Etched indelibly on our hearts and seen more clearly for being held to the light. The grooves of the lettering of my memories shadow themselves and stand strong as a sea stack in a gale. So let me remember until I am able to say a final goodbye.

But as I write the words final goodbye, the paper blurs and tears burn my face to drip mutely off my chin and I wonder again at the poverty of this language of ours that I always thought was so rich. Oh the bleakness of the word goodbye.

June 19

I give in at last and take a sleeping pill. Maybe I can break the cycle of waking at 1:30 each morning and not being able to get back to sleep. I've only slept one night through in the past twenty-two.

June 20

The pill worked. Fixing pancakes this morning I comment to the kids that I slept eight hours and feel better. Dave lightly quotes my mom, "Grandma says sleep is a restorative, Mom, and Grandma knows best."

I forget. For two hours I forget. I watch a TV show and enjoy it. I am astonished that I can forget for a time. I am so ashamed of myself and so guilty. I forgot our Dan. Lord! I am jerked like a yo-yo. Good this morning—horrid this evening.

June 21

When the alarm rings in the morning, I keep my eyes shut. The rest I just had brought no rest. My mind does not click and whir, but dully drones and makes little distinction between waking and sleeping. Dan is my first thought. I don't have the energy to rise—I don't have the desire. I see no meaning in the daily routine. It's just another demand the world makes, another senseless demand.

So I lay, eyes shut, and force myself to pretend that I want to get up. I pretend that I care that my body is covered, that my hair is combed, that the bed is made. Toothpaste I squeeze from a red and white tube onto a blue brush and place inside my mouth is tasteless and the senseless act of brushing drains me. I pretend and pretend. All is pretense and the strain costs dearly but it is the only thing that keeps me from quitting. And I seem to be fooling everyone.

A PIECE OF ADVICE: ACT AS IF

Many times this little bit of advice got me through the day.
Every morning pretend you want to get up.
Pretend that you care if you get through the day or not.
Act as if it matters.
Pretend the sun and the rain,
the singing of the birds,
the blooming of the flowers
has meaning.
If you pretend long enough,
hard enough,
with hope enough
maybe one day
you may discover
you're not pretending
anymore.

~ Mary M. Fern

One of the books I've read recently talked about sex. It advised, "Don't take a chance on losing your husband—you have already lost so much." The implication is to always be accepting of your husband's advances because he needs this release and reassurance. Well, perhaps that's true, but I need the comfort of love and tenderness without the sex. I give myself to George, this man I truly love, and all the while I wonder how he can want sex. I am resentful and disgusted, and without tears. With our eldest son newly buried I can't feel love, only pain, so what we are doing is raw and abrasive, no laughter, no joy.

With each of his advances, I am transported back through the years to our beginnings and the happiness we felt. There is the knowledge that this act of love and longing produced our recently entombed son. If it hadn't been for sex, there wouldn't be this pain now.

I am so sad when I think that no matter how much we try to

understand each other, no matter how much we love and are concerned for one another, we can never really feel, really touch, really know each other's hearts. In the final analysis, it doesn't make any difference how much a part of the other we have become, that we can finish each other's sentences, almost read the other's mind—we still and always are alone.

I don't want to lose my husband. I love him so deeply he is written on my soul. But why do I always have to be the understanding one? Be the pleaser? Do I think he's so driven, so weak that he has to have his own way? That he will leave if he is thwarted? Shouldn't I give him more credit for his strength, his understanding? Of course I should. He has proven for years the quality of his character. But at this time of all times I need him to understand that the agony we are both experiencing, I cannot put it aside so easily. I am so filled with the thought of our son, he wakes with me and he lies within me in this bed.

Chapter Seven

ENDLESS DAYS, FOREVER NIGHTS

"It is always darkest just before the day dawneth."

~ Thomas Fuller

June 22

I sit for days not writing, not even thinking. I get up and automatically do the normal things. Then, I sit. Sometimes I surprise myself when I discover I am crying—but surprise is too strong a word. It's more like I observe *that person* crying, but that person lacks any connection or meaning to me. I am outside myself again. I blink at her, recognize me in her, but like an old, old photograph that is not me anymore. Is this shock or depression or withdrawal? Or more denial? Is it another part of the healing process? I don't know.

Neighbors drive by and as I sit at my window I see them carefully avoid looking at our house, believing superstitiously perhaps that death is contagious. I observe their actions as if my eyes are not connected to my mind.

My sister phones or drops a card on a weekly basis. Today she says "You know how you asked me to keep that blonde away from you? How did I do? "

"Great," I respond. "I never even saw her at all. Thanks." We laugh, but I am a little bewildered—I never did get the smallest glimpse of that couple. I didn't think they were here. Odd. Well, maybe they were.

Dave bought us tickets to a concert show. They are a combination George's birthday and my Mother's Day gift. Of course we must go, though the effort it takes to go out exhausts us. Lines of lyric here and there make our tears flow. I wonder how many others sit here tonight in this darkened festive place racked by pain or bursting with silent joy unknown and unseen by all around them. Once again I think how often, in the midst of living, memory sneaks up and twists the knife. *Gotcha*. But some lyrics reach out and give us a little shake and we smile together.

June 23

I quit work today. I feel this deadly pity. It's too hard. I am falling apart. When I first went back, the silence could be, as they say, cut with a knife—everyone was trying to avoid the elephant in the room. Finally, I offered to share a few details with a group of five co-workers who share this small space. My boss said it might be a good idea if I wanted to do that. When I finished, all eyes were damp, but the air was lighter. Then one man made a comment that seemed so odd to me. He said it was amazing how I was able to speak so calmly. I just nodded, but thought, I'm not calm or agitated or anything. I just put myself on automatic pilot and this is what comes out. It has nothing to do with me at times like this.

June 24

I got so angry at Melisa today. She can't stop talking and I'm so tired of being careful of her—and everyone's—feelings, of being tolerant and understanding. She was mad at the friend who told her classmates about Danny and she is still complaining about it. She wanted to do it herself. At her age, there is as much titillation as there is reality to this tragedy, I know. She is still upset about the dress she wore to the memorial. And she keeps complaining because I won't go down to the cemetery. She can't understand it. I know it's her way of dealing with it. I feel her fear and pain but I have been patient beyond patience. I tell myself she is only nine and a half, and he was her brother. But I am so tired. I really have tried so hard, but...but...

A few friends have asked Melisa over to play. She doesn't want to go. She is reluctant to be far from us. The one night she agreed to spend at a friend's, she called us at midnight and asked us to come and get her. She was frightened. I tried for a second to persuade her to stay but she just couldn't. It doesn't take a psychiatrist to comprehend the problem, though understanding doesn't make it any easier to deal with. I'm sure she was thinking Dan was away and the house burned down and he never got to see any of us again, and what if, while she was away...

I try to draw her out but cannot. Today it all got to be too much for me. After hours of idle chatter, my ears, nerves, my brain hurt and I snap and shout "Melisa, shut up!" Her face goes white, her eyes huge, and stunned, she stumbles to her room.

Oh my god. We don't say these words in our house. My line to the kids has always been, "Doors shut, people be quiet." Now how can I yell at one of my children when we have so recently buried another? God, god, god. And I stumble after her begging forgiveness.

Do not comparison shop for grief
by thinking my pain is worse or less than yours.
No, no, no.
It would seem to me that grief, like love, is measureless.
It either exists or it does not.
When it exists it is bottomless
and not to be weighed and measured.
When love is, it is.
When grief is…it is.

~ Mary M. Fern

June 25

I can't remember the simplest things. It has become necessary to make lists of ordinary chores or I forget them. I can barely form a sentence, reading is as foreign as hieroglyphics, and spelling, never my best subject, is a lost art.

The main character in the novel I am trying to read right now is a man named Daniel. It takes me a hundred pages before I recognize the name.

Melisa experienced the same phenomenon right after we lost Dan. We showed her the obit column in the paper and she, an excellent reader, couldn't find his name. She searched and I kept hearing her sigh until at last, in anger, she said "It's not here, Mom!" I leaned one hand on the table and one hand on her shoulder as I pointed to the line.

"I don't want it to be there, Mom!" she wailed as she ran to her room.

I thought denial was consciously refusing to believe something when there is irrefutable proof, but it's more than that. It is your eye and mind actually not seeing what is in front of you. There was a time when this concept would have been so intriguing—I would have been interested in looking further into the complexities of the subject. But not any longer. I don't care.

Poor Melisa, if I had realized what she was experiencing maybe I could have said something to help. If we have to go through this, why do we have to take each step in such ignorance and stupidity? What is my lack of knowledge, my not knowing what to do or say, doing to my family? And why do I feel it's all up to me?

June 26

It is impossible to keep breathing with emotions at this peak. No wonder the mind stops like a tripped circuit breaker. If it didn't shut down it would over load, the circuits would short, and the tissue would fuse into a lump of worthless, blackened cells.

June 27

I watch the moon come up, full and wondrous, and I remember a night at the ocean. I remember running down the path to the dunes. This is where my Spirit breathes. Dan is at my heels as we skim onto the sand. The moon is full, the sky velvet, and the air like Eden. My arms reach spontaneously to hold it all. I am floating. Dan, about fifteen, puts his arm around me and hugs me in equal ecstasy. Wise beyond his years, he says "This is what it feels like to be really alive. Don't you wish we could feel like this forever?" I tap the beautiful memory and still detect sand in my shoes. Maybe that is what forever means.

The news tonight says the President and the Pentagon are tapping the war drums. I feel sarcastic and sickeningly smug as I think, *You can't get my Dan.* As if he's cheated death by dying. What a nutty thought. No wonder I doubt my sanity.

June 29

It's been thirty-five days.

I cannot make the floor shine though I'm using all my determination and effort. My energy level is so low. Even when I do dust a table or wash a dish, they don't look any cleaner—everything looks dingy and gray like a before ad for a new detergent. As I scrub on this sunny June day, I think of Christmas without him. Why would thoughts of Christmas come today? Does it mean I'm starting to look ahead? Am I beginning to imagine a future? Can I stand a future that doesn't include him?

My grandma kept a magazine cover for years, a picture by Norman Rockwell that portrayed the perfect white haired grandpa and grandma serving a big turkey on a platter to their eager, smiling, well-scrubbed family.

Grandma and my mom and her two sisters would share their laughter as they imagined, *What is really going on behind all those shining faces?* They would speculate and make up conversations that went something like this, "Uncle Bill is probably tipsy and Auntie Sue is steaming. And when little brother gets his mitts on that turkey leg, what do you bet he considers using it as a weapon to club his big sister."

Now I think that's what a portrait of our family might show. We look so normal—washed, combed, dressed, and carrying on with our lives. But a peek behind the curtain reveals Dave gone every night, Melisa afraid to go out at all, George totally uncommunicative, and me see-sawing between frenetic and floundering. Our personalities are diverse, always have been, so why would I expect anything else? We couldn't even agree on pizza toppings, so why would we react alike in this circumstance? Deep inside me, I know this is really important to remember.

Curled up on the couch leaning into Dave's arm, Melisa starts to cry. "I used to try and make him mad at me. I would make noise when he was trying to record stuff and he would ask me to stop but I wouldn't."

My smart Dave waits for sobs to subside, then asks, "Did he ever make you mad?"

She sniffles and nods.

"Me too. And even when he made you mad, did you still love him?"

Another nod, another, "Me too." A pause and then, "So do you think he still loved you, too, even when he was mad at you?"

Ever so slowly there comes another nod followed by a deep, deep sigh. And I'm so proud of them.

Again and again I come back to pound on this uncrackable rock that I know contains understanding if only I could break it open. I need to understand. I am so full of questions and the world is so devoid of answers. I wish I could get really angry, but there is not enough energy in me for anger. I am banked with embers of rage at wiring done with little skill and caution. Anger at manufacturing companies whose wires might melt and arc. Anger at a volunteer fire department that took forty minutes to muster and respond while three miles away a fully-equipped, trained department full of professionals were not allowed to respond due to boundary disputes. And at Dan, who slept so soundly that I used to tell him the house could burn down around his ears and he would probably sleep through it. I was always saying that. The pain knocks the wind in a rush from my body.

Jeff has told us he sees in his mind's eye an extension cord snaking across the couch from the TV. They knew better. And he told us about the lights always flickering.

And finally embers of rage at myself for encouraging...no, insisting, the now unbearable, "It is time for you to be out on your own. If you can't obey the family rules, if you can't set a good example, it is better if you leave." But if that memory comes on too strongly, I cannot draw my next breath.

What right do I have to breathe when he cannot?

Sixteen days on his own. Only sixteen days.

My headache is so awful I can't focus. I fight vomiting. The headache is always there but it gets unbearable when too much blazing memory comes in.

George's rash is unbelievably inflamed. There's another fire word—I'll try again. George's rash is bright red. He itches from head to toe. At least we finally know, after all these years and all the different doctors, what doesn't cause it. It isn't sun or grass, pets, or food, or dust. We now know if he's a little upset, he's a little broken out. Now he is more stressed than he has ever been and not one inch of his body is free from the maddening, red bumps.

All of us must make an enormous effort to sit or stand erect. We are embodying the expression, *Bowed down with grief.*

Our life is locked in place where there is no movement, no forward or reverse. Only a here, but not even a now. It's as if time doesn't exist. It is a twilight zone. The wind blows, a river flows. They don't know where or why. A river doesn't ask when it will disgorge into the sea—the wind doesn't wonder where it was yesterday or where it will be tomorrow. A mountain is simply there. No past, no present. Whatever a mountain feels must be very much like what I am feeling.

We are moving through time so I must be functioning, but I have no conscious awareness of doing so. I find myself at the check-out counter with a basket of food and no memory of having shopped or having driven to the store.

Sitting, without appetite, at the dinner table with a plate full of food in front of me that I must have cooked but I don't remember. Someone will mention tomorrow or next week and my mind can't grasp the concept. Time is meaningless.

June 30

Dave asks if he can take Melisa to a movie and we say sure, it would be good for both of you. They kiss us goodbye and go out to get into the car. Suddenly my knees are so liquid I have to hold onto the door jamb, digging my nails into the wood to prevent myself from running after them. I want to scream, "No! You can't go!" I watch them hop into Dave's old yellow Pontiac and make myself, with superhuman will, smile and wave. The two of them, all we have left in life, are going off together into the scary, mad, dangerous world in a vulnerable, flimsy piece of metal and I can only cling to the doorframe and watch. The energy I exert to stand aside leaves me weak, but someplace inside myself I realize if I don't let them go now, I might handicap them forever. A small spark of light ignites within me and I am proud of myself—I've done the right thing.

Consciously, deliberately, I go up and down the grocery aisles determined not to buy what he isn't here to enjoy. I tell myself, *Put that cereal back. Put back that soup. No one else eats that kind. Now go home, Mary. You are done.*

In the bread aisle, two acquaintances wait in ambush and I have no weapon or armor. They say, "It's good to see you out. You're doing so well."

As they start to prattle I feel myself go to that safe place deep inside me where I watch myself nod and smile as I absorb the blows. They say brightly, "Time heals after all." One says, "Can I ask, how long has it been now?"

"Five weeks." The words drop from my mouth like globules of nuclear waste.

"Well," again she smiles, "staying busy is the best thing."

Keep active.

Fill up your time.

Keep your mind off of…things.

You have to think about other things.

Don't dwell.

Don't brood.

You have to move on…let go…say goodbye…find closure, move on, let go, say goodbye, find closure moveonletgosaygoodbye findclosurefindclosurefindclosure findclosure…

Again I nod, and we part.

I want to scream. My head is so full of emotion I want to tear my hair out, rip my scalp off, break into my skull. I want to shake my head and see the bits of agony flying out, see them drop like sizzling cinders on the ground. I imagine the pieces like pus and vomit, tainted blood and offal, visceral things.

This is what I want to tell them, to show them so they might have a clue. But I'm ashamed of myself for even thinking like that. No one knows what to say and at least they spoke, they tried. How do I explain that the last thing I want is to forget? I don't ever want to forget. Terror that I might forget nightly turns my pillow to stone.

The world keeps turning around and around in space and it's momentum pushes at me but I want, I need to stay still for a while and remember.

We put our arms around our sobbing children when a loved pet dies or a first heart is broken, we commiserate when an important game or the coveted part in the play is lost. Now it is my child who has died and we are advised and encouraged to move on, to say goodbye. But I can't, I just can't. What will I do if I forget his touch, his scent, his voice, his smile? And I despise those who say I must.

I am so beaten down by this morning's encounter that I fall asleep when I get home and wake with a new insight. I hate the thought of it, but I probably will forget some things, and that's why I must stay still for a while to remember, and that is what I am going to do. And somehow, someday I will move on. But I will never, never say goodbye.

I swore I would get still and quiet, but the world gets in the way. I resent all the common place things I must do. Phones ring and clothes get dirty. Floors need washing and food must be bought, carried, cleaned, cooked or put away or eaten. George demands, the kids demand, the dog demands. Life demands, but I wish I could run away.

If only I could find someplace where I could rest, someplace where I could think and remember everything about him. I need to feel once again him moving within me, the touch of his pudgy baby fingers holding tight to my finger for the security he thought was there. I need to remember the height of him and the warmth of him, his laughter and his thrill of life. I need to be left alone to grieve. Let me remember so I won't forget, then I will find the scattered pieces. I will figure out how to put them back together again.

Please take care.
It has been said that
alcohol does not drown sorrows—
it irrigates them.
Something that could be worse than your
family and friends witnessing your grieving
while deep in their own grieving
would be to see you
intoxicated and grieving.
A drunken person is an in-TOXIC-ated person.
And toxins make everyone sick.

~ Mary M. Fern

July 1

The thirty days of June, equaled seven hundred twenty hours, or forty three thousand two hundred minutes—an eternity.

We go out to dinner at a local place where George and I often go but Melisa has never been before. A familiar waitress brings her a Shirley Temple and asks her if she is an only child. Melisa shakes her head, no, and a stricken look comes over her face. She looks wildly from me to George and then drops her head, her face now hidden behind the curtain of her long, honey-colored hair. We stare at the woman and at each other—we are struck dumb. She must have thought us very strange.

Later we're talking about going out on the boat and listing what we would need and someone mentions film. For the first time, I think about the camera, and excited say, "Maybe there's undeveloped film in the camera! Maybe there are some pictures of—" and mid-sentence, my voice halts as I smack into that emotional wall again.

He's gone. I believe it too strongly and I don't believe it at all.

Who would think that you can't shop for food because the produce aisle is too poignant? You can't listen to the radio for fear a special song will catch you unaware and you will break down. You can't go to a movie, and watching TV is an act of courage because if they show a ski scene or a fire or a young person dying in a flaming car crash, you might go quietly—or noisily—insane.

Warm days remind me of how often he wished he lived in the sun, "Wouldn't you know it, the sun is going to be out today and I have to work. By my day off the rain will probably be back." And I suppose winter days will be hurtful as I think of the skiing he is missing.

And everyone in the world suddenly seems to be named Dan. The newspaper and magazines are filled with Dans. I watch the credits run after a TV show and count the Dans.

I can say Dan is gone. I can say my first born son died. I can almost get through saying we are now a family of four, but I can't say Dan is ____. My mind stops. He is ever on my mind so when I say something reminds me of him. I just mean...I don't know what I mean. Everything reminds me of him. He is all. All is he.

I have been staring at the screen while a war movie played out in front of me. My eyes see soldiers rushing a hill, bodies and dirt exploding, contorted faces scared, hate-filled, determined, bewildered. And I wonder what they are thinking. What is it that makes them do an officer's bidding? What is it that makes them disregard our primary instinct for survival? Is it brotherhood? Is it patriotism? Or is it that you do what you have to do because there is nothing else to do? Soldiers go forward, so do we.

People say, "You are really doing well. We think it's wonderful that you are coming through this so fine."

We're not doing fine at all. We're really not. We are getting up and functioning. We have no other choice. George and I ignore so much. We just let time go by.

We have Dan's car here. George won't go near it. He won't work on it. He has lain under cars so many times, teaching, working side by side with both Dan and Dave. He can't bring himself to do it now even though it is painful to see it in the yard and we can't advertise it until some minor maintenance is done. We can't hide it, we can't bear to part with it, and we can't stand it here. But today the pain seems to have withdrawn to some far place and stupefied, and I sit and wait. For him to come back? No, I know he won't come back. So what am I waiting for?

As I said before, our minds know but our hearts don't.

July 2

The radio's every song carries a message about leaving, lost loves, and heartbreaks, and each one drills me like a dentist. I never realized how few themes run through music, whether it's rock, modern or country. I even try listening to some classical station but the violins turn my ache to a palpable thing.

I have a curious sense of unreality about most things since the death. If Shakespeare is right and "all the world's a stage," then I'm only a ticket buyer at an uninteresting play.

When I am in public doing everyday mundane things like shopping, working or dining, I see people all around me bustle by, wringing their hands about things of so little consequence. I overhear snatches of conversation, "We've got to have this ready to ship by three. Hurry!" "Strawberry or Rocky Road?" "The salad looks good but maybe I'll have the soup instead."

I overhear these snippets of conversation and want to shout, "Who cares? You're breathing, aren't you? Isn't that enough?" Their world seems to have less depth than a reflection. It's all so transitory, almost imaginary. My world is the only reality.

Each one of my kids is so special, I don't know how to go on without one of them. I would give almost anything to see him again, but there is nothing I can do. So, like Scarlet O'Hara, I won't think about it until tomorrow.

I try to work on the memory book, clippings from the paper, cards and such. But I can't do it. I'm hyperventilating again. One article's headlines: Man Dies in Fire. It seems unconnected to us—we still think of him as a boy, not a man. He had only been twenty for forty-three days.

It's still July first. Is the day never to end?

George is angry and bitter. Last night he was in the bedroom, the vein is his temple was throbbing as it does when he is holding in strong feelings and he kept his voice down so as not to wake Melisa as he paced, "God damn. It's always been safety first. Always. How many remodeling projects have we done around here over the years? And even when we were new at it, it was always safety first. Take the saw and put it away so little fingers wouldn't get cut. Is the fence strong enough to withstand climbing on? Always, always. God Damn Safety First! I spent half my life it seems at the permit department checking out the right way because it seemed so crucial to not take any chances. And no fire alarms? Christ. What do they cost? Ten bucks?"

All I can do is nod my head, I know, I know.

But in my heart I beg, please don't let us become bitter. I've seen what that can do to a person—their face grows to be like one of those carved and dried apple faces one sometimes sees at a craft fair. It's ugly. Bitterness paints a Dorian Gray portrait and it only hurts you.

As his dad storms, I feel Dan so near. I touch the corner of my mouth and truly still feel the tickle of his wispy first-time mustache. I still know his last kiss.

Chapter Eight

ON BEING BRAVE

"Saddle Up"

John Wayne was, for many years, a Hollywood actor,
venerated for his tough guy roles.
He played soldiers and roustabouts. A manly man —
but mostly John Wayne was a cowboy.
Westerns were where he shined macho to the max.
Then he was called on by Life to play his toughest role.
He was diagnosed with lung cancer.
Very ill but gracious still, he gave one more interview.
And the reporter, in a bit of awe said,
"How did you get so courageous and brave?
Aren't you ever afraid?"
To which this movie star idol replied
"Of course sometimes I am afraid.
Courage IS being afraid but saddling up anyway."

I finally slept some, so am doing pretty well this morning. Watching George last night exhausted me.

I had a peculiar thought a few days ago as I looked at a picture of the family: *Someday you will feel happy again.* Startled, I examined the words closely, turning them over and over and for one split second I saw the truth of them. For this moment, anyway, I believe someday we will be happy again. Then I see a ski commercial and the knife twists. A young man rides down the hill on his bike—he carries the same body shape as my boy, tall and lean. He has Dan's style, rides with casual abandonment, fast and free. My heart stops, and then plummets.

I think I am beginning to see a pattern—the numbness we experience most of the time is pierced by small flashes of memory that

71

bring searing pain for just a few moments. Maybe the brain or the heart only lets us feel one slash at a time with rests in between so we don't really go mad. Like a dam keeper releasing small amounts of extra water in the rainy season to relieve pressure on the structure where if it was all released at once, everything down river would be destroyed in the rush of the flood.

An old friend, Martha, drops by for a little visit. The ring of the doorbell startles me. It's rare nowadays.

Now that I am working from home, I have set up my work table in Dan's room and I must come upstairs to answer the door, my hands covered in the glue and sisal I was using to make bird nests for the soft sculpture birds our shop is producing.

I am surprised to see her. We've been friends for years but I haven't heard from her in a long while and she was in the hospital for foot surgery the day of the memorial. I considered her a real friend and I feel badly that I never sent her a get well card. I pour some iced tea and as we walk into the dining room, she notices a picture of Dan, Dave, and Melisa on the hutch…and her eyes fill.

"I've wanted to come so badly but I just couldn't. All I've thought about for weeks is your family and I couldn't face you. If this could happen to nice people like you then it could happen to nice people like us. And if something happened to my boys, I don't think I could live. I couldn't go on. I don't know what to say or how to say it. This stuff happens to other people, doesn't it? Not people we care about. I'm so scared, and so sorry for you guys."

Knee to knee and heart to heart, we weep, we weep, and we grow stronger together.

The tragedy has brought terror to all of our friends. Most of them have kids the same age as ours, and in many cases it was having the children that brought us together in friendship. Martha's boys are contemporaries of our boys. We've known them through school, clubs, P.T.S.A., hour upon hour of little league and neighborhood functions. We were just beginning to feel an easing of parental pressure as these kids of ours became more responsible drivers and left their teenage years behind. They were all starting college or finding steady jobs and steady girls. Now this comes along and every mom and dad is snapped right back to the awareness of the haunting specter that hovers over every parent's life—fear for your children.

4th of July

We are invited to a picnic and fireworks at a friend's beach house. It's so nice of friends to invite us. As I've said before, it takes great bravery to do that.

I do okay for a while but suddenly I feel smothered, I can't breathe. I use the excuse of needing to find Melisa and walk down toward the beach.

The road is steep down to a wide strip of sand scattered with large drift logs. I see her, the center of attention, perched on an old cedar log, in a group of eight kids ranging in age from about six through twelve. She looks awfully small. They're so busy plying her with questions that they didn't see me coming. Silence pounces like a cat on a rat when they notice me. From Melisa's face and the silence, the topic of the conversation was clear. She immediately scoots over on her log making room for me and exhaling a big sigh as I sit down. She leans against me and I say, "Hey, what's going on guys?"

It doesn't take long for curiosity to erase their inhibitions. The oldest boy, the son of our host, confides that they were told not to talk about Danny and to be extra nice to Melisa if we did show up.

"We really appreciate that, don't we Melisa? It's a hard time for us right now and friends help us feel better." I feel my girl take her cue from me and haltingly nod her head.

I actually feel a natural peacefulness surrounding us and I do my best to relax so I can answer the questions I know they are dying to ask. I really like kids. They aren't always kind, but there's no pretense either.

"So, what are we talking about here, Melisa?"

"They want to know how the house caught on fire," she whispers.

"Yeah, how did it?"

"We're not sure yet, but we think it might have been the wiring."

"Did the firemen have to chop in the roof? Did they carry your son down a ladder?"

"No. Yes."

A little boy named Mike says, "Last year a man fell into the water right over there when he was fishing and he drowned. Does it hurt worse to be drowned or to be burned up in a fire?"

At last we have reached the center of the conversation and all of us know this is the question we have been waiting for. This question that is too awful to ask and each of these playmates has been waiting to see if anyone has the nerve to ask the *What's it like to die?* question.

The older boy, who I later learn is Mike's big brother Chris, leans across our little circle to punch Mike on the arm and whisper loudly, "Shut up dummy."

"No, that's okay," I say. "But I don't really know the answer. I don't know which would be the worst way to die. But I know there's no pain to being dead. And it's usually old people who die. Young people can die too, but you guys all look pretty healthy to me. Now, I'm thirsty from all this talking. How about we go get some soda?"

But Mike isn't through yet. His grubby bare feet take turns burying each other in the sand and he doesn't look up as he says, "Was the wiring in your son's house the same as we have in our house?"

"I think even more important than the wires are fire alarms, Mike. You have a nice new house with strong wires and I know you have alarms, don't you?"

"Yeah," he nodded, looking to his brother for confirmation.

"I think you're pretty safe." I smile. He rewards me with a grin.

I'm glad to hold Melisa's hand and walk down to the edge of the water. We both needed to get our feet wet. Like George and me, the salt of the sea is solace for her, this wounded daughter of ours.

It would have been strange if the children didn't have questions and though it was painful, I feel more at home with their openness than I do with adults averting their eyes or avoiding us completely. Melisa hasn't wanted to talk, but she listens so intently while the kids and I chat, I felt her unasked questions being answered. That is worth the immense effort I just put forth.

For the rest of the day, I am shadowed by Mike. He is my guardian. Chris even invites Melisa and me to see the boys' private clubhouse and Melisa is allowed to sit in the chief's chair.

Now, at home, I'm so tired that the pencil slides out of my fingers.

And, God, fireworks sure are scary.

July 5

I still can't look ahead. It seems silly to contemplate the future. Why plan when there is no certainty? A plan implies control and there is ultimately no such thing. But my mind is slowly coming back. It takes forever to think about things, but I sense a definite improvement. I still put clothes in the dryer and forget them until days later. I still start to make a meal and misplace my mind and memory. But it is getting better. It has been six weeks. Am I progressing fast or slow?

The mail brought Tom's wedding invitation. Dan was to be best man. George and I exchange looks. His eyes hold all the pain in the world. My tears well up. His eyes are a mirror. We have no words.

I ask George to bring home some ice cream. Why out of all the myriad flavors on the market did George buy Dan's favorite? "Who wants some ice cream?" I ask and three voices answer, "Me."

I set out bowls and scoop...butter brickle. The kids both startle, glance at each other, but say nothing. George looks at his dish with a shocked expression and we can see he is asking himself, *What was I thinking?*

Dave breaks the silence, with a little chuckle. "Remember the time Dan bought the root beer ice cream?" We check each other's faces. A tiny smile pushes at George's lip. I shake my head and we laugh at the memory. George loves root beer and Dan, never one to do things in a small way, bought six half-gallon cartons for his dad the first time he ever saw it in the store.

Yet my laughter is still on the outside only. Inside, I—who never had much patience with criers—cry. I believe everyone has a tale of woe, so tears only seem a play for sympathy. I have a lot to learn. I never dreamed a person could hold so many tears. It's as if our skin is an oddly-shaped, hollow sculpture holding nothing but liquid, salty, and scalding. No blood, no bones, just tears. Do I leave wet footprints as I walk?

July 6

I am so tired of pain, I just want to be out of it. I miss him so much. I just want to be with him.

George and I are so far down today we can barely lift our eyelids. We decide to go see Mom and stop at the little corner store to grab some sodas on the way. I slump in the car as George runs in. Suddenly from around the edge of the building there comes a scruffy little boy, about eight or nine years old. He is pulling a wagon with a tiny little girl riding in it like a ragamuffin princess. I lift those tired eyelids and meet his clearly focused gaze. The intensity of his stare brings me fully upright in the seat and sends a shiver through me as I feel him read my mind and heart. He knows. He knows I am at my end and he speaks to me with no words, saying, "It's gonna be okay one day. Yeah. Really. I know. It will. Promise." He enters the store as George exits and turns back for a second to level his eyes with mine again, and as if we are sharing a good story, he winks.

Nothing I can think of helps make sense of it. I am still weary to death of this pain. I only know I feel, now, as if that little boy held me on the planet. And on the planet I will stay. And as I settle to sleep, my mind keeps repeating, *Angel unaware, Angel unaware.*

July 8

I answer a knock at the door. A young man from the newspaper is seeking new subscribers. He is wearing Dan's shaving lotion. I reel backward clutching my arms to my middle.

As George jumps frightened to his feet, I struggle to regain my balance. The poor boy, meanwhile, must think he has rung the bell at a madhouse. What happens next, I truly don't know. I am off in a dangerous fog, dodging lethal objects invoked by this aroma. The scent, the scent.

God! I am so angry at him for being gone so long. If he walks in the door right now I would give him such hell for worrying us so.

July 9

When we told the kids that their grandpa, my dad, had died, Dan came over and put his arms around me. It was his fifteenth birthday and in his holding, his attempt at protecting Mom, I felt the beginnings of his adulthood, a premonition of the man he would someday become. I felt, through my sorrow, such pride in him and joy in the character and strength I sensed. I know I'm selfish, but…he'll not be here when I need him.

July 10

I remember Dan and Dave racing each other down the street—always competing—baseball, basketball, swimming, pushing each other to excel. Pushing, always pushing, on the swing or the sled, just pushing, "Me first."

When Dan turned seven, George and I built him a race car out of ¾ inch plywood. Gosh, it was so heavy. We painted it Kelly green and blazoned a big white 7 on the sides. I can still see Dave straining to push it up our hill. When I went to the door and hollered at them, "Give Dave a turn." Dan started to get out but Dave said, "I like building my muscles, Mom. Besides, it's Dan's birthday. I'll take turns tomorrow."

The giggles of their baby years, the helpless silly laughter of adolescence, the teasing and the deepening chuckles of their young manhood echo in the chambers of my mind.

And, I remember the look of acknowledgment that sometimes passed between them, affirming the caring that is never put into words.

Family pictures rest on the desk in the hall. I walk past for the millionth time and today my walk is arrested. BOOM! Out of nowhere I am enraged! Alone in the house, I shout and my voice hits the ceiling, sticking like taffy. "Where are you? You come back, you hear?" My demand boils out at his unresponsive face, and sagging, I whisper stupidly, "Don't leave me alone. Please." Then, "Don't worry about me Honey, I'll be okay. It's just that I miss you so much."

I heard again today that I was doing well. Each time someone says it I wonder what they are seeing as they look at me. Sometimes I feel so out of body it is just a shell of me that I witness walking around. I can't feel or hear my heart beating in my breast. And my mind is a ball of yarn after the kittens have played with it.

At our house we try to be polite to each other, a please, a thank you are common. But I got to wondering as I lay awake last night if I ever said thanks to him just for being him. Did I give a no-strings-attached compliment? I would nag him to take out the garbage or mow the lawn and say thanks when he did. But did I ever just thank him for being part of my life? Did I ever say, "Hey, Dan, it's really beautiful the way you always unwind that six-foot-four frame from wherever you are when you see me having difficulty and say, 'Here, let me help, get, lift, hold, push, carry, pull it for you.'" How often I accepted his help with a blasé, "Thanks." But never again. My only vow right now is to never let an opportunity go by without letting the people in my world know how important they are to me.

George is moving the hanging plants for me and says, "Dan got such a kick out of being tall. I never did get used to tipping my head back to talk to him." He clears his throat. "He enjoyed watching me struggle and stretch for a minute before he offered to help."

"I know," I say. "He was pretty good about helping, wasn't he?"

"Yeah". There is a long pause and his eyes leave mine, and then he almost whispers, "I wonder if I ever would have gotten used to looking up to my little boy?"

July 11

I cut a piece of paper into a circle and fold the circle into five sections, and then tear it carefully along the folds. When I have five jagged pieces, I lay one of them aside. Now, with the four remaining parts I must form a new family circle. I can't do it. I try and try. It can't be done. I have to—I have to. But, how?

And my mind goes spinning or into one of its mad litanies.

"All the king's horses and all the king's men, and all the king's horses and all the king's men, and all the king's horse's"

I know nothing will ever, ever, ever be the same again and

somehow we must find a way to go on. But, how?

"Heavy hearts, like heavy clouds in the sky,
are best relieved by the letting of the water."

~ Christopher Morley

Dave finally shuts off his music and pounds up the stairs. Again, tonight he gives me a swift kiss, tells me he will be "out and about," and then leaves for the evening. I want to shake him, to hug him, to say it isn't possible to hold Dan by imitating him. Even if it were, we would have an imitation Dan and we would lose our Dave. I want to shout, *"Stop it! Please stop!"* But I say nothing. How am I going to help him? I curse how stupid we are in all of this.

July 12

He is the alpha thought. Into the fuzzy cocoon of restless sleep each morning comes the smashing, bashing knowledge of the presence of his absence.

I still don't sleep through the night and still resist pills. The temptation would be to take them and sleep day and night, refusing to face the truth. I need to be very careful to avoid extremes of anything— drinking, laughter, tears, for fear that once I start I may lose control and be damned to laugh hysterically forever or drink till I am sodden skid road flotsam.

Today has been my first day without total heartbreak. And that breaks my heart.

My friend Rosalyn called and invited us for dinner. I'm apprehensive but I accept. She promised no pressure.

"I really do appreciate the invitation," I say, 'but we are such bad company. We never know what might make us break down. We cry unexpectedly and we make people around us really uncomfortable."

"You know," she laughed softly, "I've seen tears before. I've even been known to cry. Tell you what, we'll do a simple barbecue and eat outside. You can come at the last minute if you want and leave as soon as you're done eating. Oh, and bring David if he's free."

"We'll try it." I say. My palms are wet with sweat—the phone slips as I put it down. I marvel at the courage it must have taken for her to pick up her phone.

Often when we start out to take a ride or eat out, we get a few blocks from home and find one of us is feeling too emotional to continue. Melisa, in particular, has been dealing with carsickness, something she never had before, and only bringing her home and resting on her bed with her alleviates the queasiness.

July 13

There was a FIRE at the neighbors today!

It isn't serious and no one is hurt, but the smell of smoke coming through our open door and windows makes me so sick, I vomit. Dave comes up from his room to be with me. We sit in the living room, shaking. There is no way I can look to see how bad it is—my knees won't hold me.

When I recognize the smell, my impulse is to check it out, but my feet won't move. "Dave? Honey, can you go see if anyone has reported it?"

He looks at me with haunted eyes, "I can't Mom. I can't."

Melisa shoots down the hill from her girlfriend's house and tries to make herself part of my body again. Yes, a person really can be as white as a sheet. She doesn't speak, barely breathes, and only blends her body to mine, holding Dave tight with her eyes and whimpering.

The fire engines scream down the hill but we don't move. The couch is a safe zone, as long as we stay still and talk only to each other, we will be safe.

We have a long conversation, Dave and I, while Melisa sits, a statue. Often when Dan is mentioned she covers her ears or goes to her room. Today she listens as Dave says his heart is anesthetized.

"I guess I just don't care anymore. Nothing seems to matter. Six weeks ago it was all so important—school, a career. Then I saw how bad my grades had become and I didn't even care."

This is scary talk, still I say, "I know, I feel like that sometimes too. But what do you do? You've planned since you were eight years old to get a degree and teach—you can't just forget it now."

"Why not? Who cares? What if I spend four years in school and

80

then something happens to me? Nobody ever knows what'll happen."

The putrid reek of smoke is still in my nostrils as I try to think of how to answer such an important question. Dave is so conscientious I sometimes tease that he was born old. For him not to care? No! Then from somewhere, the answer comes.

"You know Dave, you're right, and you're wrong. Right that nobody ever knows what might happen, but wrong that nobody cares. I care—I care a lot."

Melisa's muffled voice whispers in, "And I care, Dave."

I give her a little squeeze and continue. "What if you quit school and those years pass and nothing bad happens to you? What if you didn't do what you really wanted so nothing good would have a chance to happen either?"

"But I don't care."

"Well, maybe you have to pretend. Just pretend you do care. There are a lot of kids that will benefit from your life if you don't give up. Honey, you will be an excellent teacher. Grandma says we have to be patient with ourselves. Maybe by September we'll all have more energy."

He is crying now and Melisa, with her head in my lap, is plugging her ears and crying too. The sorrow in this room is beyond description.

July 15

George and I stop at the corner grocery and as we leave I see Dan. He is sitting in the back seat of a car that I don't recognize and it is pulling away from the curb. We make eye contact and I speak his name. George grabs my arm to stop my lunge toward the car.

"Did you see—?"

"It wasn't him Honey. I saw. But it wasn't him"

"Let me go! Where did they go? Aw, god."

The rest of the day is a blank.

July 16

I am angry with George. He is broken out from head to heels and each time he gripes about it I get annoyed. How can he think something so damned stupid is important? He jogs every morning as if he could run away from reality. At night he sleeps as if Muhammad Ali got in a

81

knockout punch. He has always used sleep as an escape. Maybe I'm just jealous.

July 18

I haven't thought of him for the last few days. He seems like a vaguely remembered dream. Was he ever real? Is any of this real?

July 19

I'm scared that sometime I'll be out somewhere and the knowledge will finally hit me and I'll scream and scream forever. I want to hide at home for fear of that happening.

An acquaintance phones and asks, as if she really cares, how I am doing, so I let my guard down. "We're doing okay. One day is not so bad and the next might be pretty awful. We miss him a lot. He could be so sweet and," I chuckle, "he could be such a stinker."

I hear the gasp through the line, "Oh Mary, aren't you afraid that making a remark like that will make you feel guilty? You know," she says in a tone dripping with sincerity, "one shouldn't speak ill of the dead." To me! She says that to me! I change the subject and put down the phone, but my thoughts roll on.

It is my heart speaking when I talk of my kids, so even in exasperation my words are a love song. I will not remember Dan in anything but the truth as I saw it. He will not, if I can help it, become over the years some pure example of heavenly light, although he was some of that. He was also an infuriating teenager. He was human with all the varied topography of a true living person.

I don't want to remake him. I want to remember him. I need to stay to the truth of the real boy, this boy I love.

Chapter Nine

I WANT A MAP, I WANT A GUIDE

"Laugh and the whole world laughs with you,
weep and you weep alone—
for the sad old earth must borrow its mirth,
but has trouble enough of its own."

~ Ella Wheeler Wilcox, "Solitude"

July 20

When I awaken in the morning there is an instant of disorientation. *Where am I?* I wonder. I lay on this bed and the memories seep in—memories of giggly, sleep-warmed little ones insisting that we "Get up! It's Christmas!" Memories of Sunday mornings when we would all read the funnies in the paper. I lie in this room and remember dozens of private heart-to-hearts. "Mom, can we go in your room? I need to talk." This room so full of living, learning, and loving.

It used to be such a special place—now it is no more.

"Give sorrow words.
The grief that does not speak
whispers the o're fraught heart
and bids it break."

~William Shakespeare, Macbeth

July 21

People cared and were so supportive the first two weeks but now they forget him. I guess I understand, but I don't like it. I'm pretty down on the human race right now. What is human is often not humane.

And then there are those two neighbors, Darlene and Joe. Every day they phone or drop in. A minute, five minutes, maybe for half an hour. I haven't decided if they are driving me crazy or keeping me sane. It takes extreme effort to visit when one doesn't know what to say. I love them for not giving in to their own fears. They will never know how much I appreciate the price they are paying to be genuine friends.

Today they showed up at the same time and they talked with each other, putting no pressure on me. They aren't afraid to mention Dan and they laugh at things that come up in our daily lives and bring me light doses of normalcy. The outside world comes in with them and they sluice it gently over me and help me keep my door to reality open. They are saying so softly that life goes on and it isn't as bad a deal as I temporarily think.

I want them to come, but I wish they would stay away. Deep inside I know they are being friends in the finest sense of that word. They stretch their hands out to me in love, though the reaching causes them pain. And we have learned one thing from this experience—the only thing that matters is love—to give and to receive. Love makes all the difference. I read somewhere, "If the end of the world were announced, every phone booth would be stuffed with people trying to call each other to say 'I love you.'"

But the majority of them have faded away like summer dew, or they go to the extreme of the longstanding acquaintance I glimpsed at Safeway yesterday. I came around one end of a long aisle and she rounded the other end, spotted me and fled, cart and all, back the way she had come. Sure makes me feel strange.

And I wonder why we are so often the ones to give the comfort? Why, when it takes such a tremendous amount of concentration and effort simply to breathe, is it up to us to give the hugs, wipe the tears and say time after time, "It's going to be all right. It's okay." But wait, it just came to me—one cannot really hug oneself. In holding out our arms, in giving out hugs, we have to be getting them back. Maybe it only seems to be resting on us—maybe all the time the consolation has been mutual and it is only because we are so far down that we don't realize we are being uplifted, and in comforting we are comforted.

I wish I knew why so many people avoid us, though I plead guilty to doing the same in the past. I was afraid I would intrude. Now there are no knocks on the door. So we are left alone when a presence might be inexpressibly helpful.

If I had the courage to sit across the table from some of you and let my words tell my heart, I would say, "Don't avoid us. We really need you now. We feel cast out of the world as it is. I know you don't want to add to that pain and I promise I don't want to embarrass you any more than I want to embarrass myself, so I'll keep control. But even if my sorrow manifests itself for a moment, even if it pains you for a moment, isn't that all right? Your little hello might lighten a crushingly heavy load."

Still, how could anyone know the right thing to do? I certainly don't. One minute we want company, the next we want to be left alone.

I know this now and I'll share it—it isn't the tears that hurt. The tears heal, for an instant, at least—they relieve some of the agony. What hurts is to be ignored. To have this most significant event in our lives discounted. To be given the feeling that Dan has been forgotten. Do you hesitate to speak for fear you might remind us of our pain? Do you really think we won't remember unless you remind us? Does the person whose right arm is severed at the shoulder and hemorrhaging feel the prick of the needle in the left arm?

And *closure*. I hear the word *closure*, and each time I hear it, I hear the words hidden within—be done with this, shut it off, shut it up, close that door. And my soul rebels.

And, you're right. It might be a really lousy day the day you've gotten your courage to phone or knock. Do it anyway. Just say, "Hi." Just say, "I was thinking about you." Just say, "I don't know what to say." And we can go from there. Maybe up and maybe down, I don't know. But I know I would never forget your effort. Just as I will not forget the evening and the bar-b-que we just had with the Williams'. Melisa and their Suzanne ran around the yard playing while George and Rod cooked and I got in Rosalyn's way in the kitchen. It was such a *normal* visit—a few moments of damp eyes as all of us acknowledged sorrow, and then moved on—as life does. I don't know what it cost them in effort, but the comfort they imbued throughout the evening was priceless to my family.

Chapter Ten

BROKEN HEART STILL BEATING

"Be still, sad heart, and cease repining—behind the clouds is the sun still shining—thy fate is the common fate of all, into each life some rain must fall, some days must be dark and dreary."

~ Henry Wadsworth Longfellow, "The Rainy Day"

July 22

Like a poor, caged chipmunk on a squeaky exercise wheel, my mind picks up a phrase and pursues it, spinning and spinning to exhaustion. Today it's been, *There are no ifs in God's world.* Repeated again and again until I have no memory of where it came from and no understanding of why it is stuck inside me. I get lost in the pattern and forget for a while.

Near the beginning I would pray, *Just let me get through today.* But the plea quickly became, *Let me make it through this next hour, this next minute.* I reasoned if I could make it through the next few moments whole and sane, things would get better. I don't believe that anymore. Now I just take what comes and don't wait for it to get better.

Losing a child, they say, is the ultimate tragedy. And this child was so strong and completely healthy. There is nothing in my experience to compare this to. All the pains I have felt in a lifetime are two grains of sand to this desert. The pulse of the house isn't beating correctly. Our kids drive us crazy. Our kids fill us and our world with warmth and love. It is so empty without him.

Fear and sorrow and loss and even death are not new to us. Very few people in this world can reach our age without having experienced a share of pain. George and I lost our innocence when we almost lost Dave as a tiny two-and-a-half pound premature baby. We've lost jobs, almost lost our house, watched friends divorce, had serious health scares, had to put down precious pets. Each of us has buried a father. I have buried a dear friend. Fear and sorrow and loss and even death are not new to us…and yet…they are two grains of sand to this desert.

And where are all the colors? I live in a sepia-toned world. No, it isn't really shades of beige. The colors are there but they have no light, no life. It's as if nothing I see from my window has depth, spark or dimension. I know the grass and trees are green, the sky is blue, and white clouds cast shadows on the ground, but it's like a bad painting. The shades are muddled and flat as the floor.

In fact, the fresh cut grass doesn't have any fragrance and as I look around, there isn't any discernible texture to anything. All the normal senses have left me. I am bankrupt of life.

I finally deposit the insurance check. Headache is truly excruciating. Pain stabs me senseless each time I think of money in connection with his death. A profit and loss that don't compute.

July 24

Tonight I come out of my numbness for a few minutes and George and I try to talk but this chasm of misunderstanding between us cannot be crossed. I feel rage that life is going on. I want to stand still for a while—he wants to race on. He is grieving hard, but completely to himself. Even I wouldn't be able to guess if I didn't know he must be. I, too, try to stifle myself most of time so I won't upset our friends and the kids.

How much pain can one show before the other children grow resentful and question their value in the family? Can I cry, scream and moan three hours a day, or every other day? How much before they say, "Wait a minute, we are still here. Doesn't our being alive count for anything?" Or am I giving them too little credit for understanding? If I don't cry will they think I don't value him or them?

Would they—could they—understand that no matter how much I love them, I hate almost everything right now? I hate the sun for rising when my son isn't here to see it. I want to scream, but I am normally so controlled, I'd scare my family to pieces if I did.

Aw, but we're already in pieces. I want to curse God for taking my boy away but I'm afraid to. Perhaps that will make Him angry and He'll take someone else from me in retaliation. Crazy thoughts. But I wonder what kind of god there is who stands back while such pain goes on in the world. My mind is consumed with death and I ask the age old questions, but there is nowhere to turn for answers.

Is death pre-ordained, with all our days individually numbered? If you come across someone bleeding to death and you stanch their wounds and save their life, have you interfered with God's will? Or has your lifesaving act been His will? Can two opposing acts both be right?

Are we ever to know the answers? And where is my Dan? And why? And all the multitudes that hate has killed in all the wars in all the centuries, if it isn't God's will, why doesn't He stop it? How He must weep at our inhumanity. Yet, He has only himself to blame, if He made us.

And that's the heaviest question of all, did He? Is He?

George is starting to fear that I am deranged, but I think the whole world is mad. To be so concerned about the mundane things, about tomorrow. What's tomorrow anyway? Thousands of people alive today don't have one. If Dan's life and his death are so easily forgettable, of what importance is anything anyone does? And that brings me once again to the eternal question: Why?

There are no answers and I miss him more each day. It is getting worse, not better. I stand at the mailbox and a neighbor asks, "How are you?" I respond with that horrible four-letter F-word. "Fine," I say. "Fine, thank you." But my mind screeches "How the hell do you *think* I am? How would *you* be?" But I smile and say, "Fine, thanks."

In the mail, we get a card from someone who has just heard. It says Dan was a fine, helpful young man, just what one expects to hear, but then it goes on to say, "…just a couple of weeks back he saw me dragging my garbage cans out to the street—you know the baby is due any day now. Dan pulled over, got out in his white shirt and slacks, told me I shouldn't be carrying stuff, and lifted them for me. I was worried that he would get dirty or be late but he said, "They'll understand.""

I doubt the store understood, but this woman does. She knows all we have left are memories and each new one we can add to our hearts is immeasurably valuable. I can't wait to tell George. I am so grateful.

I visualize a beautiful wooden treasure chest mellow and aglow with rubbing. In it George and I have placed our memories and Dave and Melisa have added theirs. And that's all we have of Danny forever more.

Each explicit event someone shares with us is beyond price. Every memory we can keep and examine is everything.

The quick step of changing emotion gives me vertigo. Hot with anger one instant, warm with gratitude the next. Wanting to shake one neighbor one instant, and hug another the next.

IN PRAISE OF OUR FRIENDS

Our friends felt ineffectual many times. They were not. Sometimes I think we are still alive and open to life because of our friends.

I have heard that some people want to slam the door on the pain and are angered by friends calling or sending notes that remind them of their loss.

We could never forget, so mentioning our son, was for us, a good thing even if we seemed saddened.

Are you at a loss for what to say?

Naturally you would be, how could you NOT be, but just try this, "I don't know what to say or do and I know I cannot fix anything but, I care. And I am here for you. In any way I can be."

THEN

Do be there in any way you can be. Try not to be afraid. Do pick up the phone just to say hi. Do drop a card or a note in the mail. And once in a while do say, "I was thinking about your son or daughter or mom or dad today and wanted you to know I care."

Do this every once in a while for a long time.

The tiny bouquet of For-Get-Me-Nots that was left on my porch a year after our son died cemented a friendship so precious that I consider the woman who placed it there my sister.

And for heaven's sake, if you have a bit of memory of the one who has passed, please share it. Use the name. Please. Every note, card, letter is a priceless link to our loved one. It reminds us that a life, no matter how short, had impact, had meaning. Try to say something personal no matter how small.

It is very scary to face a grieving family or friend. Be brave.

Remember, a true friend is one who comes in when all the others are leaving. You will be blessed for your effort and courage forever and ever.

~Mary M. Fern

July 25

George decided it would be good for me to go back to work at the shop instead of working from home. He decided I should spend some time out of the house and called my boss to suggest she ask me to come in. Unbelievable! I know what I need. I need to talk myself hoarse, to cry without apology, to mourn without constant interruption. How could he be so presumptuous? How could I be so furious? He doesn't know what is in my heart. Particularly when he admits he hasn't been too close to Dan these last couple of years anyway. And that remark rankles, no it bellows, bellows through my being though I understand where his words come from. I know they were bravado to mask pain, yet I cannot erase them—they pick at my brain like a woodpecker at a bug in the bark.

We were walking through the mall a week or so ago trying to look for some shorts and he commented, "It must be harder for you. You were around him daily, you talked with him and ate lunch with him. He was at work by the time I got home and half the time I was in bed by the time he came in. I didn't even know him the past couple of years."

I heard guilt and sorrow behind the words, yet I felt betrayed, as if he was trying to leave all this grief and pain up to me and let himself off because he didn't have daily contact with Dan. I felt angry, and more alone than ever.

We're trying to talk to each other. We're trying so hard. He's apologized. I've apologized. We've promised each other to be kind and gentle and nonjudgmental...again.

A FAMILY ALBUM

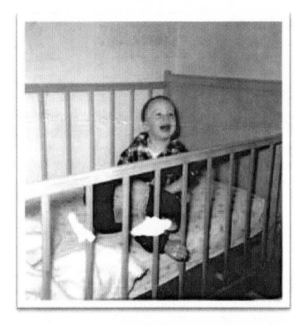

A gleeful Danny at 11 months with his lavender & black monkey

Dave & Dan

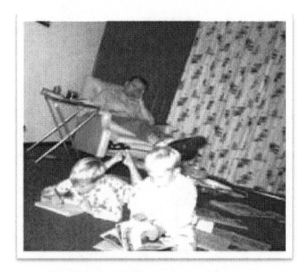

My Boys

Melisa completes our family

Oh Brother!

Dave, George, Dan, Mary, Melisa & Pepé

Dan, Dave, & Melisa, Graduation Day

I have no words...

This is a magic healing moment as Melisa asks her dad for this dance.

Melisa's turn in a cap and gown as life moves on

Melisa 18, Licorice (the best dog ever) is 8, Dave 27

The Asparagus Fern in bloom. Dan is still bringing me flowers.

High above Kauai
With a rainbow, comes joy

"Perfer et obdura—dolor hic tibi proderit olim."

"Be patient and endure—
someday this pain will be useful to you."

~ Latin from Ovid 43 B.C. – 14 A.D.

July 26

I sit at the breakfast bar with the newspaper spread before me reading obituaries. They've never been my choice of reading before this. I'm wracked with sympathy for anyone under thirty as if that is some kind of diversity line between age and youth. And the lower the age, the sadder I am.

Dave comes in from his summer job immediately calling, "Where is everybody?"

"I'm in here, Honey." I call from the kitchen.

"Well where's Melisa? Is Dad home yet? What? What's so

97

funny?"

"Nothing," I say shaking my head. "It's just that Dad asked those same questions when he came home ten minutes ago."

The door bangs open once more. Melisa's run home when she spotted Dave's car. "Where is everybody?" she pipes.

Dave and I raise our eyebrows at each other and shrug ruefully at the family's compulsion to constantly count heads, our paranoia.

July 27

Two months today. Only two months and yet it feels like an eternity. My split mind is at war, one side and then the other, attacking and retreating. *Leave me alone*, I scream silently, and then hear myself wondering why everyone leaves us alone. And, "Why don't you go out and play?" followed by an empty house and, "Oh my god, where is she?" I ask myself the question, "Why has he been gone so long?" Then instantly answer myself, imploring, "Don't answer, don't answer." Split.

The other night I told George I needed to talk and he said, "What about?" as if there were anything else in the world. I said, "I just need to talk and think about Danny." His response? "We've said everything there is to say." And he's absolutely right. But I need more. Yet if he won't talk I can't talk. Thus, I am in a state of suspended animation and he wonders why I withdraw.

George is so silent toward this loss. He won't help me or give me a chance to help him. I don't know what to do. We are very different from one another, but our strength seemed to be in our differences. We complement each other. The attributes I don't have, he has and vice versa. We seemed to grow better in each other's company. Now it seems there is a very real, basic value difference. He seems to be concerned only with the external and transitory, while I only care for the internal and enduring. It's not that he's wrong—it's only that our opinions are so divergent. If he will only vacation in the desert and I only vacation in the rain forest, will we ever get together again? I know he would like me to hurry up and get back to normal living, but nothing will ever be normal again. Normal is three kids. Why can't he understand that?

July 28

It's Saturday. My long apathetic sleep is over. For today anyway, I am seeing things more clearly. Was a two-month anniversary a turning point? Perhaps. Dare I trust?

I sleep through the hours of one until three this morning. Since the fire, I have awakened each night at about 1:20 and have not been able to return to sleep till after 3:00. Actually, it is 1:24 when I wake. I don't know if I have set my mind to that time because at some level I know that is when he died, or if my body has only become accustomed to that schedule. It doesn't matter. I've only had two full night's sleep since May 28. So it is strange to get through that critical period for the first time.

I get up, but don't head for the living room couch as usual. Instead, I curl up on the chair in the bedroom thinking of, oh, a thousand things. I glance over to where George lies sleeping, only illuminated by the faint light leaking through the drape and my heart aches at the sight of him. He is so tired. All the lines on his face are drawn down, far down. They are cut so deeply you would think he had never smiled in his life. His loved face, not very long ago, was well on its way to becoming beautiful, weathering with laugh lines that would show great character in his old age. Now it has changed. His lips are tight, almost mean looking, and turned down even in his sleep, and there is a vertical line between his eyebrows that seems to deepen with each passing day. Oh, it hurts to see. The lines begin to shimmer as I really see him for the first time in a long time and I begin to cry for him.

This morning when I get up I look into the mirror and I clearly see myself for the first time in ages. My eyes—they are a million years old. There is no animation, no life to them at all. It takes a few minutes, as I stared in puzzlement at my own weird reflection, to realize what is wrong. I must have looked at myself dozens of times in the recent past, but I guess I didn't really see myself, and my eyes are so dead.

I give myself a mental shake and smile. My mouth turns up and the skin around my eyes crinkles. My face makes all the prescribed moves. My eyes, the mirrors to my soul, remain dead.

It is so odd to see myself. My hair, that has been slowly getting some gray for a long time, is suddenly heavily woven with white. Also reflected in the early dawn grayness of the bedroom where George still slumbers, is my old husband. We are matching bookends, ancient, etched with cracks and very, very fragile.

July 29

Melisa brought her new puppy home two weeks ago. And outside of pretending for her sake, I haven't really even looked at him. Dogs are a family weakness and this package of furry bouncy blackness certainly is cute, but I haven't let myself like him. I don't want to get attached to anything.

I heard the dog's name for the first time about three days after Dan's memorial service. Melisa was still staying at my mom's house on the lake when our phone rang. I hesitated to answer as we were still getting calls from those who hadn't heard until then, and those calls could be really hard for both the caller and for us. Finally I picked up the receiver and it was Melisa on the line, very excited, saying, "Guess what Mom? I found my Licorice!"

"Your what?"

"My Licorice, Mom. He's black and shiny and he likes me a lot. He picked me out."

I had no idea what she was talking about, but it became clearer as I forced my numb brain to focus. Mom's neighbor breeds Labs and must have a new litter. But we already had a dog. Pepé is old and sick and we must make the decision soon but I was sure I wouldn't want another dog for a long while, and I didn't think George would either.

"We'll talk about it Honey," I said, "Let me speak with Grandma now, okay?"

"Okay, but don't forget. Tell Dad his name is Licorice."

Mom's voice smiled as she said, "We went for a walk and the neighbor invited us to the kennels to see the new puppies. Melisa got to hold one and right away it began licking her shirt. Most likely where she had spilled some ice cream, but she just knows it is because the puppy loved her right away."

"Can you work on discouraging this for us, Mom? We haven't gotten up the nerve to take Pepé in to the vet yet. We don't want to think about a new dog."

"I understand, Honey, but that little girl of yours is already in love."

"We couldn't afford one of those dogs anyway, even if we wanted one. Dang it! What's next?"

"I don't know, Honey. I only know Melisa is smiling today. My neighbor says they will have to give these pups away because the breeding was an accident. Now the mother dog must whelp a couple of litters before they can repaper and sell new puppies."

"Illegitimate puppies? Is that what you're saying?"

"Well, I'm sure they wouldn't put it that way Mary, but yes."

Between that phone call and today, we had found the courage to release Pepé', and Licorice had entered our life.

Today, Melisa gathers her courage and agrees to spend the day at a friend's house so I am puppy sitting. His well-being rests with me and I am seeing him, really seeing him, at last. He is darling, with feet as big as doll's plates and he walks as if he has too many of them. And my smile, though weak, is a smile. Though stripped of my indifference, I am naked and cold without the comforting familiarity of my apathy.

The South American Candiru catfish enters into its prey through
any orifice and eats it from the inside out.
I think this is bitterness and
better not bitter, is the goal.
But, how?
Ah, of course—
acknowledge and accept:
LIFE is not fair.
Whoever said it could or should be?
What's fair anyway?
Always more questions than answers.
Always.

~ Mary M. Fern

July 30

I'm feeling strong today, rested, ready to attempt a test. I'm good at tests. I can do this. I try it in my head. I stumble and stumble, but at last I can say "Danny is gone." I try it out loud, but still in a whisper, and my voice sinks and becomes gravelly, lashed into ribbons of sorrow. "I can get through this sentence. My Danny—My Danny is gone." I haven't been able to say those words. I don't want it to be so. I want it to be different. But it can't be. I've known all along it can't be, but I haven't been able to admit it. My Danny is gone. Oh my D'Mark. Poor baby.

Dave goes out in the evening and returning, automatically leaves the porch light on for Dan. I get up at about 1:20 to check on the kids and I too continue letting the light shine his way home.

Time passes.

July 31

I keep telling myself I have the freedom of choice. I can choose to hold onto my family, I can choose to blaze a trail for us—I can make all of us believe in a future. I hope I'm right. And today's mantra? From *The Little Engine That Could*, "I think I can, I think I can."

August 1

I slept again last night with only two interruptions. What a difference sleep makes. I fall off thinking of him, and each morning I wake with him wrapped tight in my mind. As tightly as I wish he was wrapped in my arms. But the crushing pain is finally easing. There are endless black hours daily, but there are some less black hours too.

Melisa and I play badminton and manage to stick the birdie high up in the giant spruce in the front yard. I go in to get the broom and swing ineffectually at it but it mocks my attempts. Melisa opens the package to get another birdie and says, "We'll have to wait for the wind, won't we Mom? Even Dan couldn't get that one down, could he?"

"No," I chuckle, "I don't think he could."

"He was really tall, huh, Mom?"

"He sure was, darn near twice as tall as you. Once when you were about two he picked you up upside down and held you so you could walk your feet across the ceiling."

"I don't remember that. Was I scared?"

"No. He used to scare you sometimes when he would get angry, but I don't think you were ever afraid in his arms."

"Did he get mad at me a lot?" The question is causal but the guilt behind it is not.

"Not really. Kids get angry at each other just like big people do. But that's okay. Does it seem to you that he was angry a lot?"

"Uh-uh, I guess not. But sometimes I was ornery to him, wasn't I? I used to make noise when he was trying to record his music and he would get mad."

I've heard this one before. It must be weighing very heavily on her. I answer as mildly as possible, "Sometimes you were ornery, sure. Everyone gets frustrated sometimes. He could be pretty ornery himself. So can I. Anyway, I don't think that matters as much as the fact that you loved him and he loved you."

"Yeah, he did." She says. "And me him." She takes a big, missing cut at the new birdie. We keep playing and we keep smiling.

Vacation time is coming! I resist making solid plans. I could easily blame this on my lack of energy, but there's more to it than that. Today I realized it's leaving Dave for two long weeks that is bothering me. That is so scary to me right now. And leaving means getting farther away from the last place I saw Dan, when what I want is to get closer. I want to go backward in time, not forward.

Thinking of time in a block of two weeks puts my mind ahead more than I am capable of doing right now, and puts Danny farther back in my past than I can bear. I don't want to go. But I don't know how I can get out of it. This is one more thing George wouldn't understand. He would consider giving up our trip a selfish indulgence on my part. Maybe it is. And maybe I do still care what he thinks. One has to pick their battles. This is one I will not pick.

August 1

Our ignorance has made us more vulnerable than we might have otherwise been. How did we get so dumb? Even though I know awful things happen, somehow I never really took it in. We all seem to think we are invincible. How many times have I heard someone say, "It can't happen here." Of course it can. Maybe it is one of those things that can't be taught but that one can only learn from experience.

I now feel that I have lived my life behind a curtain that has been thrown wide open. Pets end, days end, storms and rainbows end, bad times end, but so do good times. We have to grasp and hold the brief precious moments, for too soon they will be gone. Just as the start of any journey is the end of another, so too it must be that the end of a journey is the start of another, or as Richard Bach put it so beautifully and life affirming in his book *Illusions*, "What the caterpillar calls the end of the world the Master calls a butterfly."

Butterflies are almost universally loved
as a symbol of beauty and the ability to change.
So fragile, a rain drop can ruin them,
so strong they can beat their way
across hundreds of miles of ocean. Metamorphosis.
Emerging from a cocoon
they must work to unfurl their vivid wings,
allowing blood to flow into tiny veins,
strengthening them for a lift off.
They depend on the sun to dry the dew
on those wings so they can fly.
They depend on the breeze to help waft them
over the waves.
They depend on a certain elevation, a certain temperature,
a certain species of tree for survival.
We, too, can take time to build our strength.
Let the beauty of nature help heal.
Let the love of friends, like a kindly breeze,
waft us over the stormy waves.

~ Mary M. Fern

Darlene comes by for coffee and as I put the cup on the table in front of her I notice I have given her a mug that is much more than the sum of its parts. As I look, I can see spectral red roses and baby's breath so clearly it almost wafts a fragrance. It is a recent Valentine gift from Dan.

I want to snatch it back from her. For a moment tears flood my eyes. Quickly I say, "Sorry."

"Don't be", she smiles. Her touch on my arm says it's okay. She busies herself wiping a nonexistent spot from the table's surface while I gather the pieces of myself back together and inhale, my brain screaming for oxygen.

I don't want to cry. I'm so sick of crying, so tired of hurting. But I am so empty and nothing can absorb the emptiness. I count every card and every flower and every memory to fill the void but it remains, it remains. Like a black hole I pull in every kindness, every glance of sympathy, every gesture that tells me someone remembers, but nothing can fill the emptiness.

As I compose myself, Darlene says, "Can I ask you something that's been bothering me since the memorial? It's kind of strange."

"Sure, go ahead."

"There was a couple there, he was built like a fireplug and she had kind of ash-blonde hair? They almost drove me crazy. All afternoon every time I tried to come over to you they about tackled me. At first I thought they were just rude as hell but I tell you, I could not get near you. I finally gave up and took my family home."

I cup my chin in my hand and as the scene plays in my head I stare at this good friend's bleached, platinum-blonde hair and begin to laugh.

Darlene is completely befuddled at my laughter but one mystery has finally been solved for me as I think, my sister, my sister! And I hear the echo of myself saying to her, "If that blonde shows up, keep her away from me." A simple case of mistaken identity—this was the wrong blonde. But, good job Ellen, good job.

Chapter Eleven

A GLIMMER OF LIGHT

"If you think you can do a thing or you think you can't do a thing, you're right."

~ Henry Ford

August 4

So we go on vacation. At least there aren't any ghosts on this little Bayliner boat. Dan never had a chance to go out with us—our schedules always conflicted. He and Dave learned to water ski behind our old boat and talked of taking it out on their own to impress all those tanned young honeys on the beach.

Early August is a blur. I try so hard to be normal and that means I must not let myself think of reality. I still can't think too deeply of him. I have to skirt his absence and let only the hem brush the memories.

Today as I crowd onto our two by four deck, I look over to the beach where Melisa and Licorice are digging in the coarse sand. I smile and say, "Wow, beautiful day," and give George a good morning kiss. Then I am staggered, ambushed by tears as the guilt crashes down. How dare I enjoy a moment when he isn't here to see, hear, experience it!

August 7

I'm having terrible nightmares! Vague and misty so I can't remember them, but am left with the feeling that demons have shredded my brain with their claws. It is again 1:20 a.m. and my thoughts are ugly. I think I need to leave George. He sleeps, I do not. He wants to forget. I want to remember. I can't get him to express anything. He has locked me out and I am so alone. We are separated by a Grand Canyon of diverse emotions. I love him and he is so special and doesn't deserve to be stuck here with me.

Oh God, I beg you.
Won't you please touch my heart with your hand?
I've cried, I've grieved, I'm desolate—
I've had all the pain I can stand.
Please God, in your mercy, your love and your might
please tell me,
I NEED to know
is he with you? Happy? Free at last?
And why did he have to go?

~ Mary M. Fern

August 8

Webster's dictionary defines "vacation" as freedom, but we are not free. We have a poster on the wall of the boat that depicts a sunset seascape and quotes Emerson, "Though we travel the world over to find the beautiful, we must carry it with us or we will find it not." I guess we didn't carry it this year.

Melisa and her puppy are testing and tasting life. I watch as she and George row the dinghy to the far end of the inlet. Faintly, I hear her giggling voice, "Here Licorice, here boy. Look Dad! Did you see that? Watch dad." I can't make out George's words, just a soft rumble, but Melisa, excited, has yet to learn how well voices carry over water and we have little heart to modulate her.

I peer through the binoculars as the two of them entice the pup into the water for his first swim. I hear the sounds of their blended laughter.

I feel nothing.

Later I hear, "Mom! Mom we're back." And I step onto the swim step to steady the dinghy and retrieve the soaking little retriever.

"You should have seen him, Mom. He can swim. Dad, get out. I want to show Mom how good I can row now." Her exuberance clangs in my ears but I smile as I check the buckles on her life vest. "Dad says I'm really getting good. Push me off, watch, watch!"

I watch. I grin. I pantomime wild applause. I praise her. I hope I'm fooling her.

We get lost when we leave Matia for the marina at Anacortes. Melisa has a stuffed walrus named Fuzzyface who sits on the dashboard and acts as our lookout and navigator and takes the blame for any boating errors. George, steering the boat, is frowning and Melisa asks, "What's wrong, Dad?"

"Well", he says, pointing at the small mass of land off the starboard side, "that should be Decatur, but it sure doesn't look like it."

I pick up Fuzzyface and ask, "Where are we fella?"

"Take the wheel, will you Pumpkin?"

"Okay, Dad."

George is still studying the charts when Melisa says, "It's James Island. We're back at James Island."

"Impossible. James is west and we are heading east."

"But it says so on the sign, Dad."

Sure enough, the sign posted on the dock is easily read with the binoculars.

George looks so puzzled, "You can't be reading it right."

"Dad," she says in her preteen tone that says she is being patient with the idiot, "it says James."

"Well old Fuzzy sure blew it this time, didn't he?"

George and Melisa go into gasps of laughter and I join in with wonder. Have we managed to forget for a while?

August 11

It is so good to see Dave, but not so good to be home. The old place just isn't home anymore. And I have some decisions to make.

Dave let the hot water kettle burn dry. It's ruined. Last year Dan ruined a kettle the same way. Last year I said, "How could you be so careless, you could have burned the house down."

This year I said, "Déjà vu, huh? Don't worry about it. They're on sale at Penny's." And I meant it. Don't sweat the small stuff. Another lesson? I hope so.

August 18

Our friend Bobbie has invited Melisa and me to go with her and Paige school shopping. We chat over iced tea as the girls stroll the mall. Suddenly, Bobbie's face is clouded with pain and her warm brown eyes search mine as she speaks. "I've wanted to tell you how much I admire your family for the way you are holding together through this entire trauma. I've been ashamed of myself for avoiding the issue with you. I can't even bear to think what it would be like to lose one of my kids and I never know what to say to you."

I am so surprised by her words. "Oh no, you of all people don't need to apologize, please. You're one of the very few who still take the trouble to call and include me. It's so hard, most people don't even try."

"But the memorial? You have so many friends. Don't you see any of those people?"

"Only one or two."

"What about the rest of your family? George and Dave and Melisa?"

"It's the same for them. Each of us has a couple of friends who try and stay in contact with us, and you? You are one of them and I just thank you."

We let it rest. It pains others so much to be with us that I try not to allow myself to speak. I make myself go still.

I guess people can't do anything right for us right now. The only thing we want is Dan and nothing anyone does could truly satisfy us. I don't know, but it might help if friends would call more often. Three or four people have called to suggest some sort of outing but have called on a day when I just could not contemplate visiting and declined. I guess that put them off but if they had said, "I'll call again in a couple of weeks to see if you feel more like it," or that they would call again soon, that might have helped, but how could they know? When I have learned of a death in the family of an acquaintance I have often sent a card or made a call, but don't want to be intrusive so I do understand, but from now on, I will give it three calls or three cards before I let myself be counted out.

August 19

It's been three months.

August 20

Tom brings his wedding pictures to the house for us to see. Another young man stood as best man in my Dan's place. Tom tells me a beautiful story—he and his new bride stopped by the cemetery after their reception and placed a flower from her bouquet on Dan's niche.

It is a hard, hard visit. Dan will miss the joy of his own marriage, the beginning of a new life with someone who means the world to him. And we won't touch the future through him.

I manage to get through the visit without expressing any of my feelings of anger and injustice. I have to remind myself constantly, it isn't just or unjust, right or wrong. It is nothing in the eons of things, yet it is everything. And bad things just happen.

Right now, the only thing that holds me on Earth is knowing all the people who love me would suffer if I weren't here, and I couldn't do that to those I love so much. Likely, they would suffer even more because I wouldn't be here to try to blunt some of the wretchedness. More confusion, more angst.

August 21

I love words. I am now shocked at how sadly inadequate is our language. We use the words *heartbroken*, *empty*, *grieved*, but they are only words until one lives them. Living them is the difference between a medical textbook description of a fractured leg, and actually feeling the fracture happen. Between seeing a film on childbirth or laboring to bring a child into this world. Between hearing the statistic that one in eight women will get breast cancer and having that breast be yours.

August 22

I can't stop smiling.

Through the night, I can't sleep and at four, I finally give up trying and go to the kitchen to make some coffee. Suddenly, I get that odd feeling that I am being watched. I turn to face the sliding glass door, and staring back at me through bandit eyes is a raccoon. A big guy, about two-and-a-half feet tall, well, two feet anyway.

Our neighborhood is so long established that a squirrel is considered big game around here. But this raccoon and I sit and appraise each other until darkness fades and he ghosts away in the gray dawn.

At breakfast I tell my skeptical family, and George gets the oddest expression on his face. "Strange that he would come around here where he could smell the dog." He pauses, and then goes on, "Do you remember when Dan took that awful fall when he was a little guy and blacked both his eyes? The bruises lasted and lasted and people looked at us if we were some kind of monsters. Remember what we called him? Our raccoon baby. I wonder where that animal came from," he mutters as he turns away.

August 26

That goofy raccoon has become a nightly visitor and all of us are getting up at dawn to see him. He plays hide and seek around the edge of the patio and we laugh. Even the dog doesn't mind him. They accept each other completely, though the pup is only three months old and doesn't accept so much as a strange leaf in his yard.

This creature is so pleasing to me. I'm the original city girl, but I can reach out and stroke the wild thing's fur. Why don't I have any fear?

August 28

It's been ninety days, is that short or long? I don't know—but I think I've made a quantum leap forward. At least for today, at least for this moment, the bleeding has slowed.

Like a whirling dervish, I clean the house and rid it of accumulated clutter. George and Melisa want to hang onto things I say they don't really need.

George got annoyed at me recently and told the kids "Hide it if you want to save it guys. Mom's on a mission." The kids started to laugh and we had to join in. It felt good. Still, I do want to simplify, to throw out everything that isn't pertinent to love and understanding.

August 30

It is the end of August. George takes Melisa to work with him and gives me a full day without interruptions. I hope to use it to put into some sort of perspective this ugly lost summer. To see if I can find the new heading we can take as we start gathering the bits of our shattered lives. The pieces of a family minus one-fifth of its circle.

The quiet is wonderful—I've been able to think. I can't even express how I miss him but I can see now that we will be able to go on. I am at the very bottom of the sea but I've ceased struggling and that in itself is restful. Suicide never really was an option for me, just a wish to stop the pain. I want to see Melisa grow. I want to be there when Dave finishes college. I want to see George smile and mean it. I want those things.

One thing that was holding me back was the lack of opportunity to really feel the loss. I have been very strong for everyone's benefit and have not often allowed myself to break down. I have relearned this about myself now—I am one of those who must escape to a cave in solitude to lick my wounds. That is how I respond when I have some illness. I need solitude to ponder when any big issue enters my life. Then I must write to make sense of it. Of course that's how I would react to this. And now I can understand how George needs to fill every second so he could avoid thinking until he could put some space and time between himself and this tragedy.

My grandmother, a feisty, strong backboned British woman, was a major influence in my life and I loved and admired her. Brave and liberated long before the fashion, Gram was a great believer that everyone has a *cross to bear*, and the airing of troubles only put an unfair burden on the listener. So it's tough for me to cry much in front of anyone. We sure do carry those early formative years with us as we grow.

I thought I might cry today while I was alone. I try but I can't seem to cry on cue. I can easily accept others emotions, but somehow I don't give myself the same respect.

I keep hearing that this is the most terrible thing that can happen to a parent and that sure feels true. I'm so sorry for everything he will miss. I'm sorry for his father and for his brother and sister who will miss him for the rest of their lives, for the world that will never know him, for the deeds that might have been accomplished, the songs that he might have written. And I'm sorry for Danny, this kid of mine who didn't want to skip any experience, yet will forgo most.

Reading is a passion for me and yet this summer it takes the strongest concentration to read even a line. A great book is water and I a sponge. When I am near the end of such an absorbing book I will often put it down and make myself leave it unfinished for a while because I hate it to end. When I finally do read the last page I close the book and savor what was written. A phrase or word picture will come back to me helping me to see more clearly the world around me. I really feel the need to understand. Closing the book on Danny's life seems to be like that—only indescribably more so. I didn't want it to end. I could not close the book. Now maybe I can, but I need to lean back and savor what was. I was barely seventeen when he became part of the core of my existence—it's unrealistic to think I can put him out of my mind.

I am spending much time in introspection. Life has seemed so senseless that I have been trying to sort out what has genuine value from that which we only imagine does. I need to find something good and strong in this world that has so much hell. Are we here for a purpose? Is it to love, to learn, to help one another, to have fun, to enjoy? Do we have a task required of us and once it's completed, does our life here come to an end? Is there a place after this of peace and beauty? A place without wars and displaced persons, without starvation, ghettos, earthquakes and murders, a place where none ask, "What's in it for me?", a place where it would be unthinkable to destroy the Amazon basin, where it would be unthinkable for a child to starve or an old man to sleep on the street. A heaven I guess? Is there?

I read a comparison once of birth and death that questioned whether a baby faces birth in the same way that we face death, with fear at being thrust from the only world it knows. Is the child's crying at being born the same as our tears when someone dies? Yet, at birth there are usually parents with arms open joyously awaiting their little one. Is there a power, a god, lovingly waiting for his child to come back to him?

It's tough to know what to hope for or believe in—so I am just going to continue to believe in love, though we sometimes must pay a high price. We have love here in this house. We still have that, and I believe our family will survive.

Chapter Twelve

WE WILL SURVIVE

*"I like living. I have sometimes been wildly, despairingly, acutely
miserable, racked with sorrow. But through it all I still know quite
certainly that just to be alive is a grand thing."*

~ Agatha Christie

September 1

Back to school time for Melisa. Dave starts back in two weeks. And it is time for me to get back to living. I want to go to the cemetery—it is such a short walk from here. When we first got married and moved into this house, I was scared of the graveyard. One night I got up to go to the bathroom and from the window I could see ground fog that my imagination formed into ghosts. I stubbed my toe running back to bed. I was so young and so steeped in Hollywood's mummies and goblins.

But as a mommy, I learned the joys of that beautiful, peaceful spot. We've spent pleasant hours there watching the seasons through their cycle. Mallards stop to rest at the pool and the stream brings fairy music to my ears. The kids and I picnicked there. We would sit under a big willow and eat and read. It has the only paved lanes around, where better to push a stroller, or to be taught to ride a tricycle, or bike, or practice driving for the first time? Over the years it has become an idyllic oasis in the midst of our bustling life, but I can't go there now. I've only been twice. Each time I hyperventilate and can't bear to stay.

We bought a space in a columbarium there for ourselves, and now his remains rest there. We made the purchase because we figured if anything happened to us it would be one worry off the kids' minds when they would have too many hard decisions to make. Then like a top, life spun us around.

September 6

Our 21st anniversary and I forgot all about it until I dated this page.

I was working downstairs this afternoon when a friend of George's stopped by to ask for a favor. George came down and said, "Denny's here and I'm going to go with him for a few minutes."

I didn't hear Denny—I heard Danny. Danny's here. I bolted to my feet exploding, "That kid! How could he stay away so long?"

George rushed to my side as I melted, my bones turning to liquid, to the floor.

Not seeing him has made it harder. George and I still don't believe he's gone. We tell ourselves a thousand times a day, but we don't believe it.

September 18

Oh those clichés. We look at sayings such as, *Time heals all wounds*, disparagingly. But why are they any more stale than *I love you*? Most of our expressions come from folk wisdom, rooted in cultural history and used to ease the Spirit. A shopworn, old saw is better than nothing, isn't it? It would be nice to be Browning or Teasdale with their passion for words, using them in ways that are balm to the soul. But we are not those glorious poets, so we search our minds and memories and offer what we find—platitudes. But, washed in the blood of new sorrow and coming from the heart, they are a straw to cling to and as I begin to gather and bind those straws together, they are starting to support me.

"O Memory, thou bitter sweet, both a joy and a scourge!"
~ Mme.de Stael, French Novelist

September 20

As a couple we have lost touch with each other but we are still reaching out, still trying. Maybe we are improving. We have tried to be ever so gentle with each other at all moments of the day and night, but there are cracks, deep ones, in the foundation of our marriage created by the violence of the earthquake that has rocked us. The upheaval found every old flaw and opened new ones. We see it happening to us and it is so frightening. We've invested too much for too long to stand by while our love bleeds to death.

Two days ago I approached George with the idea of us taking some time off from work and going out on the boat alone. No phones, or pagers, no obligations. He agreed with an eagerness that surprised me. Yesterday he walked in and said "it's all set." Now it's my turn to ask my boss for time off during this incredibly busy season for us. Neither of us ever wants to impose on our fellow workers but my co-workers were enthusiastic in their desire to *be there for us*.

Then I asked two of my newer and fast becoming irreplaceable friends, Bobbie and Rosalyn, if they would be willing to pick up Melisa and take her to their homes till Dave got off work each day. Both burst out, "Yes!" before I could even finish the request. I guess they had been waiting for the chance to do a favor. I am humbled by their kindness and lifted by their love. Dave was amenable and Melisa excited to prove how responsible she could be. It is scary to leave them but it is the most necessary thing I think we have ever done for ourselves. We must find out if we still have *ourselves*.

So George, Licorice, and I are back on the boat in relatively stress-free solitude.

It seems to me one problem has been that our society won't allow a show of human emotion unless it is anger or laughter. So all day, every day, we bottle up all our grief and pain. When we come home we either let out the anger or dissolve like molded Jell-O salad left too long in the sun. Either way, we give the best of ourselves to others which leaves us with only the worst for each other.

We have gotten to be such fine actors but hate the masks we are wearing. Honesty is such an important value of our marriage but now my best friend won't talk to me and won't let me talk to him and we are rudderless when we ignore or refuse to explore our feelings together.

We discuss it and come to an understanding—we will be together or go off on our own as we choose. If we want to talk we will, and if we don't, we won't—and we need not explain. We will bend to whatever breeze blows. The only supreme effort we are going to ask of one another is if one of us desires to talk, the other will try their hardest to simply listen.

One early morning while mist still rises from the surface of the water, we are on the deck, coffee in hand. I decide to ask him how he gets through his day.

"I can't imagine," I begin, "how you go off day after day to a job that has suddenly become meaningless? How do you match a tie to your shirt when it doesn't seem to matter anymore? Or write orders when…oh, you know what I mean."

He is quiet for a long time, and then he says with a hard shake of his head, "I don't know. I'm almost frantic when I'm away from you guys. I hate to leave in the morning because everything I care about is in that house. Then sometimes I hate to come home. It is so empty now. I hate the hollowness."

I fight tears at his tone.

I've tried to imagine his drive home from the plant after his boss gave him the news that our son had died. The plant is less than a mile from home. Was it the longest mile ever driven or the shortest? "When you did make it home at least we were together," I say, "but for that awful mile you carried this burden alone. I'm so sorry."

We talk and talk and begin to cry together. We don't have to pretend for each other anymore. We are so tired of pretending.

September 25

We take a long walk on the beach, empty but for the gulls and little sand crabs. We are so sad. We sit on a log and watch as the waves sweep in and out on their eternal journey. We weep. We weep and we talk. George says our house will be as forlorn as the gulls cry until Dave and Melisa leave home, too. "It is so empty now. His being gone is so huge. Maybe when they are all out of the house it will feel as if they are all grown up and life is normal. Maybe then it will be okay."

"I know what you mean and I've wondered the same thing. If we could lock it up and walk away, I sure would."

He looks so confused and lost. We both feel there must have been something we could have, should have done to protect our child.

We touch hands and I hope we will still be together, hope we will still want to be together when this time of sadness passes. And someday it will. I know.

September 26

I write long letters to the kids. My note to Melisa is full of what the islands are like when they are empty of people:

Oh Little Bear,

The islands are much prettier when they are quiet like this. The moon glade is a fistful of shiny coins tossed like confetti by a mischievous hand. In the early morning it is so silent you can almost hear the sun rise. The birds and deer, raccoons and seals are much less skittish now that the trails and bays belong to them again, and the deer are coming right down to the shore. And your puppy, well, Licorice shivers when he sees them, but is getting used to it and doesn't bark.

I don't dwell on Dan in my letter. Let her have fun this week. I mention that the quietness is doing Dad and me good, and we hope to be less sad when we come home.

I just wanted you to know, our precious girl that we are so proud of the way you are growing up. We love you my Angel Geese.

I know she'll smile when she reads that goofy word, as I smile now writing it. I use to sing her a made-up song about her being a little angel girl who slid down on a moonbeam to bring joy into our lives, and one day I heard her singing it and she was saying in a two-year-old voice, "I'm a wittle angel geese slide down on a moonbeam."

My letter to Dave is entirely different. Those boys lived in each other's pockets for nineteen years. They were babies and little boys and adolescents and teenagers together. Now they will be together no more. My god, what do I say? Should I even try to put into words this terrible trial? I think of how much my brothers have come to love and support each other over the years. They've turned into such good friends as they left youth behind. Dave will not have that. My head splits and I have to put this down for now.

I want to rekindle his extraordinary courage. He's having a lot of trouble settling down to school and school has always been important to him. It would be a terrible loss if he quit and I can't believe he would, but he did so poorly in his finals last semester. He went from solid A's to B's to D's on his finals. I told him to make an appointment with his professors to *explain about Dan*, and he did. It took so much courage for him to speak up back there in June when we couldn't say Dan's name without tears. Dave was so deep in grief but somehow he choked the words out. But for all his anguish, his instructors showed little inclination

118

toward compassion or taking his proven record into account. One professor in particular sickened me. He said, "I know just how you feel. When I was away at college, years ago, my father died. But, if I let something like your grief influence my grading where would it stop?" I listen to what Dave is saying—I look at our heartbroken son and have nothing to offer but my arms.

Dear Dave,

I hope school is settling down for you. It would be hard to discipline your mind to books. Summer was so unhappy. I know I can barely concentrate. Even light reading is hard to comprehend. And retention? Laughable.

I wanted to thank you for your help in letting us have this time away. It is peaceful here. Now as your dad walks Licorice, I sit and listen to the waves slap the boat and begin to feel somewhat...better, I guess. You're making it possible by keeping an eye on your little sis. Dad and I have done a lot of laughing and crying, talking and remembering. We've brought some of our guilty feelings into the open so we can start to deal with them. Just giving them voice is amazingly helpful.

I've been so furious with myself that I insisted Dan move. None of you pointed the finger of blame at me—still, I've been tormented. Now I am far enough away in space and time to examine my feelings. I wonder daily if things had been different and he had stayed at home, would he still be alive? The only perfect vision is hindsight they say, but I have had much time to think in the last couple of days and I am getting some perspective. I want to share with you what I am discovering as I know you are fighting some of the same demons and we've always respected each other's thoughts.

So here goes...

The things Dan did that we, as parents, found intolerable are so minor now that he is gone. If he were still here, and we were still trying to make a home for all of us, his transgressions would still have to be addressed. We couldn't let him continue to flaunt family rules, to come and go as he pleased, when he pleased. He was not being fair to you or Melisa. Yet those things are inconsequential now. If we had known he was to die at twenty, we might have lightened up. But we were trying to instill a sense of responsibility and maturity into someone we loved. We thought we had every right to assume he would live a long and full life. I thought tough love was needed. But now I know that wasn't tough love—this is.

When my brain replays my words now, "Dan if you can't behave like part of the family then it's time for you to move. We can't take it anymore," I am crushed by guilt.

Still, there is some peace in knowing how hard we all tried. You've heard the saying, "You did the best you could with what you had at the time." Well, we have to engrave that on our hearts if we are to go on. We are human. I guess we can't escape some regrets. We are supposed to be striving to be perfect, not perfect yet. We get angry, at times, really angry, but that makes us normal, human. Not saints. There are billions of people who don't drive us crazy because they've never touched us enough to make us care. It doesn't matter to us if they are mean-spirited or wonderful—it is only the ones who touch us and mean a lot to us, who can make us very angry or guilty.

Ah, Dave, I've been concerned about you. I know you have been feeling some guilt, too. I want to point out what is so self-evident to Dad and me that you seem to find obscured right now.

Dan loved you. Always.

You know if he could, he would forgive you for anything you said or did to him that you perceive to have been wrong, just as you would forgive him. He was so proud of all of us. I've been told of how he bragged of our accomplishments. He was so thrilled when you decided to go on with your schooling. Higher education just wasn't for him but he was so proud of your decision.

And though he knew you hated some of his choices, he never doubted you loved him. He knew it. Honey, I know about the times you loaned him money, the times you tried to cover for him when he would come in late. You were good to him and he knew you cared. Giving advice is easy, but Honey, we have to take this advice. We have to think about the good times we had together, the times you helped one another. The times you spent pushing him up the hill in that heavy old race car and when I'd holler from the porch to take turns you would reply, "It's good for me to build my muscles," and Dan would steer and grin. And about the countless hours you practiced baseball and basketball together, forcing each other to improve. I'll never look out at the hoop again without seeing Melisa on Dan's shoulders, him acting as stilts for her as you and she played one-on-one basketball. How delighted she was with both of you. Remember him taking the day off without pay because they wouldn't give him time off to attend your graduation? And the horror shows we used to watch and the time we got so scared we ended up piled together on the armchair laughing like fools? One of the happiest times for me was five or six years ago when you guys were trying to teach me the crazy dance steps of the NOW generation and in exchange I was giving you lessons in how to hold a girl when you slow dance. We have a lot of good memories, don't we? And those are the ones we have to keep.

I don't know why it is that our brains keep feeding us over and over all the things we think we did wrong and seem to hide all the fun and good times we shared. All the good things we did for him. I don't know. I just know it's important to retrieve that good stuff because if we can't find the balance we may tip over and not be able to get back up.

And how have we been treating you throughout this whole tragedy? Have we given you the impression that we don't care where you go, what you do? When I told you we didn't care if you went to the memorial we simply meant don't concern yourself with what anyone else thinks is proper. I know that was a strange message to convey but we felt if it was less painful to skip the service we would understand. And when night after night we've said, sure go out, have a good time—it was only because we are feeling such a sense of urgency about time. We weren't saying we didn't care, but time seems so short and precious we wanted you to do what you wanted to do. We are not insensitive to you—our motivation is 180 degrees the other way. Our hearts were saying, "Let him be with his friends if that is best for him." But I have to tell you it wasn't always easy to watch you walk out the door.

In such an unbelievable nightmare with no knowledge of how to help each other, some things were destined to go wrong. I only hope we didn't do anything to cause you more heartache than you already had. We are such a reserved family, keeping as treasures our deepest thoughts. It's been a high honor that I have treasured over the years that you or Dan would often come to me and bare your hearts. Please, my Davey, please continue to do that. We can

121

speak of how painful all this is and we can speak of other things too. Hey, how about those Seahawks?

Our reserve must be a legacy either from your British great grandparents or a throwback to the stoicism of Dad's Danish heritage. The cooler northern countries have put their stamp on us. We come mostly from indemonstrable stock. No Italian or Spanish temperament here, eh? And we temper our wild Irish. We definitely lack melodrama, for better or worse. But let's keep on hugging, okay?

I am having a difficult time overcoming my reticence. I've had it proven to me many times that, "A joy shared is doubled and troubles shared are halved." We need to voice this tragedy. But it is tough to change a lifetime habit of privacy. Only when I am writing can I be this open, even with you, your love for me and your listening to me make me feel much honored.

You are so like your dad in many ways and you know how much I love your dad. You're gentle with your humor, wonderfully bright, introspective. And sometimes, like Dad, you stun me with your perception. Oh, thinking about how perceptive you can be...if you have been scared about Dad and me, you can let that fear go. We loved each other yesterday and still do today and somehow we will keep on loving each other tomorrow.

We're so proud of the man you are becoming. You know, it's really funny Dave, no one prepared me for the most exquisite experience of parenthood—I knew always that I wanted children, I knew I would love them and nurture them with all I had in me, but I did not know that when I looked across the table at a child I had birthed and watched grow and loved so deeply, I would see a person like you, a person I would be proud to choose for a friend.

I love you my friend.

Love,

Me

Absent in body, but present in Spirit.

(I Corinthians V. 3)

"How many kids do you have?"

"Ah," I clear my throat, "ah, excuse me…um, we have two kids. Our, ah, third child died recently."

Horrible. I feel so awkward and they feel terrible and everybody stutters. It's dreadful. Yes, dreadful, and it happens all the time.

It just happened again. I'm chatting with a woman on the dock and she asks so innocently and I'm stuck and in my mind I ask how many kids *does* it take to make my family?

For most of our years, we've had three kids, and then, in the space of a blink, it all changed. Now there are two here, alive, but the answer is still three. In my heart there will always be three. This is the only answer I can ever be comfortable with. I have three children. If the conversation leans that way I will mention that we lost our eldest son and have two still at home. If I can answer that question without pause or tears I probably won't have to elaborate and the moment will pass.

Funny how one can have such a huge fall from such a little stumble. Saying two seems a denial of him. I won't do that anymore.

Well, look at that, I have made a decision. A firm decision.

One of our children is a little farther away than the others, that's all. From now on I will state this distinctly, and if that causes discomfort, so be it.

September 28

Heading home. The boat sways on the trailer behind us. We're a little rested, a little sunburned and we drive along holding hands.

Home. It is so good to see the kids. But home doesn't have the same feeling that it used to. It doesn't surround and draw me into the warmth of familiarity as it should. There is a different sense of strangeness. It's like looking into a dusty mirror at the reflection of each room rather than at the room itself. I have read that many people who lose a child find they must sell their house because they can't stand the pain of each room without that special presence, each stair without the beloved step. I find that easy to understand in these rooms that are too full and too empty.

The divorce statistics for bereaved families are also astronomical and I can understand that, too, but I don't think they will include us. This last week we connected again. We can talk, we can share. And both of us want to remain together. George healed us a lot when he opened his heart to me and said, "I'm going to try to be strong and gentle. I've thought about what you said about the difference between tough and strong. Tough is on the outside and strong is on the inside, is that what you said? Tell me again what you mean."

"It's just what I think. For example, a bully can scare us because he seems so tough and intimidating, right? But I think a bully is really just a person who is scared inside. Always ready to pick on a weaker person. Always ready to knock you down because they are so afraid that if they don't hit you first, you'll hurt them first. What an awful way to go through life. But a strong person doesn't need to prove anything to anyone. They are secure within themselves so they can be gentle as they walk through the world. Think of my mom. The most gentle person you will ever meet, but oh, so strong. She's been tested and tested by life— she knows what her character can withstand so she can go through life just being kind. But you'd be a fool to imagine her kindness is weakness. There's an old expression about steel being forged in the fire, made stronger by the flames. I'll look it up when we get home."

"Back to the books, huh? A good sign?" he laughs, then goes on. "I'm going to try to do better from now on. I'll even try to listen, but it pains me so much to see you cry. I'm not used to it, you never cried, and I feel like I have to do something to fix it. But there's nothing I can do. Nothing. I can fix anything. I can't fix this."

And with his words, of course I cried again, but this time I explained, "The tears make me feel better, but just knowing you'll listen to me already makes me better. I wish I could fix this, too. If you think it's been easy to see your pain or if you think I can't see it, you're wrong. This can't be fixed, Honey. It can only be lived through. If we're real lucky."

Melisa seems to have grown inches in the week we were gone and is getting long and gangly. It feels like Heaven when she wraps her arms around me and gives me a kiss before she turns her attention to the dog. Holding Dave is a joy. For better or for worse, we are here. Do I feel hopeful? No, that's too pretty a word. Determined? That requires too much energy. So what is it I feel? Able, I feel able. Don't know what's coming, don't know where we're going, I just know…I will be able.

October 1

I wake this morning not instantly thinking of him. It is the first time he isn't first on my mind. Time and space must at last be taking their toll. Is this the true beginning of healing or just another "stage?" He is still an all-day accompaniment and my last thought as I fall asleep each night.

October 2

I just remembered! A recording of Melisa's last slumber party. Maybe his voice is on it.

October 4

Still haven't looked for the tape. Still avoiding disappointment if he isn't on it, or anguish if he is.

Melisa likes her teacher this year, though her grades are down a bit. She has been through so much and is still so fragile I don't have the heart to be too critical. I expect she will improve before too long. Dave says his concentration is still bad—I'm sure that is her problem, too.

October 5

It has been four months. Today I notice it is a pretty day. I work hard and it feels good. I've been doing what's necessary but haven't cared about the results. Now I notice I actually take some pleasure waxing the fine grain of my favorite table.

Each day I take a long walk just to get out of the house. Then in the afternoon when Melisa gets home, she and I take Licorice and walk the neighborhood. Over the summer, I almost let myself drift away like a released helium balloon, getting smaller and smaller as it rises, and I don't want that to happen. Our Melisa is such a neat kid and so special to me. I love her confidences and silly jokes and I love how she can make her daddy laugh.

October 6

I intend to straighten the few mementos we have left from the fire.

125

It seems to be the right time, but I find I can't do it yet. It still hurts too badly. Sorting and putting away his things is one more finality when the thing most abhorrent is finality.

What is the time table supposed to be in all this anyway? When is it ever going to be *better?* Why is it in our society that it is more virtuous to have an unruffled exterior, even if it is dishonest, than it is to be emotional? To get angry, but not sad. To laugh, but not cry. I know I've said this before, but I just keep trying to understand.

October 8

George is a salesman and part of his day is often taken up with business/social meetings. Tonight, he comes home looking bruised. "Did you have a tough day, Honey?" I ask.

He nods. "I had to go to lunch with a couple of guys and after we ordered they started talking about their families just to get acquainted and pass the time." He let out his breath with a sigh that would have sounded theatrical if it wasn't so darn sincere. "I just hate it when that happens. I wait for them to turn to me and say–"

"I know," I say. "They ask how many kids do you have?"

"You run into it too?"

"Not as often as you. But yes. And it's hard, I know."

"What do you say? How do you handle it?"

So I tell him what I discovered while we were in the islands. We do have three kids and that's the way it is. I guess we shouldn't be surprised that our feelings are alike on this hard issue.

October 9

A deep, beloved voice rumbles beneath high-pitched little girls' giggles. He was there, as I had remembered, helping organize the party. So few words. Damn! I am so mad at myself. Why didn't I record more?

October 10

We had plans for the evening and so did Dave, but he wasn't happy that we had a sitter for Melisa who he did not know. He has become even less trusting and we get the third degree about how well we know this young lady.

I convince him she is trustworthy.

She doesn't know us too well, so I warn her that Dave might be home before us. I don't want her to be frightened when he lets himself in with his key. She responds, "Oh is he the tall one? I saw him at school. He's so cute!"

I manage to hang onto the threads of my composure as I answer, "No. No. The really tall one was Dan. Dave is not so tall but he's just as cute." Then I read her stricken face as she remembers, and I smile that all is well and head for the kitchen to point out the evenings treats.

How many ambushes can there be?

If you are trying to read and the words
make no sense,
if you find yourself staring at a page
for long moments and it just doesn't compute,
let me suggest you try children's books for a while.
It sometimes helps to tip toe
slowly into mental exercises when your head
is so overwhelmed with sorrow that your brain
seems to have left you. There are some very good
books on grief for children. They are filled with the kind of
information an adult can actually absorb when they
cannot manage to understand anything else.
Children's books usually display challenges
and how they are overcome. They remind us that every
age of life has problems to solve, life skills to learn.
You and I have already learned many skills.
Maybe this one is greater, maybe the hardest ever,
but just one more.
Remember, The Little Engine That Could?
"I think I can, I think I can."
I know I can. I know I can.
~ Mary M. Fern

Chapter Thirteen

THE KALEIDOSCOPE OF LIFE

"'Tis better to have loved and lost,
than never to have loved at all."

~ Lord Alfred Tennyson-"In Memoriam"

Is it better?

Perhaps I'm beginning to believe it. I need to find some way to go on only it's so hard to want to when he can't. No sane parent would tell their child, "You wait back there. I'm going on without you. I'm going to walk away and live the rest of my life without you." But that's what it seems I have to do.

A cross section of my brain would be layered like the walls of the Grand Canyon. Only the top most level no longer seems to hold much pain. That feels hopeful to me.

Here's a simple example: Dave tells me he is planning a ski trip with some of his friends later this year. My reaction starts something like this, first a lightning strike of fear at his leaving, all the attendant fears like driving conditions and avalanches, then the thought I actually express, "Good for you, I'm sure you'll have a good time." This is followed by a twinge of sorrow as I think, *Too bad Dan isn't here to go.*

So far I'm okay, but the next thought unsheathes the knife as I remember how much he loved skiing. Then, going deeper I enter that splitting place where my brain separates with the stress. After Dan's last ski trip he came home illuminated. He could hardly wait till the house got quiet so I could really listen to what he wanted to tell me. He was rapturous as he talked about being close to paradise when he stood on top of Seventh Heaven, his favorite run at Steven's Pass. I think of his joyful face, his excited hug and his words, "Oh, Mom, you have to go with me. I have to show it to you. Maybe we could hike up there some day. It's awesome. Remember how you felt that night at the ocean when the moon was so beautiful? Well, this is my ocean." If my mind pauses there, in that moment when he shared his elation at finally being skilled enough to make that scary ski run, to reach that dream, I ache with bleakness. My thoughts blind and blur, lost in a snowstorm of emotions swirling, and my frozen heart feels as if it is chipping away. I guess I should be happy that he got to do it once, but all I can think about is that he will never get to do it again.

I think of the future without him and that future becomes unbearable. If I continue to spiral into the depths and imagine all he is missing, it is crushing. He appreciated this world and was so eager for it. The sun and snow and excitement, family and flowers and pretty girls in snug jeans, ambitions and dreams and desires. If only, if only.

October 14

Melisa and I make cookies. When it is time to stir in the chocolate and nuts, I mentally turn to Dan whose strong arm did this step of the recipe so many times in return for licking the bowl. Don't focus on the death they say—celebrate that he lived they say—but who do they think will stir the chips into the dough?

October 16

Today I ducked around a corner in the grocery store to avoid talking to someone. It's my turn to play that silly game. Today I wasn't up to the effort of chatting. It isn't pleasant to know you are the catalyst for someone's distress.

October 17

We go shopping for ski clothes for Melisa. She is so excited. This is she and George's second year for the slopes and they are looking forward to their time together in the snow. In the parking lot I will myself to smile and tell myself, *You can do this Mary. There will be no hyperventilating.*

We're surrounded by bright colors and shoppers' happiness and I hold my emotions by a string while they bounce above my head like a kite in a high wind. This is Danny's spot in the world and I can't stand that he's not here.

Suddenly, I know I'm going to be sick. I make some excuse and catch George's angry expression as I dash from the store. Melisa's words follow me out, "Don't you want to watch me put on the red ones, Mom?" But I can't. I just can't. At the car, I open the door to use it as a cloak, and lean over and vomit.

129

October 18

The tension in our bedroom last night was strong and sharp. George joins me in lying awake. It's unheard of for him to be sleepless. He often escapes problems by sleeping. It's driven me to distraction for years as we learned to adjust to each other over time. But last night he was upset and wide awake. He tossed with his irritation until early this morning when in a raspy voice he says, "You know it really was unfair of you to leave me to pick out Melisa's clothes. Didn't you hear her call you to stay?"

"Yes. I heard her but I couldn't stay. I really couldn't."

"It was just as tough for me to be in that ski shop you know. The memories are as strong there for me as they are for you, but I faced it."

I want to scream, *Face it? You faced it?* Instead, somehow I speak softly, "I don't think you do face it. I think that's why you're mad. You were forced to stop denying it when I left you alone yesterday."

"That's not true and it's off the subject. It wasn't fair for you to leave us."

The guilt he heaps, hurts. I have to bite my lip to restrain myself but somehow I do. Somehow I know that this could easily be the beginning of a blame game that would destroy us. Somehow I find the strength and sense not to fight back, only to say, "No it wasn't fair. I'm sorry."

Somehow I refrain from mentioning the daily aloneness I face in this house while he fills his time out in the world. The meals I cook where I have to throw out the extra portion. The bedroom I have to walk by every day. The plants I water that were his. The mail that still comes for him. The questions I must answer for the kids. The courage and encouragement I must somehow find so I can fill my family. The millions of memories that stab me every minute of every day. And I keep my mouth shut for once, only opening it long enough to say I am truly sorry. At last exhausted, he falls to sleep while I, sleepless, remain sorry. Sorry for everyone and everything everywhere.

October 20

Some women are attracted to muscular chests, chiseled features, or derrieres. I love eyes and hands. Clear, kind, intelligent eyes and the story to be read in hands. I was thinking about his hands today, thinking of all they had done and all they won't ever do again. His beautiful, long-fingered hands. They will never again grasp a tool or form a fist in righteous anger. Never slide in awe and joy over his wife's body or reach to let his baby grasp a finger. They will never applaud at another basketball game or grip a steering wheel or gracefully flip one of his treasured records. Those hardworking hands will not pause in wonder at the silkiness of an infant's skin or reach out to shake a new friend's hand. They will not add their strength to lighten someone's task or be thrust, open-fingered into the excited air at Dave's graduation. Never again a high-five. They will never pat Melisa's back or gently wipe a tear. They will never touch us again. His beautiful long-fingered hands.

October 24

Forgot again.

I am at the grocery store and buy his ice cream and a package of Fruit Chews. I don't realize until I start to put them away at home that what I have here are his favorites. How can I still be forgetting? It's been one hundred and fifty-one days. At first, it made some kind of sense to set the table with too many places, to bake too many potatoes and strain my ears for his car pulling into the gravel driveway. But after this long?

October 25

I finally get around to organizing a box of his baby clothes, Cub Scout shirt and badges, a brown polyester tie, half-melted—one of the things I picked up at the rental house. The few papers he kept in an old steel box. I find his drivers training report card, a complimentary note from one of his English teachers, his wallet and some pictures. A note from the vice principal his junior year, "See me." There are two notes from me. One is a list of the people who had phoned him one particular day. I think they were planning a party—my motherly intuition was on alert. The other is full of tributes and praise for his specialness. I love to send these little notes to friends and family.

There is his diploma and a half-full bottle of aftershave, its fragrance mingles with smoke. My eyes itch with unshed tears and the lump in my throat is sandpaper covered. I can't rub my eyes because my fingers are smudged with soot and each time they approach my face the smoke odor forces me to thrust them as far as my arms can reach. I want to condense the box of artifacts from the fire with the bits of his history that I have kept over the years but as I open one box, I am knocked sideways by the smell of smoke.

October 28

It's almost Halloween. He loved every holiday. For Halloween we'd put together some cool costumes out of stuff we had around the house. Never one to do things in a small way, last year he brought home a pumpkin so large I couldn't encircle it with my arms. It weighed eighty pounds! Every year we would carve a face on each side of the pumpkin because no one could ever decide if we should have a scary Jack O' Lantern or a friendly one. We would roast the seeds and...

October 30

The loss of a child is so huge it's like the national debt—a sum so vast it makes no sense. We can't comprehend the vastness of it. But I am learning I don't have to gobble it all up till I am ill. I can take it one tiny bite at a time.

Melisa brings home an elephant joke—they are the latest grade school fad. "How do you eat an elephant?" she giggles.

"I don't know Honey, how?"

"One spoonful at a time, Mom."

November 3

"What's that?" I ask Mom in a panic. I can hear a strange crackling sound. I'm instantly nauseated, fight sickness and nerves, hyperventilating and sniffing like a child with a cold. I check inside and out and discover Mom's neighbor is raking stiff, dried leaves. I feel like a total fool as I sit on the stairs breathing deeply, trying to clear my head of images.

Mom and I talk a little about Christmas and I tell her that we couldn't stand to be home during the holidays without him. "The kids want to leave. We'll fly to Tahoe. Dave and Melisa and George can ski. That way we won't have to get a tree and stuff. All those traditions we've built around the children's lives. It's too hard."

My mom nods, understanding.

"You remember" I say, "that since Dan's first Christmas we've let them pick one ornament a year. They each have their own box. I couldn't stand to put them on a tree." I end with a burst.

Mom nods again and her words are so accurate, "Can't stand to put them on and you couldn't stand not to."

Most of all we won't have the fatiguing chore of acting *fine* before all the relatives to try to save them discomfort. There is no point having Christmas be depressing for everyone.

"Whatever is easier for you," she says. "I just wish you wouldn't feel you have to be so protective of the family's feelings. Your brothers and sister would be more supportive if only they knew how. They will understand, but we will all miss you."

HOLIDAYS

I don't want the holidays to come,
but they will.
I don't want to see twinkling lights
and hear carols playing,
but I will.
I don't want people to say Merry Christmas, Happy New Year,
but they will.
I don't want to feel lonely and sad,
but I will.
I don't want folks to try and cheer me,
but they will.
I don't want to miss you so,
but I will.
I trust time will make it better.
Will it?

~ Mary M. Fern

Melisa is acting up and so is David. Both of them are studying for finals, and though Dave is in his second year of college and Melisa is only in fifth grade, both are under lots of pressure. I do what I can for them, making nutritious meals and trying to see to it that they get enough rest. I can still make Melisa go to bed and can sit with her while she reads herself to sleep, but bedtime is out of my control for Dave and has been for a long time. I see him getting more tired and grumpy and worried about tests.

I get up in the middle of the night and notice the glow of his light under his door, so I go down. "Are you still up, Honey? It's almost three."

"I have a clock, Mom."

"Oh, okay. It's just that I hate to see you working so hard."

"I have to do this. You should understand. You're the one who always says how important school is." His voice is crisp and snappish but it's belied by his weary face.

I go upstairs trying not to be hurt and fix him some soup and crackers. As I knock softly again, I hear his put-upon sigh, "Come in." But seeing me with my hands full, he gets up and takes the tray with a real, "Thanks, Mom."

I give him a hug. He hugs back.

Melisa isn't so cranky but is sometimes so carefully composed she might be a mannequin. She has taken to walking with her head down so her long, honey-colored hair makes a curtain for her to hide behind. She rarely wants to be touched, but also wants me very near. I guess I have to give her more time.

November 8

The yellow mum from the memorial has bloomed. It is so late in the season. I can clearly see that the flowers are yellow but I see them as if through a thick screen, the color somber and dulled.

November 12

I see a woman on my daily walk. We smile—nod and female-like give a compliment. "I love the way you've frosted your hair," she says.

My face smiles as my heart lurches. I remember Dan buying my first bottle of coloring for me. Each time he teased me about going gray I told him I had earned each one, many thanks to him, and someday he was going to pay. I would hold up a strand and say, "This, my love, is the first time I ever heard you cry. And this is when you lost your tooth on your tricycle. This is when you went over the dirt cliff on the motorbike, and this is when you broke your leg. And all of these are for the times the school has called wondering when you are going to favor them with your presence." Darned if with his very first paycheck he didn't buy me a bottle of medium ash brown Lady Clairol. Now how could I use ash brown? Besides, without him here to tease me there doesn't seem much point to keeping it colored and it has grown out. Frosted. Ha.

On the phone last night, Mom and I laugh at the frosted hair story and she asks, "Are you starting to find a few things to smile about? I think those are the things that will begin to fill that empty place you speak about, though it may never be completely full."

"You could be right, but I don't know. Do hearts really break and leak until they're empty or do they burst like an overblown balloon from the hurt? I don't know if I even have a heart left."

"Oh Honey, it's just that you feel so empty inside but I know you. You still have a heart, yes you do."

As I look around, there is so much emptiness. In his room, in my head, in the house—and at our dinner table, the empty chair.

We are reluctant to gather at the table for a meal. It's so hard to swallow when his absence lumps our throats. We're all so busy that the only catch-up time we have is three or four times a week at dinner. That is where we connect. We tease each other and talk about everything. Usually it's about work and school, sports, music, and drag racing. And me, ever the teacher, trying to throw in a little politics, world affairs, art, history, and manners until the kids just roll their eyes. We have made it a point to avoid arguments at the table. I like a good debate but I don't like cooking enough to want the meal spoiled by squabbling. We sometimes do our share of that, but we do it elsewhere.

Now all conversations simply sputter out like a lawn mower running on its last fumes. We all try, but even Melisa hears the effort in our attempts to feign interest. George suggested we switch places so as not to stare at the empty chair. The kids were not about to buy that, Dave quietly against the idea, Melisa more vocally so. We've taken to eating most meals at the kitchen bar. I am a good cook but now everything tastes rancid on my tongue, and I notice that Dave is often *busy* somewhere else at dinner time.

November 13

It is almost too much to resist being pulled into to the vortex of the whirlpool that is grief. I have to let the current do with me as it will. And for a while, I have no desire to resist. But here we are in mid-November, five and a half months of almost unrelenting pain, and at last I feel a real change. It's as if I had plunged to the depths of the deepest ocean valley where all was blackness and the pressure made it impossible to breathe. Now, somehow I have surfaced. The sea is stormy, the wind wild and capricious, and yet the water is no longer icy, cold and dark.

In my pain, I resented getting Melisa's puppy, Licorice. Only because she so desperately needed something to hold on to did I let him in.

Puppies are a lot of work. This new dog could not replace our Pepé. He certainly couldn't take up any of Danny's space. He was trouble at a time when I wanted to be left alone. I, who love animals, was determined never to like him—however, I could remember so well what my Collie, Rocky, meant to me when I was Melisa's age.

I wouldn't recommend a puppy as a cure-all, but it's hard to concentrate on your sorrow when a little Labrador is playing tug-of-war with the belt of your bath robe as you try to walk down the hall.

One afternoon when Licorice was about two months old, we were alone in the house. Getting up from my work table, I didn't see him lying stretched across the doorway. I tripped over him and fell flat out, sprawling on the kitchen floor and landing hard with the poor puppy under my legs. I can still hear his cries as he ran screaming to hide in the dark depths under my bed. I thought I had killed him. I hobbled as fast as I could toward my now silent room. I lay on my belly and coaxed and coaxed and apologized. He crawled out at last and snuggled onto my lap. He was fine. And he was forgiving. And we were friends.

One day a couple weeks later he ran from the kitchen to the living room. Galloping under our big philodendron, the bottom leaf slapped him on the head. Instantly spinning around, he counterattacked taking a large bite out of the offending opponent. And wonder of wonders, George and I...laughed out loud.

Since I am the family insomniac, it has become my job to answer his whimper at five a.m. and let him out. Wrapped in a blanket, I sit on the steps in the backyard, watching him explore and watching dawn break.

This morning ritual has become a place of peace for me. Each day I have watched as the pup becomes braver. He started out, back in July, looking over his shoulder with every other step to reassure himself of my whereabouts. I can still see his expression the first time he went around the edge of the shed and lost sight of me. He came scampering back, running so hard as he looked for me that he went tumbling as he rounded the corner. When he picked himself up and snuggled to my legs his little heart was pounding so hard. Now, older, stronger, and braver, he bumps his head on the door, eager to get out and he never looks back.

That puddle of black squishiness has continued to drag me out of myself. He was one of the healthiest things we could have done for ourselves. Somehow Melisa knew what she needed and in helping herself, she helped all of us.

November 21

Melisa talked to me about Dan today. These spurts of conversation seem to have no rhyme or reason. But I welcome them. Laughing and crying, she remembers the fun times she had with him and admits the not so good ones. Again, I tell her that it's natural to get mad at your brothers or your mom and dad. Sometimes we think hateful thoughts about one another. It doesn't mean we wish anything bad on someone, and even if we did wish it, we do not have the power to make wishes come true. "If we had the power to fulfill every wish, Little Bear, we could look out that window right there and we would see a swimming pool, some horses, and an emerald green Corvette."

Melisa looks pointedly at our front window and shrugs her shoulders, "No green Corvette Mom." And we laugh.

I've noticed this odd phenomenon before. Each of us has touched on it. No matter how we search our minds, we have been unable to remember the kind, fun, gentle, family times we had with Dan. The only memories we have, seem to only be about the things we are sorry for. Yet, each of us can readily point out for the other their positive interaction. There is a huge lesson in this for me. Regrets are no fun. So when I err, and I know I will, I want it to be on the side of kindness.

I see relief on her face as I remind her of the hours they played basketball together, the water balloon and squirt gun fights, building sand castles, fishing at Uncle Bob's, her *riding* on his bike for miles while he held it upright and pushed it. And, the 111,111 games of Go Fish.

It feels good to know she is beginning to remember happy times rather than beating herself up with silent guilt.

I am beginning to learn that talk can be healing. And look at me talking about healing.

I see a lightness reappearing in Melisa that wasn't there before. She hides signs of emotion that might call attention to her and I was concerned that it might be becoming a problem. At a school conference yesterday, her teacher told George and me that Melisa broke down and cried during a discussion on death in the classroom. I know she must be holding a tremendous amount of pain inside. Crying in front of your peer group—well, that's simply not done at ten years of age unless the agony is overwhelming.

Apparently there is no *right way* to get through to her, no right way to help. I can only hope what we are doing won't turn out years from now to have been too much the wrong way.

The school principal came in while we were at the conference. When she heard that Melisa had cried she said, "Shouldn't you folks be getting over this by now? It's been a long time, I think, to still be so emotional, don't you?"

I don't remember what I said but her words propelled me into that deep place where I can observe myself. Nodding, and then standing, I held a hand out to George, who rose, white faced with a vein throbbing at his temple saying, "I guess we're done here."

November 25

We go to the ski shops again. It isn't so hard this time. We need a sweater for Dave but I am surrounded by reds and blacks, silver and white. All Dan's favorite colors. I can't find the greens, yellows, or turquoise that Dave likes.

November 26

A sad day today. Tomorrow is Thanksgiving, six months since we have seen him. Six months that have been an eternity, yet in comparison to the time to come, it is only a drop of rain in a deluge.

November 27

Thanksgiving Day

I'm trying very hard to feel gratitude for the years we had. Both Dave and George had a horrendous day. I hear Dave quietly moving around his room and it is as if the air wafting out is full of woe. He doesn't want to come upstairs to be with us—rather, he keeps avoiding us. I search for and find George. I beg him to go down to talk to Dave and he does. He is down there a long, long time. George tells me later that they both cried.

Chapter Fourteen

CHRISTMAS

*The light was gone, and there wasn't a sound
But the roar of wind through the pines and firs.
I came to a clearing at last and found
That I'd lost my way in the universe.*

~ Maurice Lesemann

November 28

We go Christmas shopping and when we return home Melisa wants to go through some of the Christmas boxes. Like so many women, I have a bunch of Christmas treasures stored away.

I am peeling potatoes and actually placing them in the correct pot when I hear her call as she runs upstairs to show me, "Mom can I keep Dan's Christmas stocking if you don't want it?" My heart sinks a little as I realize she's beginning to accept the fact that he's not coming home. I guess she wants a tangible, happy part of his life to hold on to.

I remember Dan, Dave, and me making those stockings, their excitement and sparkling eyes, their sweet clumsy hands as they cut felt pieces for Santa's beard and clothes and glued on the nose and eyes. My logical mind understands and applauds her healing, but part of me is silently protesting, "You can't have it. It's Dan's!"

I hug her and say, "Of course you can have it. He would be happy to know you want to keep it, Honey."

I go to Melisa's room to tuck her in around eleven. She is sleeping with his old Christmas stocking cradled in her arms. It is so beautiful to see that I go get George and Dave. We stand at her door and hold each other. We smile.

November 29

We are invited to dinner with the couple who lost their son the week after Danny was killed. Their daughters are about Dave's age and the youngest girl is a year older than Melisa.

As we sit down, our host says, "I was afraid this was a bad idea, but now I think it was a good one."

"I was worried too," George responds, and all of the kids nod.

I wish Dave could have come, but he is working. I had hoped he and their girls could have talked about their shared sorrow, having all lost an older brother.

Dinner progresses in sporadic fashion, just like at home. They speak, we speak in partial sentences. We lose our train of thought, search for words, stutter and stammer, and slow to a stop, mumbling, "I guess I lost it." And when the others nod and say, "I know," they really do.

Our hostess rises again and again. She forgets the salad, then the sugar, then some utensils, then to plug in the coffee.

As our minds lurch with our thoughts and words, so too do they lurch with our actions.

At first, the kids are silent. They watch us closely, but as they begin to see all of the parents are expressing themselves in similar ways, the oldest girl breaks the quiet. Speaking for all of them, she looks directly across the table at me and says, "I haven't wanted to talk about my brother. I was afraid it would hurt my folks even more."

Melisa ducks her head behind the curtain of her hair as we all dab our damp eyes and I nod. "I think our kids feel exactly that way too. But maybe we have to talk to somebody and who else would really understand?"

Her sister breaks in, "But it's just so hard." And every head around the table nods.

George raves about the pumpkin cake we are served for desert and asks our hostess for the recipe. She smiles a little and answers, "I don't mind writing it down but only if you are going to use it. If you're just being polite I'd just as soon not take the trouble."

How I love that honesty. Time is too precious to waste jotting down a recipe unless it will be used. None of us will ever again be as likely to waste our time in the future. Use it in crazy ways perhaps, but not waste it. Time is for us, clearly finite and much too important to waste, so don't just be polite, be real.

Later the four of us sit with coffee and conversation and she brings up a well-known support group for parents who have lost children. "We went to a meeting, but it was too painful and we left. We might try again later."

I say we haven't even thought about counseling, "It's so hard for me to speak to anyone about this—I can't imagine sharing with a room full of strangers."

"I know," she says, and much more wise than I, she smiles and gestures at us, "but we were strangers."

There is a rainbow today. As it fades into the gloom of the gray Seattle sky, my heart lifts. For a moment, there is sun and with that sun there is hope.

December 1

Rosalyn and Bobbie invite me along to shop for Christmas gifts for the teachers at our girls' school. There is a designated amount of money and these friends are the designated shoppers. It's hard to go, but they're brave to include me and it's good for me to try. It takes lots of energy and if something I see catches me off guard, I tear up. And sure as rain in Seattle in winter, something sneaks up and stabs me.

At the men's cosmetic counter I am attacked by the scent of the after shave Danny loved. Odors have an unbelievably powerful, visceral impact. It is a body blow. I stumble, almost knocked off my feet. I start to hyperventilate. I cling to the counter. It takes minutes to remember where I am, but thankfully no one notices my weird behavior.

Kindred spirits, these friends and I used to laugh together as we vented. Now I hear myself saying as we talk about one particularly challenging teacher, "We have to understand and be kind. This teacher, she's a weak human being, just like us. We have to love one another and everything will be alright. Only people matter," I say, "not all the petty politics of school."

I am sincere in my words, but later, reflecting on the day, I think I must be pretty hard to take. These friends of mine are loving and kind and were only complaining to blow off steam in a way that is healthy and harmless. It's okay to gripe with our best friends. They ask me along with generous spirits on what should have been a fun shopping day and I get all holier than thou with my preaching. I should be hugging them in gratitude for still coming around. I must remember it is me in this rarified atmosphere, and be careful not to alienate one of our few lifelines. They cannot possibly know this state of altruism I'm in. They cannot know what it's like. The only way to really understand would be for them to live it and I don't want them to ever, ever know.

I pour some spice tea and get out a new green pen and the Christmas cards. Now the tea is cold and the cards are still unsigned. How do I sign them?

Christmas is getting closer. I'm crabby and full of tears. My neck is in a constant cramp. My shoulders are so slumped. I sigh and sigh. I hear myself and am surprised. I ache in my muscles and wonder where all the tightness comes from. Consciously, I straighten my back and neck. I pull my head up and take a deep breath. Shame on me for letting others see me like this, I scold myself, and then remind myself of thousands who have it so much worse. Still, before too long, I hear myself sighing again, as soundlessly and slowly as hair grows, the weight of the world descends.

Are we stupid to grieve so? Is it a waste of time when life is so short, or is it simply a hard, hard lesson in patience?

Dave says the hardest thing about Christmas is trying to think of what to buy for Dan and then remembering he will never give him anything again.

December 3

George comes home tonight looking beaten and bewildered. "Everyone accuses me of being a grouch. I don't think I'm different. Am I?" I go silent and wait. He sighs and continues, "This afternoon I ran into a friend who kidded me about my frowning. He called me a Scrooge. I got so mad I had to walk away so I wouldn't hit him. When I calmed down I realized that's exactly what you guys mean when you say I've changed. I used to be so easy." I hug him and hold this friendly person that everyone likes and I love. After a minute I let my body stiffen—and I very carefully step out of the embrace.

"What's wrong?"

"Well," I deadpan, "if you're as unstable as nitroglycerin I'm going to be walking real easy." My small joke reaps a laugh, more than it warrants, but just what we need.

This is the second time he's gotten so explosive. A couple of months ago he did blowup. It is still the talk of the beer salesmen circle. He and a number of his competitors were at a major grocery store revamping the cooler. Most of the men keep their rivalry on a friendly basis, but this day, one sales manager was getting unnecessarily pushy. "Damned if I didn't roll my sleeves up and invite him outside, as if we were in junior high again. I was so mad I was shaking. Two other guys were holding me back while the rest just stood there with their mouths open. I don't know what got into me, he hadn't said anything special. He was just being his normal jerky self. I couldn't believe my own actions. The fellows made him leave or I think I would have tried to kill him. God, Honey, you wouldn't have recognized me."

Yes, I would have recognized him as he is these days, but there was a time, not so long ago, that I would not have known him if he were frowning or angry.

December 4

The kids are going skiing with George tomorrow and I'm scared. I had a horrid daydream with everything in slow motion. Their car slid, agonizingly slowly, while coming around a curve as they were coming off the mountain. Pieces of white guard rail splintered and floated before the car as it fell and fell and fell into the deep green trees far below, and all of them tumbled like clothes in a dryer. They were scattered across the forest and caught in limbs of trees until the branches broke and they fell farther and landed and died. I swallowed a scream. Like most moms, I've been known to be precognitive when it comes to my family. I want them to stay home but I say nothing. I don't want them to be afraid to live.

December 5

I would have gone crazy if I had stayed home so I spent the day with Mom. My mom. She just lets me talk. She is so totally non-judgmental and the world's best listener. Her advice comes mildly in little suggestions that you only recognize as advice when you ponder later. When I was a kid and someone would tell me I was just like my mother, I used to get annoyed. Now I can't think of a higher compliment.

I try not to over burden her...Oh my goodness! That thought just hit me like a big wave. That is just what the kids said when we were at our friends for dinner last week. *We try not to add to the agony.*

Poor Mom. I know how I feel when my kids hurt. Now she has lost her firstborn grandson and in her pain she must watch her beloved daughter and family grieve while she is helpless to do anything about it. Mom has lost her own mom and my dad in the last five years. And when she was twenty, her beloved big sister died of TB. She knows Dave and Melisa's grief intimately and sees George and me going through what her mom went through.

"How did you do it when Daddy and Grandma died in such close time proximity, Mom?" I ask.

"I take it to the Lord and talk and leave it there as much as I can."

"I envy your faith but I don't have it, and I don't know what to do."

"Patience Honey, patience. Maybe you don't have to do anything right now. Maybe we just need to visit and have our coffee."

And so we sip. And soon I talk—a lot. I discover inside myself things I haven't realized before. I was so angry at one family member who had been pretty hard on Dan. Mom helped me again see that being family doesn't guarantee loving feelings. "We're just all trying, Honey. Trying and stumbling and failing, but trying again."

It seems when I am able to articulate the things that have been bothering me, they begin to get lighter. Time after time in conversations with George or Mom, I find I am given a boost over the hurdle that is in my way. There is something about expressing thoughts out loud that is healing. This is new to me, difficult and new. My life role has always been the listener, the advisor, not the one to be speaking my deepest thoughts.

December 8

Talking to Mom really did help. I slept well last night. Of course being weak with relief at the safe return of my skiers may have had something to do with my relaxed state. They had a good time and their faces reflect that. I'm so glad I kept my mouth shut.

Sleep is a wonderful thing. Now that I have had three nights in a row, I remember how nice it is. Maybe all this rest has helped me. Someone asked today how we were doing and I said, "Pretty well, thank you." And for once it wasn't a lie.

I phoned a new friend.
She lost her son a couple of years ago.
She's been very kind to me.
I felt good enough today to try to
give a little back.
It was my turn to say,
"How are you doing?"
"Oh," came the answer, "I'm pretty whelmed."
"Whelmed?"
"Uh-huh. Some days now I'm almost good.
And most days I'm pretty okay.
And I'm rarely overwhelmed anymore,
Often I'm just whelmed now."
So in my calling her she again helped me.
I am learning a whole new vocabulary.
I'm not happy about it
but all those grief words don't overwhelm me anymore either.
I, too, am just whelmed.

~ Mary M. Fern

December 14

The family has always gone together to pick our *Charlie Brown* tree. It's usually a woe begotten waif of a tree one of us feels sorry for that ends up to be *the most beautiful tree we've ever had.* Picking a tree this year is a dreaded idea. But sometimes the fates step in to ease the way. Melisa wants to help Shenan bake gingerbread men at her house. Dave chooses to stay home and watch a football game. So it's just George and me. There is more than Seattle's famous rain on our faces as tinny tones from the speakers hung high on poles around the tree lot assault our ears with "Rudolf the Red Nosed Reindeer."

145

December 16

George keeps putting off hanging the outdoor lights. I finally realize he simply doesn't have the heart to do what had become Dan's job. So today Dave does it. We debated putting them up at all. Everything is such a big decision.

"Oh, let's go ahead," Dave says. "Melisa needs to see Christmas coming no matter how false it feels to us."

He is one smart boy.

Dave is reluctant too, but today his friend Jack is over so I take advantage of them and bring out the lights. As far as Jack is concerned, it is just a simple little job that has no reminders. We say nothing and let him take charge.

The first thing they do is explode a bulb. And what a mess to untangle! There is such agony in Dave's tone as he says, "I don't even know where to start—this is Dan's job." As we fumble with the spaghetti like strands of colorful glass and wire, I can almost hear Danny laugh. I feel him near, longing to lend a hand. We don't even know where the outside receptacle is to plug them in. But determination gets us through.

At last they are up with perhaps a bit of divine intervention. A number of bulbs are burned out but by that time we are too, and we don't care. Melisa is so surprised and pleased, so it is worth the immense effort.

The lights cast a dab of luminosity into the dark night. We have taken another step up the mountain. Yet, I feel like a yo-yo never knowing from one second to the next where our emotions will be taking us, up or down.

It is the 17th

It is my birthday.

Today is the 18th —Melisa's birthday.

Melisa enters double digits today. We take her to a movie and as we walk in, there are all the little girls in her class—a birthday outing for one of her classmates. Only Melisa and one other girl were not invited. The mother of Melisa's classmate stares at us in shock as some of the girls rush up to greet Melisa, thinking we are there to join them. Faces are red, voices stammer, and we are so hurt for our little girl we could explode. I know everyone has the right to invite whomever they wish, but with only a handful of girls in the class it seems rather unkind to rebuff only Melisa and one other little girl. Melisa's face is a question mark, but she carries it off with tremendous composure. We are fierce with pride.

December 22

Who doesn't love Christmas? But thoughts of this first Christmas without him have haunted me almost from the first day. You have to go to Mars to escape the hyperbole. I think George and Dave like Thanksgiving best with five kinds of pie, all the relatives and football. And our Melisa loves any gift-getting occasion. But Dan was ever my helper on holidays. He knew Christmas doesn't happen by itself. The family touches that make it wonderful take work to be brought to fruition. He willingly accompanied me singing carols. George and Dave complain that they can't sing and don't understand that it isn't the tune, it's the sharing. Dan wouldn't quit when there were still five dozen cookies to bake and ice. He couldn't get enough of shopping and wrapping. He would stand near a Santa Claus line to warm himself in the joy of the excited little ones who waited. Then he'd come home to share the stories and make me laugh.

I knew this day and tomorrow would be two of the hardest in my life, so I planned them to be completely different than any we had previously shared. We would fly to Lake Tahoe and the three of them could ski and I could read. There would be decorations that were not familiar, a holiday meal that I didn't have to cook. This would be everyone's present all wrapped in one. Building memories is important and that seemed the perfect solution for some of our pain. An entirely foreign environment, skiing, and no strain to make Christmas happen. Not to get out the old ornaments the kids had chosen, now worn and scratched with memories gathered over the years and saved for them to take when they started their own families. George and I have saved for years for a rainy day. Right now it is pouring.

It didn't snow in the Sierra Nevada this year! Our apologetic travel agent can't believe it and has to refund our money. I don't know what to do. Then from somewhere, it all becomes clear as I realize traditions aren't written in stone. They're not commandments. If one thing we always do is too hard, we just won't do it this year. The heavens won't come crashing down.

Instead of waiting for the family to gather so we can get out the ornaments as we always have, I suggest to Melisa, "Why don't you invite a friend over and you can get out the ornaments." She is so excited! She and Shenan ooh and ahh as they carefully lay the fragile treasures out on the blanket covered table. It takes a lot of the strain out of what is my favorite, holiday task. Normally, I love the memories that flow so strongly as we unwrap each special decoration and everyone has a *remember when moment.* I can't face that now.

Another day, we have three of Melisa's friends in for lunch. I teach them how to miter corners of packages and how to make simple bows. They have a great time and it feels pretty good to me too. The girls' moms get some free time, we get my wrapping done, and it's good to hear laughter in the house.

Then there is trimming the tree. "Just us tonight." I reassure the family. This is every bit as hard as we feared and we share the trauma. Tears start time and again while one memory after another drifts with the scent of pine through our house. Melisa tries so hard. She keeps a running dialog of happy past times as if by speaking fast enough, she can keep her tears at bay. Each of us sounds as if we have an awful cold with husky voices, red eyes, and constantly blown noses, and for the first time in memory, no one says it is the prettiest tree ever. It is an exhausting chore and we go to bed whipped.

December 24

Tonight's dinner is a waste. We sit down, prepared to do our best to make this night a good one, but none of us can eat. The food is dry and dusty. It can't be swallowed. Blinking rapidly to hold back tears, we really try, but soon give up.

We decide to open gifts tonight instead of doing our traditional morning unwrapping. Melisa, still trying, is the only one even close to normal, though she is subdued. After she opens her gifts, we just slow to a stop.

Each year, Danny would buy Melisa the biggest, craziest looking stuffed animal he could find. Last September when George and I were up in the islands, we went into a little dockside gift store and saw a giant, beige, brown, and white coyote that we couldn't resist. From his fluffy soft tail to the tip of his big floppy ears, he is as big as our little girl.

In a note attached to the present, we explain why we bought it for her as if it were from Dan. We call him Kemo Sabe remembering the name from our long ago Lone Ranger radio days.

"It is supposed to mean trusted friend, at least that's what we remember," I say. "He's someone who won't ever leave you. You can tell all your secrets to him and trust him forever, no matter what."

Buying Melisa a gift from Danny is most likely a onetime only thing. It seemed important this year for her to have one last gift from her biggest brother.

Licorice brings us a laugh or two as we teach him how to open packages, but all in all, the house echoes emptiness. Sometimes I feel that forced laughter is worse than no laughter at all.

At last we call it a night. Dave ghosts down the stairs to his room and Melisa, who hasn't stopped hugging her coyote, heads to bed, Kemo Sabe's tail dragging on the floor behind her.

George and I collapse on the couch, arm in arm, exhausted.

It is after midnight when we hear a loud knock on the door. My crazy thought is, *Why would Dan knock?* We jump to the door and open it. There on the porch is a brightly wrapped box the size of an apple crate. George runs down the stairs and into the yard, but can't see anyone. We bring the box in and hunker down on the floor next to it. It is filled with gifts for each of us—candy canes and apples, cheeses and various gaily-wrapped little mysterious packages, and there was a note. In hand writing we did not recognize the note read, *"We're thinking of you and hoping your Christmas will be filled with sweet memories."* The note was signed, Santa Claus.

As hard as I try at this moment, I cannot describe the feeling as George and I sit, cross legged beneath our lonely Christmas tree holding these gifts of love. We laugh and cry as we try to guess who cared enough to plot and plan and stay up this late, giving up their Christmas Eve to say, "I love you in this way." I'm not going to open my gift ever—it will hang on the tree every year to remind me of the true meaning of Christmas.

It's now very early Christmas morning and everyone is asleep. I know it's irrational, but I sit on the couch waiting for Dan. "No matter where I am, no matter what I am doing, I promise I will always be home for Christmas with you," he would say and I would laugh that he was so serious.

"Don't make a promise like that, Silly," I'd say. "You will get married some day and your wife will want to spend Christmas Eve at her folk's house."

"That's okay," he would laugh, "She will know right where to find me."

So here I sit. And here I wait.

Dave and Melisa love Santa's box. Playing the guessing game brings lightness to our day and as we color in Melisa's new book from Santa with her new crayons from Santa, I think this is the best gift of all.

Christmas day has past. At last.

December 27

George, Melisa, and Dave have gone skiing again. I'm okay with it this time. I'm glad to have the day alone. I want to write to Danny and tell him about our first Christmas without him. I write to say:

Well Honey, we did it. I'll never know how. We got through Christmas Day without you. Should I try to explain the emptiness?

We rearranged everything in hopes of making it easier on ourselves. I don't know if it helped. All of us sort of played the game for Melisa's sake, though I doubt we fooled her. In fact, I think she was playing too, for us. We didn't read the Christmas story, our voices were too cracked. We didn't carol. Dave and Dad were never gung-ho about singing anyway. You were the only one to help me carry the tune, with Melisa's sweet tones in the background.

We can't convince ourselves you are gone. It's like—it just isn't so. I don't think we are deluding ourselves, but even when we try, we can't force ourselves to believe it's true.

For two days I tried to hang the stockings—I couldn't do it. I pushed the job off on your poor Dad. Just as he had pushed hanging the lights off on Dave.

Dad and I took a rose down to the cemetery for you. One red rose. We went alone. We didn't ask your brother and sister and though they knew where we were going, they didn't ask to go along. It was really hard, Honey.

Such an obvious thing sounds stupid to say, but we all miss you so much. We all wish we could tell you face to face that we love you. You are so much here, yet not here enough. There is a space inside us that nothing can fill no matter how hard we try. Sadness is a constant companion, almost comfortable in its familiarity.

Nobody can wish us a Merry Christmas. Thoughtful friends have sent cards, sensitively chosen and carefully worded not to say it. They say things like, "Peace Unto You," or, "May Love Be A Part of Your Holidays."

Your friend Riley brought us a dozen yellow roses and his little girl sent me a clear glass ornament etched with a flying bird. She found it at a garage sale last summer and insisted on buying it for "Danny's mama." She is three now and she still remembers you and how you would play with her.

We had dinner at Grandma's house with all the family. It went okay. Aunt Patty gifted me with an acrylic medallion carved with gulls skimming in wild waves. I hung it in the hutch that is slowly filling with relics of the sea. Gulls, shells, whales, dolphins in crystal and...I remember the night we danced, you and I, to the sound of the waves on the ocean.

I love you.

December 31

It is New Year Eve day. The day starts out okay and goes slowly, slowly, down, down, down.

We are invited out and truly appreciate it, but we are too raw to go. Melisa is excited about going to Grandma's for the night—she gets to stay up till *Twelve O'clock midnight!*, and have hot chocolate with Grandma and Zeke, their dog. Dave is at a friend's cabin. They are spending tomorrow skiing.

We stay home quietly and weep again, but now we weep together. We try to talk, but there is nothing left to say. It's all been said, time after time. Yet we still try to make some sort of sense out of a senseless thing. We know we must acknowledge the thing we most wish not to acknowledge. But this is something we have learned—it doesn't matter from which side of the goblet you drink—the glass contains the same bitter brew. It's a solution of pain and sorrow, guilt and grief,

151

helplessness and hopelessness, tears and tempest, agony and fear. Love or faith can hold your hand while you down it to the dregs, but love and faith can't do it for you. As you slowly swallow the searing potion, you are alone.

George and I have made many great strides since the end of May, a seven-month eternity ago. Maybe the biggest step is finally understanding that even though each of us is alone, it is possible to be alone and together instead of alone and apart.

Death:
The act or fact of dying—permanent cessation
of life in a person, animal, or plant,
in which all vital functions cease permanently.

Grief:
Intense emotional suffering caused by loss, misfortune,
injury, or evils of any kind—sorrow—regret—as:
We experience grief when we lose a friend.

Guilt:
The act or state of having done a wrong or
committed an offense—culpability, legal or ethical—
(I am still alive. My child is not. I am guilty.)

Mourning:
The actions or feelings of sorrowing or expressing grief—
lamentation—sorrow—specifically,
the expression of grief at someone's death.

Sojourn:
To dwell for a time—to linger: as a traveler to a foreign land.

Chapter Fifteen

HIS AND HER GRIEF

"If I should pass the tomb of Jonah
I would stop there and sit for awhile—
Because I was swallowed one time deep in the dark
And came out alive after all."

~ Carl Sandburg

The seven months since May seems like a hundred years. The holidays are behind us and there was one pleasant surprise. There has been no post-holiday letdown. I find little things are beginning to matter again. Like Melisa not making her bed or drinking her milk. I've been functioning without any direction for so long now, as shadow not a substance. Am I now coming back? Could this be healing?

So many people still can't be comfortable around us. Christmas day with the family had some awkwardness. We missed Dan's bigger than life laugh and his teasing. Dan's peers, cousins John and Colleen, seemed most at odds without him. Dave, of course, is still floundering but acting more normal and looking a bit better.

Everyone else was treading so carefully, trying to pretend that all was normal. But it was such a sham. I'm just glad it is behind us and I'd bet we all feel that way.

I wish I could dream him or feel his presence.

Sometimes I wonder if he was real. There, I've said it.

Sometimes I get mad at him and I want to shout, "Where are you?" Wherever your Spirit is, are you too busy *out and about* to get back to your mom? Other times, I think there isn't any such thing as a Spirit. I can't visualize his face anymore and that is a torture, although when I think of him the corner of my mouth feels his last kiss.

January 1

We all know intellectually that bad things can happen to anyone—now I know it in my heart. It is so irritating to hear people say "This is such a nice place I didn't believe it could happen here." (Kidnapping, murder, etc.) "It can't happen to me," is a lie! But you can't know what you don't know, can you? I thought I was starting to climb the mountain. Again, an avalanche has buried me and I must dig my way out.

I have been told, in a tone of surprise, that I am taking this tragedy so well. It is as if by trying to continue functioning, I have shown myself to be less grieved than I *should be*, an unnatural mother. If I were prostrate, that might be faulted too. So I go along being me, without worrying about others' perceptions. Who among us truly knows another's heart?

I have a friend who said about Jacqueline Kennedy, "She couldn't have loved her husband very much, she didn't even cry."

My friend couldn't see the courage and dignity that helped hold a trembling nation together. All she could see was the lack of demonstrative grief. It's that old *book by the cover* thing.

January 2

Oh, those kids of mine. I want to stop loving them so much. I go from wanting to hold them in my arms day and night, never wanting to let them out of my sight, to not wanting to feel any closeness at all. If I don't love them so much it won't hurt so badly if I lose them.

January 3

Curious to see how Hollywood handled a movie about a household in the aftermath of one son's death, we go to see a movie called *Ordinary People*.

George and I get irked when the audience laughs in all the wrong places. When we talk it over later, we realize their laughter is a statement of their own lives. It means they don't understand. They have been blessed by never having been in the situation. George thinks the couple could have tried to be easier on each other. "That marriage mustn't have had much love," he says.

How do we think Hollywood handled a death in the family? No better than we did. But we're not quitting.

January 4

I go to another movie, this time with my women friends. I enjoy parts of it. It is a comedy, but there is a scene with a death and a corpse and I hold tightly to the armrests so I won't flee. Later we stop for dinner and I actually find the food has a taste. Conversation means something. The cotton is out of my ears. I can feel and taste and hear and chuckle. The fog lifts for an evening.

I come home and crawl into bed. George is half asleep. I form myself like polish on a nail to his back and am really glad for him. It's bizarre, to be able to feel again instead of being blank. I guess I'm like a chick coming out of an egg, smelling the air and letting its feathers dry.

So when the guilt hits, it smashes me hard enough to leave bruises. How could I, how dare I, have enjoyed myself?

January 5

Maze, labyrinth, roller coaster, merry-go-round, yo-yo, all this and more. How do we get through? Am I not giving the kids enough attention? Is it time to shut the door on the past? Would that bother Dave and Melisa even more if they thought we could let go that easily? What do they need that we aren't giving and what are we giving that they don't want or need?

And George and I. What's happening to us? I One day we turn to each other and the next we turn away. It all takes so much effort as we have to learn and relearn each lesson.

January 12

I let myself get too tired. That's a serious mistake. I've finally recognized how important rest is. If I don't get enough, I can't cope nearly as well. This grieving takes a lot of energy and hard work. When I'm tired my defenses are down and I slip more easily into the despair. I know I'm not healed yet, though I'm so tired of this grief business.

Forgive
To give up resentment against or the desire to punish—
to stop being angry with—to pardon as in: forgive yourself.

Healing:
To grow sound—to return to a sound state—
to get well, as a wound heals.

155

Living:
(Through) To experience and survive—to endure.
(A ship) To remain afloat under trying conditions.
To remain alive, to last, to endure.
To maintain life. To have life. To enjoy life.
To LIVE life.

January 19

Why do we grieve so very differently? I know, I know, I know. Men and women are biologically, historically, culturally, inherently different. I know. But why? Is it because biologically a man can spill out their sperm anywhere and go on about his life while the woman is left to give birth to that life? Is it that men left the cave to wander around silently hunting using only grunts and hand gestures while we stayed behind barefoot and pregnant, nursing and nurturing the young, the ill, and the old, keeping the home fires burning while chatting and gathering? That seems to make sense, but the failure to communicate could be killing us right now. Even our vocabularies are different. I don't think of war as playing war games. I don't think of killing animals as a sport.

Sometimes I think men are crazy. I mean really and truly mad. Today I heard an Army general speaking in a smug but rational tone about *acceptable casualties* in a *limited nuclear exchange*. And I thought, *No wonder George and I can't talk. No wonder we don't understand each other.* I would like to tell that general that the human race may not be as resilient as he believes. One is gone from our home and we function as automatons. Imagine if every family lost one member tomorrow and were in the state of emotion we are experiencing. The human race stumbles on, but at what cost? We are so much more animal than any of us are willing to admit.

George lives so much in the here and now—today's work merits a paycheck tomorrow, instant gratification. He seems to see only his immediate link in life's chain, the link that includes me and the kids. I too work for a paycheck but that's just a job. My life is far more about delayed gratification as I raise the children and reap rewards through them someday. I see myself as one link in an unending chain back to my grandmother's grandmother and beyond and forward to grandchildren's grandchildren and beyond.

George and I love each other. We keep reaching out for one another but can rarely touch and I ask myself, is the reaching enough? I have no answer unless the answer is inherent in our stubborn willingness to keep trying.

Death and grief have been an obsession for months now. I find myself comparison shopping in a shop of horrors. Which, I ask myself would be worse? Watching a loved one wither away as my mom's sister did years ago of tuberculosis at only twenty-three? She had contracted the disease while working at her nursing profession in an age where the only *cure* was fresh air and wholesome food. Grandma and Grandpa erected a tent in their front yard and cared for her for over a year as she died. I cannot imagine the pain of that—only know that my mother's voice changes all these years later when she speaks of her *big sis*.

Still I wonder, is this instant unexpected death of a vibrant, healthy, young person worse?

How do families cope with a murder? Or a suicide?

How stupid of me to try to weigh or measure. The truth is there is no such thing as better or worse, harder or easier. Ultimately, there is only the unchangeable fact that a person who laughed and loved and planned and permeated every facet of our lives, a person who got his very life from us, is gone. The questions—who, why, where, when and how—do not matter in the end.

He was the fire and ice. If there was excitement to be found, he would be at its core. Larger than life from his six-foot-four frame to his laugh and his growl. Dave is my sweet clown, his humor refreshes. His single-mindedness of his life's purpose and his insights are amazing and we've always been able to speak more as contemporaries rather than mother and child. Melisa, our Little Bear, so far she is all cuddles and confidences and her giggles warm the house with love.

Each of us brings something so special and important to our home but a big chunk is missing—and though it is calm and predictable around here now, it is also colorless, dull. We are like a soup with neither salt nor pepper, flavorless.

Still, life is going on and our family is going on with it. Melisa and Dave are looking better, the dark circles are fading from under their eyes, and they are less nervous and are starting to laugh a bit again. George still looks beaten and I, I still cannot see myself at all. No reflection, no shadow.

February 7

Mummy-like we still need to wrap and wrap and wrap the strands of reassurance around us. Of course he slept. (Did he call for me?) Everyone knows he could sleep through anything. (Were they trying to protect us when they said they weren't sure if it was him they saw at the window or only a shadow?) The toxins in the smoke must have been instantly fatal. (But did he know, if only for an eternal minute?) The house went so fast. (Did he feel pain?) He probably died in his sleep—but probably is not enough. (Did he call? Did he hurt? Was he scared? Did he wonder why? And where we were when he needed us? Did he know???) And if I knew the answers, what good would it do?

Often it seems I can feel him right behind me. If I could turn quickly enough I would see him. I can almost feel his hands rubbing the tension out of my neck. I draw my head in, turtle like, knowing he is going to tickle the sides of my neck to tease me and watch me shiver. Melisa has started rubbing my neck just as he used to. Her hands are so little and her gesture so bittersweet, and yet her love is gold and I am humbled by the power of my love for her.

The heavens drip their tears on my window today. The barren branches of the trees are charcoal against the pewter sky. And my tea grows cold as I think and think.

There is not one best way to deal with loss. Our own lifetime experience dictates how well one is equipped to cope. When I think of the times we tried to shelter the kids or assist them at tasks we thought *awfully hard* for them, I'm sorry. Every parent knows how hard it is to stand aside as your child tries to deal with any tough job or emotional pain by themselves, but it is the only helpful thing you can do. We must stand by with love and encouragement, but not attempt to take their work or their pain over for them.

Life is full of hard places and each time we work through one, we add to our strength and coping skills. Then, when a colossal agony comes along, we will have earned a tiny bit of armor. I imagine this should be written in stone or on the map we parents receive when our children are born. Oh, that's right, we don't receive a map. We have to learn that the hard way too—by living it.

"i carry your heart with me (i carry it in
my heart) i am never without it (anywhere
i go you go, my dear—and whatever is done
by only me is your doing, my darling)"

~ *e.e. cummings, i carry your heart (i carry it in my heart)*

Grief is losing its momentum and muscle. Mourning is beginning to raise its head. It wears a gray cloak rather than grief's black garb. I read somewhere this quote: "Grief no longer possesses me. I process it." And that, I believe, is the difference between grief and mourning. Grief was the sinking to the bottom of the sea. Grief was the slow ascent to the storm-wracked ocean, no life boat, no life jacket. It was about being tossed like a seal in the jaws of a Great White.

Mourning is calmer, not so terrifying, and the waves, though still enormous, now are just scary. The winds seem less capricious—the troughs between crests stretch wider. You still do not know which direction you are floating or if another storm is on the horizon, but you seem to be able to catch your breath and maybe…maybe even swim.

Now you have the grief—it does not have you. Now…you are mourning.

It might be wise to have a universal mourning sign, some visual whisper that says *go gently please*. One could wear it on those days when it was particularly important to subtly let the world know your emotional status. Not so much as a selfish or sympathy-inducing ploy, but a reminder for you and them that others are sharing the same experience— you are not alone. Maybe we would be reminded to count our blessings and be more inclined to hold out the hand of compassion to the next sufferer. Maybe the healing, understanding, and love would flow a little more freely.

In England in the late 1880s, when my grandmother was a little girl, the mourning custom was for all family members to wear solid black clothing for one full year following a death. Even the children were not exempt. The following year, one wore gray edged in black. Letters were trimmed in black. Hankies were edged in black.

Gram remembered spending what seemed to her to be years in dull dresses. As the daughter of a church deacon, the family had to be more than averagely decorous. She once told us in her spirited style, "About the time I got to put on a colored frock, another relative would up and die." She never liked to see her grandkids in gray or black.

With stories like that in my background, naturally I don't advocate a return to those old customs, but if there were some ritual, some way to tastefully acknowledge each other's pain, it might be a helpful healer.

Sackcloth and ashes. Hair shirts. Painting your face with lines of black ash to announce to the world that you are in intense grief. Rending your clothes. Throwing oneself on the funeral pyre. I guess we've been doing strange public displays for centuries. However, in present day, American grief is not allowed. Publicly letting your pain be known is frowned upon. Grief is embarrassing. And embarrassment is not fine. Vulgar humor, yes, anger yes, rudeness, drunkenness, all kinds of self-indulgence, yes—but no tears and no grief.

I was watching a show, "Believe It Or Not" that portrayed a tribe in Africa that has a strange, albeit, most intelligent method of handling grief. A new widow was surrounded by her fellow tribesmen who were putting necklace after necklace of beads over her head. There were some strings for every person in the village. Every evening the widow would remove one necklace. As the days passed and she removed each succeeding chain she would be compelled to focus her grief. Think of the positive aspects of such a ritual. Being able to physically carry this burden of sadness day after day and lighten it just a bit night after night might tend to ease some of that sadness. And the tribe, reminded constantly of the one no longer in their midst, would be free to mention and speak of him, in itself a healing thing. Daily, in a tangible way the widow's burden would lessen. At first the easing would not be noticeable, but slowly, week after week, the weight she carried would lighten until, with the passing of time, she would begin to feel the air touching her skin again, to feel the load lighten, and instead of being guilty as she started to come back to this realm, she would have a sort of psychological awareness of having carried her grief. And her Spirit might rise with the lifting of the beads of death. What remarkable insight this tribe's forbearers had into the healing process.

And I like the idea of Mexico's Day of the Dead where the family picnics at the cemetery and speaks of the one who is gone so they can't be forgotten. It has been such a fear for me that if others forget him I might forget him too. Even being able to watch the children play among the engraved stones so everyone can see even in the midst of sorrow that life, vibrant life, is going on, would be a healthy healing thing.

In our country in the past, we did much the same thing, honoring our ancestors on Memorial Day by going out to clean up the graves, put new flowers on, and tell the family stories. Now we have become such a scattered society, so many of us moving away from the old home towns, that those traditions seem to be dying out and in a way that's a shame.

February 20

Music is memories. I love it and I hate it. Both music and memories almost always hurt. I still slam my hand at the radio dial when certain songs fling their melodies out to pierce my brain. But I want to keep his music with me regardless of the pain, so I take up the guitar. I try. Practice, practice. But my fingers are like the legs of a newly-foaled colt, wobbling and unsure. I never could rub my belly and pat my head at the same time.

Melisa has begun to play too. She is a natural with easy rhythm and style. She learns all the chords so quickly and is able to sing along in her sweet voice to her own strumming. I love to watch her as she perches on the edge of the couch, head tipped beneath her long darkening auburn hair.

I can still click off my deepest feelings and thoughts at the mention of Dan. It is that out-of–body, three-way split my mind does. I can speak of him, I can listen to him being spoken of and only the outer layers of my mind are touched, but music can catch me without protection. The unexpected scent of his after-shave lotion can bring me to my knees, incapacitated. The exhibit of his favorite toiletries and its attendant aromas block the door to my favorite store as effectively as a Doberman.

February 27

When I am down, I forget I was ever up and when I'm up I think I can stay up, but I cannot. The quick elevational changes are so confusing. Then around Christmas I got a great idea—I started putting numbers on my calendar. I am using that familiar scale of one to ten to rate and chart my daily progress. Some days I may put three numbers on the same calendar square. Now I can actually see that last Monday was a four or five, though Tuesday was a terrible two. Or Wednesday morning was a four-and-a-half, not too bad, but Wednesday evening was even better at a five. In the last two months there have only been five squares with a one on them and squares with four or five are becoming more common. It helps me when I can actually see progress being made. It gives me hope.

It's been almost ten months now and I guess this is healing. It seemed to start in December and now even more clearly I see I am coming back to this world. I've been away in a far place where values are different from the newspaper's front page. I seemed an alien here. But petty things are again infiltrating their way onto my list of priorities.

I begin again to act and react less thoughtfully. Our society is in such a rush we can't seem to take time to care. Modern living pushes us so fast we forget that we are in charge and could slow down if we wanted to. It's a McDonald's society—fast food, fast cars, and fast fads. And I am finding myself rejoining that traffic.

For months I've been protected by a limbo state of grief in which I have been full of kindness for all. I couldn't stand the thought of anything hurting or suffering. We were doing enough of that for everyone. There's so much pain in this world that one can't do anything about. So it has seemed to me criminal, clearly a moral deficit, to cause anguish to another living being.

The compassion I have felt has been a nice cushion, a plus to helping me come out of all this agony. The world is a tough place right now, probably always has been. We seem to hold caregivers in low esteem. Teachers, volunteers, nurses and counselors—those who give of themselves in the hope of making the world a better place are often looked down upon. This land of ours seems only to be about bigger, better, brighter, and most importantly, richer. We talk about how wonderful the caregivers of our world are, but honestly, who are our idols? Munitions makers are high on our list of heroes because they are wealthy enough to be listed in Fortune 500. And sports figures are there. We pay them an unbelievable amount of money so we can watch them crush one another on the field or court or in the ring. Always making life about winners and losers, never about being fellow travelers on a sometimes rocky road. And Hollywood legends? We put them on a pedestal. We want them above us and pay them well so we can titillate ourselves with scoffing at their foibles or envying their exploits. Our priorities are topsy-turvy and like the luckless turtle on his back, we can't get anywhere as long as our values are upside down.

I want to hang onto caring. I ask the heavens to keep my heart and mind open.

March 9

There is a picture in the paper today. I can barely move my eyes from it long enough to pencil my thoughts. It shows a freak snowstorm in southern California and two children are playing in this most unusual gift from the sky. Two other young men are watching them play. One of the observers…one of the observers is Dan. He is my Danny. He wears the same pale gray ski coat and pants. From the crepe-soled work shoes to the crease in the newly-acquired, straw cowboy hat, it is Dan. The same shrug of the shoulders and leaning stance. I thought I had become shockproof. I was wrong. I go to that deep place, now so familiar and as I reel I again wonder, *when will he be back?*

March 15

Over twenty years ago, when I was in high school, my older brother had a good friend named Dennis. He was killed in a plane crash shortly after he graduated. I rarely hear a small plane go by overhead that I don't think about Dennis. He is clear and present and warm in my memory and he is on my mind today. I find it comforting to think that somewhere in the world there are people who will remember Dan as I remember Dennis.

March 19

I can't stop thinking about Dennis. I didn't know his parents though they were highly connected in our city. I also didn't know how much cards and letters mean to a bereaved family. They mean a lot. I wonder if they are the kind of family who feel that the sadness of losing their son is best forgotten. Would it be unkind of me to write at this late date? Still something is driving me.

March 24

I fight the impulse as long as I can and then I give in and pen a note. I tell them how and why I remember their son. I write about the pain I felt at his death.

I write:

The point of this letter is to tell you how often I have thought of your Denny over the years and seen his face so clearly in my memory and warmed myself in his smile.

One of the things that has been so awful in our loss is the thought that our son had so little time to make an impact, to be remembered by any but ourselves. Then, like a blessing, your Dennis came to mind and I realized if after all these years the thought of him still brings me pleasure, perhaps there are people, of whom we have never heard, who twenty years from now will think of Danny and be happier because he lived.

I took great comfort from the thought and felt compelled to pass it on to you. Dennis, though he is one of those who had so little time, certainly did make a profound impact on me and I am better for having known him.

March 28

Today I received a letter in the mail from Dennis's parents. Tears run down my cheeks as I feel the warmth of their thanks. How often, they say, they still think and talk about Dennis as if he were a recent part of their lives. They say he has never gone away from them and they too feel the world has been made a better place because our sons lived.

I am touched beyond words and I wonder if this has in it another lesson, a teaching that shows it is never too late if you are motivated by the instinct of kindness to reach out to someone and say "thank you" or "I'm sorry" or "I remember and care."

March 29

Funny how each of the extended family reacts differently as time goes by. My sister drops notes in the mail every couple of weeks to say, "I'm thinking of you." Brother John calls to chat on his lunch hour, "How're you doing, Sis?" and his youngest son writes me letters and poems. George's mom searches for cards and sends them regularly. But so many family members and friends seem helpless. They want to do something to fix the situation and can't. And we are helpless to help them help us.

My brother Bob has, what I find to be, a strange philosophy. It is one of complete acceptance, so cut and dried it is hard for me not to be resentful. Is he displaying true feelings or bravado in fear of examining his real emotions? He is one of those who can't seem to understand why we aren't *over it yet,* why the holidays hurt, why we don't just know Dan is better off and let it go at that.

Each of us thinks the other is bizarre. He is a best friend to me and this difference is a wide river. Maybe he is closer to the Spirit than me, more aware—and because of that is more sublime. I know he and I need a boat or a bridge and right now we don't have one. I also have a cousin who writes notes to us on every occasion and with each note our pain is alleviated by a fraction. And I have an aunt who gets annoyed when anyone mentions Dan because, "They'll never be able to forget him if everyone keeps bringing him up."

How different we are. A person in grief can empty a room awfully fast by expressing their pain. No one wants to hear it and most will go to almost any length to avoid it. It is almost comical—if someone can't physically leave, they escape by changing the subject with a jerk.

And we do all we can to help them.

Shhh, don't say a word.

I am on the phone with Mom and I say, "My poor George. His beautiful face lines have changed, maybe permanently. The smile creases around his mouth have started to turn down. There is a slash between his eyebrows where pain has drawn them together so he looks angry. It makes me sad."

Mom makes a sympathetic sound and says sadly, "Your face too, my Mary, your face too."

March 31

"Oh Mama!" Melisa shouts this evening as she runs into the kitchen where I am scrubbing pans. She throws her arms around me, her voice was so full of emotion it frightens me.

"What's wrong?" I ask, but she won't answer, just keeps clinging. Then George comes in and says, "Didn't you hear yourself, Honey? You were singing?"

I look at him and his eyes are full and I realize I haven't sung in almost a year. Music is to my soul what air is to my lungs. That is probably one of the reasons Danny loved it so. From lullabies to silly, made-up songs and on up the scale to include rock and roll and almost everything else.

"Sing my song for me, Mom," he would beg.

"Oh, Danny boy…"

Our house has never been without music until this year. When I would start to hum a tune I would hear him saying, "Sing it again, Mom," or "Come listen to this, Mom," and my throat would close, my voice would drop to a gravelly depth and fade like twilight into darkness. What pains us most is often what we have loved the best.

But another page is turning. I am getting stronger.

Chapter Sixteen

MOVING ON

Tempus fugit, nonautem memoria.
Time flies, but not memory.

~ Vergilius Mora

April 2

I have a friendly acquaintance that I see weekly at the grocery store. About a month ago she broke her ankle. When I found out about her accident I sent her a get well card, then I forgot about it until I saw her the next week. Each time I see her I am startled anew. Every day her cast is her burden and isn't in my mind as I go about living my life. Now, I am thinking that grief is very like that cast. Only the person wearing it can be aware of it every minute of the day and night. Only they can know how it drags at the body, how awkward it can be, and painful, itchy and hot. How awful it is to be bound by it waking and sleeping, and when they bump it occasionally it causes an instant of fresh agony.

What a wonderful revelation for me. Now I understand how our friends can be so forgetful, and when I can understand something it does bring a little relief. I realize that the folks who knew him won't think of him every day, but will always be reminded by whatever special incident triggers the memories they hold. Even if I am not aware of it, others will remember. I know they will.

When I come home from the store, on the front porch there is a small, potted plant of Forget-Me-Not's with a note from Rosalyn, one of my newer friends who has shown herself to be extraordinarily courageous, kind and compassionate over the past year. The little card that accompanies the bright blue flowers reads, *I don't remember the exact date but I remember it was Spring and I'm thinking of you.* I sit down on the sun-warmed stairs and hold this love for a long, long time.

April 11

There was a strong wind storm today but Melisa, Suzanne and Paige ask permission to go into the cemetery and put some flowers on the grave. It still is a terrible effort to behave as if a request to go to his grave is fine and normal, but she needs this. There must be something cathartic about showing it to her friends. I wish I could understand what goes on in her mind. Kids seem to be so much more pragmatic than we adults. I wonder if their acceptance and realism is healthy or cold or perhaps just too young to understand? I guess it doesn't matter.

The girls come trudging into the house laughing. Red-cheeked and starving, they relate the hard time they had getting the flowers to stay put. Dan's niche is high up on a marble wall and it is necessary to use a long-handled pole, twelve feet in length, to reach it. You must then slide the metal ring on the end of the pole under the vase and lift it directly up which releases the vase from the clips that hold it to the wall. Then you lift the vase down, fill it with water and flowers, and replace it. It is awkward and difficult for anyone at the best of times, but for these little chicks to do it while fighting the wind must have been close to impossible. Melisa laughs while telling me about her thoughts, "Dan would have to hold his stomach he would have laughed so hard," she says, "but then he would have scooped me up high so I could reach the vase and put the flowers in, wouldn't he, Mama?" She turns to her girlfriends, "You should have seen how high I could go in his arms!"

I have to blink and swallow hard. I turn away glad for the excuse of sandwiches to cut. I can tell they've been practicing as they proudly singsong in unison, "It was really hard but we did it!"

My smile is real as I look each girl in the eyes and state, "You've proven one more time that with determination you girls can do anything."

April 12

George jogs with Licorice in the cemetery every morning. His path takes him twice by the columbarium that holds Danny's niche. He says the flowers the girls worked so hard to present to Dan are Scotch Broom, a hardy bush of a weed known for its bright yellow blooms and its innumerable black bugs. His eyes are damp as he chuckles and again my smile is real.

April 15

Today there is no number on my calendar square. Today is such a contrast to what should have been. It is Dan's twenty-first birthday.

Dave comes in with his shoulders slumped. "I was over at Northgate and all I could see in every window display was something Dan would have liked. It really hurt Mom."

I hug him to me. I know. Oh. I know.

Melisa comes in from school. She gives me a paper circle with a small face that says BE HAPPY. I laugh as she pins it on me, smile side up. I need a pinned-up smile—my own sometimes feels stapled down in sorrow.

I went to work this morning but requested the afternoon off. I needed to be alone.

Today I want to tear my flesh and let the pain escape. Instead I force myself to go to the cemetery. As I get out of the car and walk toward Danny's grave, it starts to rain—not unusual in Seattle, but until this moment it had been clear and sunny. Fat splats of water strike me and the wind begins blowing fresh and unexpected. I feel as if the heavens are crying and wonder, are they crying for him or for us?

I bring him a red rose. I bring him a celebratory bottle of beer. I always promised I would treat him to one glass of beer. He would have come of age today. But the rose has no scent. And I can't swallow. I have to wish him a birthday wish and tell him what I tell each of my babies every year. This time it is, "I'm so glad you were born twenty-one years ago today, my Danny." And suddenly I know I am glad, really glad, though my voice cracks and strangles with the words.

Throughout this agony I've wondered over and over if it truly is *"better to have loved and lost than never to have loved at all"* and at last I know the answer. It is. Yes, yes, yes. I am so glad my life was blessed by this son. Even if for such a short time. And I hear myself whisper, "Oh, how I love you my D'Mark. Happy birthday, Love."

Last night I dreamt about Danny. We were together in the burning house. I was so panicked, truly terrified. I was whimpering, saying over and over "We have to get out!" And I heard him clearly and softly say, "It's okay Mom. I've done what I had to do. You go on now, Mom. You go on. It's okay."

Then I am awake…but…it is not okay.

THE HEALING

A year ago I didn't think I'd ever smile again,
today the postman brought to me a letter from a friend.
Speaking FIRST of sympathy my friend went on to say,
"I just want to tell you my friend of the fun I had today."
Fun thought I? What's fun thought I?
as my eyes slid down the page.
How dare he speak of fun to me in my grief I thought with rage?
But he wrote of how he visited with his two-year-old grandson.
With wit and love he detailed the silly things they'd done.
He touched in me deep memory of OUR kids when they were young,
And the good times we had shared when their lives had just begun.
First I felt a little smile that turned into a grin,
then a chuckle crept out of me. I couldn't keep it in.
I felt the warmth of laughter somewhere near my toes,
and it melted all the ice of grief as it rose and rose and rose.
Water from its melting streamed out of my eyes,
down my cheeks and from my chin while I in great surprise
heard the laugh burst from my lips and startled looked around:
to discover it was ME who had made that glorious sound.
And as I reached for a tissue to wipe my nose and face
I realized my heart was not so heavy in its place.
And of the word bittersweet? I truly knew the meaning,
For bittersweet is what we feel when we finally begin
the healing.

~ Mary M. Fern

April 18

Spring has returned, time has passed. Time is a terrible tailor and doesn't mend worth a damn. Perhaps time would do all right with a smooth clean tear, but when a heart is ripped from a breast, stomped on and thrust rudely back in, it doesn't mend well. Certainly, it beats again. It even resumes loving again. To all appearances, it is healed, but the lacerations that deface it will not be sanded away. And I guess that's okay. Just as a soft, smooth blanket will warm you, so too will a patchwork quilt. Our hearts aren't smooth anymore, but they still are beautiful. Maybe even more beautiful for all the love in the stitches that we and so many other people who love us have put in. All those stitches now hold us and our hearts together.

April 25

"Mom," Melisa shouts, "where's my baby book?"

I smile as I go to the shelf where all three of the books reside, holding their medley of memory until a moment in the now begs to be infused with the breath of the past.

"Here you go, Honey"

"Can I look at all of them? Come sit with me and help me look. Please?"

How can I refuse such a nice request? I steel my heart against the arrows that I know will come and we snuggle together, my daughter and I, to make a pilgrimage to yesterday.

The cliché about baby books is sure true in our house. Danny, the first born has every breath carefully recorded in curlicue cursive. Each move he made was such a wonder, never experienced before. Even our parental mistakes are there to glare out in the spotlight of hindsight. Like this line, *I just can't get you to eat liver, not that I blame you but you have to have it for your health and it makes mealtime so miserable for both of us.* Why wasn't I smart enough to know that spinach was a great substitute? He loved spinach. All first children deserve some kind of award for being guinea pigs to totally unseasoned parents and trailblazers for subsequent siblings.

Dave's book records only the highlights—first haircut, first steps and words—there was so little time with Dan, just nine months older, and Dave, being such a high-maintenance baby, just feeding him every four hours day and night for the first three months had me worn to the bone. Plus, the second time around, things don't seem quite the miracle. What a shame.

Melisa is pleased with her book.

"I have lots more than David, don't I?"

"Yes you do."

"Why, Mom?"

"Well, there are ten years between you and Dave, so everything you did seemed new again. I also had more time and I was better organized. And maybe because I was older, I had more self-discipline and sense of family history."

"Nah, Mom. I know why there's more about me. It's because you like me best, right?"

"Well, I can tell you this, my Little Bear, you are my very favorite daughter."

"Oh, Mom," laughs my girl. "I'm your only daughter!"

I laugh with her.

Later I reflect on our nice afternoon as I tell George about this goofy kid of ours and he says something that has crossed my mind also. "Have you wondered what the lineup of our family is now? Without Dan, is Dave first? And, you know, Dave is now older than Danny was."

"I know. It's all very bizarre isn't it?"

May 2

My brother and sister-in-law have a big party for their twenty-fifth wedding anniversary. Their kids do such a great job of putting together food, friends and favors. Our little group does much better this time than we did at their daughter's graduation party last spring. We still stick together so closely, trying not to cling, but still needing to be visually adhered, as if together we are more of a family. Dan was the family extrovert so without him we are quieter.

Two or three people ask, "How are you folks doing?" with that particular tone that lets us know they have not forgotten and are thinking of him. We say we are "hanging in there." Everyone gets wet-eyed with quick, hot tears, and I quietly say, "Thanks for asking." As we move on, I am saying "Bless you, bless you for remembering, it is so important to us that you remember."

May

Mother's Day

I wish we could have seen him. Perhaps that would have made it more real. If I had insisted, George would have forced himself to come with me—he wouldn't have let himself stay behind. It makes me angry that because he couldn't bear it, I had to deny myself something I really needed. I watched my baby come into this world all bloody and covered with waxy, white vernix. I hugged him to me when he rode his motorbike over the dirt bank and came home so muddy and bloody I didn't recognize him. I can understand the funeral director's denial of my demand. I can understand George's reluctance. But, I wish I could have seen him. It must be because it is Mother's Day that I am lost in this old quagmire.

I visualize his gold chain and the litany starts. All that glitters is not gold. All that's gold does not glitter. His chain no longer glitters. His heart was touched with gold but it doesn't glitter either. The fine things I remember, the golden things he did for me from his youngest years, noticing something pretty and bringing it home so Mom could enjoy it too, a feather, rock or leaf. Roses for no reason, only the thought that I might need special attention. Or his way of saying he loved you even though he might be breaking the rules. Roses even when he had to carry them home on his bike in the bitter cold. And why was he riding his bike to work in the frigid degrees of winter? Because he had gotten another ticket for speeding and we took away his car privileges (not that that helped—he's the only person I ever heard of who managed to get a speeding ticket while riding a bike). I remember one cold night so well. He came in about 10:30 p.m. His hands were blocks of ice. He pulled flowers from out from the front of his jacket and whispered, "Sorry Mom. I do love you," and immediately plucked up a gray streaked hair saying, "Hey, what's this? Time for Clairol Mom." And I hit him a little and hugged him a lot.

I am such a lucky mom—I have the best kids ever and am blessed with such a special, unique bond with each of them. I smile as I hear my own mom saying, "Kids are goats, Mary, we have children."

May 13

Dave informed us a couple of weeks ago that he is going to move into an apartment the first of next month. He thinks it's time he tried making it on his own. I'm doing the best I can to hide my terrors but stupidly, the first thing I ask when he says he has found a place is, "Does it have smoke detectors?"

I stand in the sunlit living room and dust the hundreds of leaves that now cloak the fig tree and let it do the weeping for me. How can he even think of leaving us now, so soon?

I won't let him see my tears, know my fears. They are for me to conceal. I will let him go with excitement and the positive knowledge that he can make it on his own, that he will be a successful adult.

I think of how important David is to our family, to me. Even today he comes to me with sincerity, with apologetic determination, honesty, and courage. Where Dan bent rules until they broke and heated us until we exploded, Dave comes quietly, reasonably to say "I know it's hard and I'm scared, but mostly I'm afraid if I don't do it now, I won't be able to."

He will do well on his own but I do worry for Melisa as he is her best friend and she is going to be very lonely. Dave will take, as he leaves, and Melisa will keep, as he leaves, this gift from Dan—the knowledge that we are covered with incredible new armor. We may not know much, but we do know this—we are all survivors.

Jeff comes by today. It is good to see him. What a hug he has! He's been remarkably loyal about coming around though it can't be easy for him. Each time he sees us he has to be reminded of all of his losses in the fire, his possessions, his innocence, his youthful sense of omnipotence and of course, one of his best friends.

His life is very full and it must take an effort for him to make the time to visit. He puts a lot of adults to shame. We rarely discuss the past when he drops in—his present and future are of more interest to us, and we don't have to feign. If Dan is mentioned, it is with little discomfort and that is such a pleasant relief.

May 15

George and Melisa are enthused at my idea of throwing a going away/housewarming party for Dave. It is the first time I have thought about inviting a large group over since we lost Dan. George seems to see it as an omen and I have to admit that seeing a genuine smile on his face has given me the dollop of energy I need in order to plan and carry out a party.

May 19

The family is responding with excitement to the housewarming party idea. We are keeping it a secret from Dave, but everyone has promised to be here. Patty, my friend and sister-in-law, in particular, thinks it's a great idea. She has been buying little things for Colleen over the years as I have been doing for Melisa, but neither of us thought to build up a hope chest for our boys and when they leave home they will need everything.

I have wanted to look forward to something. I have pretended to look forward to something. Now I am looking forward to having all the family here. Melisa is about to burst with the secret. It is so exciting for her! Dave has promised that she can come up and visit whenever she likes and she tells me with eyes sparkling, "He might even get MTV." Poor Little Bear doesn't realize how very lonesome she will be without him.

May 23

I decide to serve an easy spaghetti dinner and save myself some work by ordering a decorated cake. I am getting tired again and my emotions are too close to the surface when I'm tired.

At the bakery counter in the grocery store an acquaintance from school walks up to me to say hello.

"You're ordering a special cake? What's the occasion?"

"It's for Dave. He's found an apartment and is moving next week."

"Oh, how exciting. Another of your sons moving out."

It's been awhile since I have felt that sense of detachment, but here it is again and I am glad.

She goes on about how she remembers leaving home. "It's so important to let go," she advises. "David will grow if you let him go and you will not heal until you let go of your other son. I see by your tears that you haven't said goodbye yet. And I know Melisa is still having a hard time. Her grades are down and she's not very bubbly anymore. It's up to you as the mother to help your family heal."

I fight vomit and see myself watch her as she strolls easily away, unencumbered by the knowledge that she has left my slashed body bleeding on the cold tile floor.

Now at home, I sit cross-legged and write a letter I will never send.

Dear Mrs. -----,

Please don't minimize my grief by preaching to me that I must let go.

Don't worry about trying to "fix" the situation—it can't be fixed. But you could help. You could offer to give Melisa some study help. You could take her out for an ice cream and tell her you need her advice on how best to make her feel better. You told me you are praying for us and that's a lot, but while you pray at night you could also reach out in a practical way during the day.

We all want to remember Danny. Fear of forgetting him nightly turns my pillow to stone. I am panicked that I might forget one tiny little thing about him, and yet forget is what you and others advise us to do.

And please tell me why most people are so afraid of tears? Don't you understand that the crying itself doesn't hurt? Why can't you understand tears for what they are: glue for the broken heart?

In recent studies scientists are finding chemicals in the tears of bereavement that are toxic. So crying rids the body of these toxins that might cause havoc.

Working as you do in a church school for young children, you should realize that tears aren't pain. They are a symptom of pain and when my grieving tears upset you, I find myself in the position of feeling the need to apologize. But this problem, this fear of tears, does not belong to the bereaved—this problem belongs to you. I see the person who will not allow weeping as selfish and concerned not with my feelings, but with their own.

When I hear people talk about the grief-stricken and comment about crying, I often think they are not truly being solicitous. In fact, it seems to me they are mentally wringing their hands and if one could overhear their true thoughts it might sound like this: "I can't stand it. I feel helpless and uncomfortable. I don't know what to do. So, you must stop crying and make me feel better."

That is what I hear when I hear someone say, "Don't cry. You have to let go. Forget." I hear childishness and I hear fear because I too have been in that position. We are a culture that hides quaking from death. For that matter, we shun anything that might cause us emotional discomfort, or actually, any kind of discomfort. Think of how we Americans "rough it" when we are

176

camping out. There we are out in the wilds of an RV park with our TV, stereo, electric barbecue, and hot and cold running water. Yes, we do like our ease. And dis-ease upsets us whether it comes in the form of a slow moving elderly person, a retarded seatmate on the bus or a crippled child. We simply don't like it. We expect the limbless Vet to make all the right gestures to give us solace. We want our homeless to stay well out of sight and not make us feel bad about their predicament. We want our old ones, sick ones, grief-stricken ones to be unseen.

Why are we like that? Is it cultural or human nature? Or fear? Which is the worse handicap, the obvious physical one or the hidden emotional one so many carry?

When someone hushes my tears by subtly making me feel as if I am a burden for crying or overtly tries to stop me by directly insisting, "Don't," it is not my actions they are concerned with but their own.

I know this is harsh but it's honest.

Sincerely,

Well, I sure can't send that. But I feel better for having expressed it.

"As is a tale, so is life: not how long it is
but how good it is, is what matters."

~ Lucius Annaeus Seneca

May 25

Twenty members of the family gather for dinner, cake, and presents. Dave is really surprised and happy. It seems to me the laughter and teasing are easy and genuine, a perfect touch to send him off on his own. The day is good. I'm tired now, but it is a satisfied tired.

May 27

Today is the one-year anniversary. We've all been gearing up emotionally for it, expecting…what? A lessening of pain or an even weightier, more depressed Spirit? I don't know, but we seem to have been trying to put a tighter rein on ourselves in anticipation of this day. Our society makes such a big deal at the passing of each year. The very word *anniversary* brings to mind happy celebrations and it has grown repugnant in my mind. Surprise! I find today a day no more or less painful than the 364 that preceded it. George says it best, "Every day has been a year long. Today was just another year."

Time has gone crazy, it lurches and glides so we don't measure time in the conventional way anymore. In fact, the subject of our ages came into the conversation recently and we had to laugh. Portions of our Spirits are so ancient that calendar age means nothing. As for the calendar, the only thing a year did was take us, without him, through every occasion he would normally have shared. That agonizing first time is now past. No family days will ever be *the first* again, with the exception of those little occasions such as Dave or Melisa graduating, getting married, having babies, things like new jobs, special trips, big family reunions and any of the myriad milestones so important to a family. It hurts so to think of him not being here as the future stretches on. We may get through this, but I can't imagine we'll ever get over it. After today, occasions will be just another birthday, another Christmas— just another day without him.

May 28

I imagine every family dates their lives not only by the calendar, but even more by the personal important events and happenings in those lives. In conversation, someone will say, "Do you remember when the Smith's got that big old car with the fins like a shark's dorsal?" And you say, "Sure, it must have been late in '59, I remember it was right after we got married," or, "It had to have been before '70, Melisa hadn't been born yet." That's how we do it, and nothing is more significant than the date when your first child is born. Dan's death has destroyed my mental calendar.

A horrible thought just came to me. Will we now count time as just before or after late May? Yes. Of course we will. We will say "Licorice must be seven or eight or nine. I remember because we got him right after Dan..." God! It gives me shivers.

May 29

"I imagined one of the reasons people cling to their hates so stubbornly is because they sense, once the hate is gone, they will be forced to deal with their pain."

~ James Baldwin, Notes of a Native Son.

Does this explain George's bitterness?

May 30

We've been so busy at work the last two months I've not had the time to think and for now, I need this. I've gone from not wanting to go to the shop to now filling every waking moment with frantic busy work. I'm avoiding the house as much as I can. I've said before I wish I could just walk away—instead I work, driving myself to unthinking exhaustion.

Melisa and Dave are off to a movie so George and I go out to a favorite place for pizza. Driving home, we pass the exit sign marked with the name of the unincorporated town where Dan had his rental and I am startled to find my face awash in tears. It's been quite a long time since I've cried.

The night is windy, the moon almost full. Through the windshield I watch the torn and tattered clouds racing across its bright face. I watch the light and shadow play over George's face, obscuring then revealing his features, and I think about the old saying about not telling a book by its cover. All of us live in light and shadow every day, revealing a little, obscuring a lot.

There was a time in our lives when we saw the patterns of our days as sharp and defined. It isn't like that anymore it never really was. Where we were penning our family story, the wet ink has been blurred, smudged by the finger of fate.

Chapter Seventeen

A New Understanding

"There is no death! The stars go down
to rise upon some other shore,
and bright in heaven's jeweled crown
They shine forevermore."

~ John L. McCreery, "There is No Death"

June 1

Once or twice a year when the kids and the routine get to be too much, I run away from home. I run to Mom's. I love talking with my mother. She's smart, wise, insightful, and unafraid. Whatever depth or height a conversation takes, she will go there with me. It is a treat to have her to myself today as she is so universally loved that she often has someone at the house seeking her counsel.

Mom's chair angles so the arm touches the arm of the couch where I sit, legs tucked under me. She has already raised her eyebrow and clicked her tongue to remind me that I should not be sitting like this, "It's too hard on the spine and knees." And I've already said, "Yes Mom," but haven't changed position.

We reach simultaneously for our coffee and I look into the calmest most beautiful gray eyes on the planet and say, "Can I tell you a hard memory about you?"

She smiles a little.

"It's a sad memory," I say.

There comes the slightest peaceful nod, so I start.

"A couple of weeks after Dad died, George and I came to visit. When we were leaving, going down that long driveway I looked back to wave. It seemed to me the driveway had stretched, a block at least. At the end, there you were in the open door of this big house." I pause, my eyes burning while mom simply waits. "You looked so tiny, Mom. So alone. I never saw anything so lonely."

"And," she quietly responds, "That's how you feel."

I inhale fast. I didn't realize I had been seeing myself in my mother. Dan had been such a part of the music of my soul, part of what made my Spirit dance. When we buried him, the melody became too muffled to be heard.

"How do you do it, Mom? Is it still that lonely? Does it ever go away? Why, if I'm feeling so lonely, do I need to run away from everything and everyone who might comfort me? Everything I have left?"

All of a sudden, Mom starts to laugh, and when Mom laughs, she laughs all over, so I have to start to grin too. "Oh Mary," she says, "It's my turn to ask you a question."

"Okay."

"Do you have any idea how often I have asked for the strength and wisdom to answer your everlasting questions? Other babies' first words are 'Mama' and 'Dada' and 'Bye bye.' You were born asking, 'What is the meaning of life?'" Her worn hands spread in front of her as she chuckles and I laugh. Then, serious, she answers me, "How do I do it? Just like you are doing it, Honey. One day at a time. In the morning I ask for strength and guidance for that one day and in the evening I say thank you. The next day I do it again. There are still many days that are lonely, days when I have to remind myself that tomorrow will be better. I have learned to temper my expectations of myself. I dropped expectations of others long ago—now I'm learning to be that forgiving of myself too. Now I can accept my own bad days, give them a little pat and let them go. I know tomorrow will be better."

I sip and digest her words, needing to hold them, trying to hold the peace I feel all around me, all inside me.

Mom breaks our long quiet by saying, "Lonely is a funny thing, I think—it seems to me to be a state of mind, perhaps even an intention. I'm often alone but rarely lonely. Some folks, your aunt for instance, need people and noise and busyness. If she's alone, the TV or the radio is always on for company. I'm the opposite and, you know Honey, so are you. Your brother goes off by himself on long motorcycle rides to 'blow off the cobwebs' and your sister hikes the remote streams with her fishing rod. Our family seems to be okay alone and to understand the difference between loneliness and solitude. How often have I seen you curled up with book or pen in hand a million miles away?"

"Solitude is peaceful for me," I say. "I guess it isn't a want, it's a need. I need empty space and time to think so I can get perspective."

"Maybe you need to honor that. Recognize that your Spirit needs some silence. We live in such a noisy world. You can explain to George and the children. It won't shock them you know. They will understand. They love you so. Why do you think are you so hard on yourself so much of the time? You give such good advice to so many others—I wish you would take some of that advice for yourself. Be kind and gentle and honor yourself. Forgive yourself, Honey. You didn't do anything wrong. Life just happened."

I let her words wash over me and wash me clean.

"Mary," she continues, "Are you ready to hear this now?"

I nod.

"We know, don't we? The greatest joys and the greatest tragedies open us to the greatest metamorphosis. That's what is happening to you. You will never see the world the same way again. And you shouldn't. This must change you. But patience is required. The cocoon doesn't just break open one day and let the butterfly step out. That fragile, tightly-wrapped, wet creature has to work to break out. Then it must look for the sun to dry it before it can spread its wings and fly."

Dust motes swirl in the sunny patch of the well-worn room where the dog has disturbed them on his way over to me for an ear scratch. Mom's words swirl too, gently dancing in the air, and feel to me like aloe on a sunburn.

Driving home I feel relieved, released, re-created, almost as if, butterfly like, I could fly.

June 2

Today is my dad's birthday and though he passed a few years ago, I whisper him birthday wishes.

We've just finished moving Dave. His tiny place is clean and convenient to work and school and it's only about five miles from here. He is equal parts excited and nervous, and George and I are trying hard to be happy for him. We're so very proud of him but know we will miss him and probably be afraid for a while. Melisa can't wait to get to spend time with him in his new home.

June 5

This process of grief we have been forced into makes me think about watching the kids learn to walk for the first time. How I marveled at their single-mindedness and determination. I often wondered what compelling force was driving them on. They would pull themselves up so slowly and ever so tentatively let go of the support they had used to stand. I remember the look of mingled surprise, delight and fear before they plopped to the floor again. Then they would gather their courage to try and try again. There is a mysterious force in the human Spirit that kept them trying. Those tottering first steps so wobbling and the child so delighted to be upright only to fall unexpectedly when they thought they had conquered this skill. But as they got stronger over the months the balance improved, the task became easier, and one day they were running.

I'm not running yet but not falling as often either. I don't think it will ever get easy, but it is getting easier.

June 10

Dave comes over today to pick up some treats we made for him. The house is quiet and we have a little time to visit. I am so glad I kept my thoughts about his move to myself. When he leaves, he hugs me and says, "I was kind of scared to do this, Mom. And I think if I didn't try it right now I might not have had the nerve to leave. Thanks for not making it any harder."

I say, "We're a little scared too and that's okay. We don't doubt your ability for a second, you'll be fine. It would be strange if we all weren't a bit nervous. Getting out into the big world on your own is a giant step, but we're just stretching the bonds between us, not breaking them."

"Right. And I'll be back once a week to wash my car."

"That's fine," I tease, "just as long as you don't bring your dirty laundry."

Hours later, I'm still feeling Dave's hug. Both my boys are great huggers. I am holding these moments in my heart, savoring them. That is another good lesson. Stay very present in the moment. I'm not morbid about it anymore, just conscious of never knowing when each hug might be the last hug.

It is now over a year since we last saw our Dan.

June 28

I shuffle the papers in the drawer and flip through my notebook and I'm still not ready to re-read it or the cards or the memory book. The many blank pages in the spiral-bound book I've been using as a journal are a mute testimony to the parts of my inner life that are a wasteland. On the outside, all appears normal.

I don't ask why it happened to us—after all, why not us? Still, I do ask why any family must lose a child? This random and violent cosmos we inhabit with stars exploding to give off light, and volcanoes exploding to create new land, and these little explosions in a family's life sometimes give off light as they too create something new. But I don't yet know what is being created.

So, fate, design, randomness? And if every cloud has a silver lining, doesn't it stand to reason that every silver lining will have a cloud? And why do I question the dark time? I never questioned the bright days when we lived them. More questions without answers.

Perhaps I have answered one question for myself though. One clear, albeit weird, philosophy has come to me in the months since he died—life here on earth would be lived pretty much in the same way whether you believed in a god or not. If you are a believer, you would try to obey what you are told are his tenets while you were here. You would love one another, help one another, and be a good steward of the earth in order to reap your reward in Heaven. Conversely, if you did not believe there was a better world coming in the hereafter, what better way could you choose to live this one life then by loving one another, helping one another and loving and enjoying this world to the maximum while you were here. So a believer and a non-believer might have an identical philosophy. That makes sense to me…somehow.

July 1

It is the second summer without our eldest boy. I am noticing many changes in our emotions. For example, we spend the weekend on the boat at Blake Island and enjoy it.

Now, there is a simple little sentence.

No one reading it would know that behind those thirteen words lie thirteen months of grief so dark I doubted we would see the light again.

Maybe this will be the year to strip the blackness from my soul. Is

184

that something one can simply decide to do and proceed to do it? I won't know till I try. I'll try to make some sense out of my child being gone. I'm still at that strange place where I can't say the final words. I can't say his name in the same sentence with the word *dead*.

Wait. I'm going to try. I take a deep breath. Danny...Danny is...My head cracks. I hyperventilate. Tears swoosh down my cheeks like a monsoon and I cannot say it, I cannot.

I discovered months ago that I can say Dan is gone. I can even say he is dead. But I still can't put the word *dead* in the same sentence with his name.

There is a change though. The tears that wash my face today do not scald and burn and turn my eyes aflame. These tears are just tears— clear, salty, wet, no longer painful. How odd is that?

Later I try again. This time I don't pant, I don't cry, but I still can't speak the words. I chide myself, *Come on, Mary. You must do what you can't do if you want to get on with your life.*

Is the desire to get on with my life in me yet? I am beginning to wish it was. It seems to stand to reason that once you begin to wish you cared, pretty soon you will be caring. First you desire, and then you plan, right? Or is it the other way around? Or both?

Some of the fear of contemplating his death is gone. I think I am becoming resigned. In some ways, the grief is easing, though I'm afraid to touch the sore spot in case the *better* is only an illusion. I sometimes go a couple of hours without thinking of him. Though that is not a relief either, for then I torture myself for forgetting even a short while. It is all so very confusing. But to get over this sadness is to get beyond Dan, and I can't bear to think of leaving him behind alone.

My family can't really go on unless I do too. Just as I don't want to go on without Danny, they do not want to go on without me. But, they will if they have to. Life always moves forward, with or without you. They must move forward and, so...will...I.

Remember Me

"You can shed tears that he is gone,
or you can smile because he lived.
You can close your eyes and pray that he'll come back,
or you can open your eyes and see all that he's left.
Your heart can be empty because you can't see him,
or you can be full of the love that you shared.
You can turn your back on tomorrow and live yesterday,
or you can be happy for tomorrow because of yesterday.
You can remember him and only that he's gone,
or you can cherish his memory and let it live on.
You can cry and close your mind, be empty and turn your back,
or you can do what he'd want: smile, open your eyes, love and go
on."

~David Harkins

July 7

Every painful memory I feel, every irritation or crisis, seems to have some of the pressure defused as soon as I speak of it aloud. The key seems to be the verbalizing or writing. Maybe because it takes a decision and an act to bring it out of myself and into the air or onto the paper. But in this case, there is no one to talk to who isn't already feeling too hurt and helpless. I should look into some counseling, but if I can't expose my feelings to a loved one, how could I tell them to a stranger? I like to consider myself enlightened, but there is that part of me I carry from the past that says only the weak seek outside help. Though when I turn that around, I think how courageous are the seekers of counseling as one must be very brave to admit they need help and ask for assistance. Maybe the real coward is the one I see in my mirror.

Friends with whom I might have chosen to speak have been so uncomfortable I just couldn't do that to them. Here is another truth I have learned: someone who will listen, just listen, is someone to be absolutely treasured.

When we get through this, I will know how to be even better as a listener and I will reach out when I think I see a need. It is risky, but I'm going to try.

Well look at that, I said, "when"...

I am so fortunate to have George. We've almost always been able to say anything to each other. He is more than my heart, he is my best friend—but he is in such pain too. I wonder if most couples are like us—for him, any words dealing with emotion are too many, and for me, all the words are too few. I have taken to verbalizing when I am alone. I talk out loud to myself—sometimes I talk to the dog. Often I speak in my heart to D'Mark.

Another lesson. I think his death has left me less fearful. I still worry about the kids of course, but that's pretty much all I fear anymore. When life has hurt you this badly, you can't believe anything could hurt this much again, so there's nothing left to fear.

I used to think I had some control in this life. Now I believe everyone is at any given moment open to tragedy in this random universe. When I accept that as fact I must accept life as it is. Don't ask, "Why?" Ask, "Why not?" I am not sure if this a true personality change or simply another temporary *stage of grief.* And how I hate that phrase.

And discovering that tragedy can happen not only to the other guy but to you also changes everything. But here is another lesson: if you're surviving this, though you cannot glimpse the sky from the depths of the pit, you can live through anything.

My neighbor Darlene is very ill. She is in the final days of a valiant battle with esophageal cancer and is, at last, exhausted and spent, almost ready, I think, to let go. I am doing what I can for her and her family. It was Darlene who my sister–mistakenly—kept away from me after Dan's memorial. It was Darlene who helped drag me through the quagmire of the first year of grieving.

It is Darlene who is helping me relearn a lesson. She is one of the most independent people on the planet, a fighter who wants to battle alone. And though I am good at it, I am the world's most reluctant nurse. Mom was a nurse, grandma was a nurse, but that gene skipped me.

Darlene has allowed only me into the intimacy of her dying and we both have been elevated because of her gift. Reaching out to help someone else really does help you. Still, today coming home from a terribly hard session at her house I am so depleted, I find myself standing at the center of the quiet intersection of our neighborhood streets shaking my tired fist at the heavens and shouting, really shouting, "No more lessons!"

July 19

Today we put some down money on a piece of property overlooking the Strait of Juan de Fuca. In a year of strange coincidences, this was yet another. Two insurance checks were sent to us after his death. Those checks have been very hard to deal with. The idea of monetary gain coming from this tragedy is abhorrent and we haven't known what to do. First we thought Dave could use it for college, but we decided that the hard work of attaining a degree was a vital part of that education. In our lives, we've found that the appreciation we have for our accomplishments is in direct proportion to the amount of work we must do to achieve it.

We banked the check, tucking some away for a David emergency and some for a Melisa emergency, and after a year's debate, decide to purchase some vacation land that should hold value. And all of us can use it for the future.

So, on another excursion, we moor our little *Nameless II* in Friday Harbor on San Juan Island and climb the hill looking for a real estate office. There are many to choose from and we choose one with the logo of the soaring gull. Still not completely convinced we're making the right decision, our hearts are heavy and hesitant. The salesman offers coffee and when he leaves the room, George turns to me to say, "You really think this is what we should do?" As I shrug my answer to him, the radio playing softly in the background begins playing "Freebird," Danny's anthem. We stare at each other in amazement as our eyes fill and George's question is answered.

The agent shows us a couple of places before we find ourselves standing on a piece of land without a tree in sight. I can't believe we're even considering a spot without trees, but it is about him, not us, and he would love this openness.

It is a thistle-strewn slope open to all the buffeting the winds of nature can hand out. It overlooks white-capped water and off to snowcapped mountains. It is without question the right place. I can almost feel his arm around me assuring me as I gaze off sightlessly. I am not tearful or depressed, but it is oh so poignant.

July 20

Sometimes insomnia is my friend—sometimes it is my enemy. Tonight is not good. Tonight the imaginary chest I have locked deep inside springs open. All the speculations and questions that are too hard to look at are exposed once more. Did he feel pain? Did he sleep through? If I hadn't insisted he move would he still be alive? As it is with so many moms, our children's souls intertwine with ours. How could I not have known he needed me? If I had seen him, would my mind be clearer, would I better understand the permanence of his absence? I saw a picture in the newspaper a couple of months ago and it was a picture of Dan. Each time I looked at it I could swear in a court that it was him. Same coat, same big old cowboy hat, lanky, handsome and heart-wrenching. And I ask, "Does he forgive me?" I ask in my heart all the things I cannot ask with my mouth, then I write it down and I put it away.

When I wake in the morning I am drained. There is so little of me left. Again. This is such an erratic journey, back and forth, one moment free, the next in chains.

August 10

I reread my last entry of three weeks ago. What a difference those three weeks make. We are back in the islands and they are good again. I am almost good again. I'm not feeling impatient or exhausted. There are multiple days of blank pages in the journal as I skip ahead. The obsession and compulsion has lifted. We are laughing out loud as we play our thousandth game of UNO, smiling as we marvel at how competent our Melisa has gotten as she captains the boat or rows the dingy.

Slowly, I have gotten back to normal sleep patterns. Fourteen months ago I could not sleep at all. If someone else had told me they had gone two or more weeks without any sleep, I would have doubted it, but it can be true. After a while, I started sleeping from 11:00 till 1:00 a.m. only to waken and be unable to fall back off. The last six months I wake from 1:00 till 3:00 a.m., and then sleep the rest of the night. Now I know what *the dark night of the soul* is all about, but lately it feels as if dawn is just below the horizon.

August 20

We're home from vacation and as we walk in the front door, a gush of sweet fragrant air rushes out to greet us. Looking around, Melisa discovers that the asparagus fern, Dan's last gift to me, is cascading tiny star-like blossoms of the purest white. Amazing, I didn't know ferns bloomed. I am so warmed with the blessing—Dan is still bringing me flowers.

Melisa startles me today at lunch with her accusing tone as she snaps, "Mom, why don't you ever go down to the cemetery? Do you just want to forget him?"

Her question swooshes the air from my lungs. "Wow! Bear, that's a question!" I say as I perch on the bar stool across from her and inhale. "Of course I don't want to forget him but it hurts me too much to go down there."

I can see in her eyes she thinks that's an excuse, and of course it is, but I can't explain any better than that to a ten year-old. She knows what love is—she loves us, she loves her dog and she loves her brothers. And someday if she has a child who she carries and plans for, births, nurtures in all the myriad ways a mother does, teaches and preaches and prays for and pays for and loves with a love that is holy, well, someday she might understand. I do only pray that she and Dave never have to learn to understand the losing part of love.

I never feel anything of him at the cemetery, I don't think of him as being there. When I go down there, all I can think of are the hundreds of hours we spent watching as he and Dave played little league baseball. The cemetery owned the land the ball field was on and allowed us to build a diamond there. In fact, when George and I bought our plot, one of the things we laughed about was being where we could oversee the old field and feel the ghosts of excitement and fun that still seem to impregnate the air.

When I am ready, I might haunt that place like a specter, but not yet. And I have a regret that grows larger each day, but I don't know what to do about it. I am sorry we placed the ashes in this crept. Nothing of him should ever have been confined. Even this part of him should be free.

YOU WILL OFTEN HEAR, "BE GOOD TO YOURSELF," BUT WHAT DOES IT ACTUALLY MEAN?

All the hints your mom told you and all the instructions your doctors advise,
all those things we know by heart and too often fail to do,
all those things that were good for you before:
enough sleep, enough hydration, enough exercise, enough nourishment,
are good for you still.
But now they are harder to remember and even if you do remember, you often no longer care.
Do them anyway.
This is a good time to use your calendar as a tool.
Sharpen your pencil and make a note,
keep it simple:

1) Start with sleep, you may do too much or too little—make a note to keep track.

2) Hydration. Most of us don't drink enough water at the best of times. Fill a pitcher in the morning and sip a bit all day. Try to empty it by day's end. A slice of citrus or a drop of mint to freshen it might help. By the way, alcohol doesn't count as hydration, neither does coffee.

3) Exercise. Again some do way too much, trying to outrun the demons of death. Most of us do way too little. It doesn't have to be calisthenics or madly dashing to and fro. Maybe you like to walk or work in the garden. But remember in grief our sense of time is skewed. It helps to set a timer because if you overdo today your exhaustion tomorrow will exacerbate your grief.

4) Nourishment. This one is not so easy. You have to eat. Even if you cannot stand the idea. Again it is often a case of too little or too much. I gained 20 pounds eating all my son's favorite foods that he was no longer here to enjoy. Fast food can lead to fast ill

191

health. The modern deli has many good choices. Six little meals rather than 2 or 3 big ones.

The goal is to keep the body feeling as good as it can while the Spirit heals.

Right now the Spirit is a little wounded child and the body is the parent who must nurture and care for it until it can again care for itself.

~ Mary M. Fern

Chapter Eighteen

OH DANNY BOY

*"Out of the strain of doing,
into the peace of the done."*

~ Julia Louise Woodruff

September 28

There are now stretches of days and sometimes weeks between my writings in this journal, but today something heart squeezing occurred. Brushing lightly across my mind, touching as softly as a butterfly, comes the thought, whole and complete, gentle and painless: Danny is dead. My son is dead.

For months that have seemed like years, every thought of Dan has been accompanied by such tearing agony that in order not to bleed internally, I've thrust them out of my mind time and time again. That was my way of handling this horror.

So it is with wonder I examine my reaction to this gentle thought. How is it that the words don't crash, tripping and stumbling in my brain? Has acceptance sneaked up on me while I tried to keep myself busy with other things?

I notice something else. Something truly extraordinary has happened. In my words, in my heart, I put my son in the past tense.

Now I weep, but these tears are so different, so cleansing. As they splash on the page, they seem to affirm the finality of his Earthly existence. I crumble to the floor and crouch there, my paper on the hassock, watching the ink spread—and I know I am beginning to believe the truth. My Danny is dead.

November 28

Making peace with myself and forgiving myself for all the wrongs I felt I had done him was something I didn't know how to do. If I could talk to him I would say that none of the hurtful things we might have said to each other in the course of growing up mean anything and that above and beyond, under and through it all, we loved him. Nothing else matters and the funny thing is, if we could talk to each other, he would say and mean as sincerely as I, the same words. Why was it so hard to remember the thousands of days of laughter, days of fun, days of joy, the ordinary days of a lifetime?

Yet I struggled to forgive myself. We had a really typical relationship: sixty percent just fine, and thirty percent just wonderful, and ten percent frustrating. Pretty much what most families encounter, I imagine. So I guess the guilt could only be my whole-being belief that it was up to me to protect this child and I couldn't do it. That failure has been so immense, it's been crushing. Now I am starting to get a more clear perspective.

January 1

Twenty months

It is the start of a new year and perhaps a new understanding. A truth only becomes a truth when you absorb it and make it your own. Before that it is nothing more than words to the wise and you might not yet be wise yourself. Getting some of that wisdom takes time.

And, oh those clichés, all the words spoken to us after Dan's death—how thankful we were for the people who tried to express comfort, but how awkward and hard it was for them. We did so appreciate even the stuttered attempts. But those trite phrases could be so infuriating.

God had called him home. (This is his home.)

God needed him more than we did. (I would like to see that proven.)

Only the good die young. (What? So every senior citizen is bad?)

He'll never know any more heartache of life. (True, but he won't know the joys either).

At least you have other children. (Yes, and they're priceless, but that does not change the fact that this child is gone.)

It could have been worse, what if he had a lingering illness? (That would have been terrible yes, but we would have had some precious time.)

And finally, *Aren't you glad you had him for a little while?* (No.

Certainly I wasn't glad at the beginning. The pain was so all-consuming there was no room for glad.)

Enough time has passed now that I have come to a place where the well-intentioned words no longer scrape my flesh raw and sound meaningless. At last I recognize them for what they are— time tested truisms coined to help us better understand and cope with this life. Somewhere, people began to discover that those old words would come softly back to act as a bit of a cushion for the rock bed of grief.

We don't know that we can come to the bereaved wordlessly. We are so uncomfortable with death in the first place, so we gush with words to fill the distressful silence. We think we must say something. Yet too few of us are eloquent, so we come with mouths full of triteness. But, make no mistake, it is better to come that way than not to come at all. These old truisms are like fine wood, rubbed to a deep sheen by caring hands that have passed them down time and again, year after year.

May

The second anniversary

More time has passed and we are still here. We are still sad but still together. Weeks go by between my journal notes. Melisa is losing the gawky awkwardness of childhood—Dan would be proud of her. What an occasion he would make of today with his little sis in her first young lady dress with grown-up shoes. She would have received flowers or something. We could count on him to mark the tiny milestones of life. There are images he would have particularly wanted to hold. So today, Melisa, at the edge of womanhood, brings memories and for me a happy tear and an admonishment to myself: Remember this.

November

Two and a half years have passed

It is another gray-sky winter and I am frozen in place with people bumping into me and George standing in puzzlement at my side.

We have been given a gift of tickets to a Seahawks game, for us a rare treat. The crowd is excited and so are we as we rush toward the entrance gates. But coming toward me, with a big smile of delight on his face is a tall, honey-haired young man who causes my knees to go weak and my heart to nearly stop beating. Dan?

Of course not, you fool.

Now the only thing I remember about today is that young man. Am I still denying? No, I don't believe so, but when will I reach the top of this mountain and stand safely on the summit with no chance of sliding back?

March

Thirty-four months

Dave and I talk. It still seems to him as if the sparkle has gone from the soda of life. The good times are coming back in a much more natural, healthy way, but we seem to have lost whatever the catalyst is that pushes normal happiness over the edge so joy can flow.

It is a long time now. We have taught ourselves again how to smile and laugh. But that delicious tickle of life that we took for granted touches us no more and we wonder if it is still out there waiting. Perhaps it is gone forever. We each have an emptiness inside us that refuses to go away. It would be odd, I guess, if we didn't. A part of us has gone and the void can't be filled.

I don't think we are particularly unhappy, quite the opposite, in fact. We have learned what is important in life so we really experience the small, worthwhile moments that make life beautiful. I guess that makes us sound as if we are made of spun sugar and we are not. Each of us is capable of the full range of human emotions—we still get mad or cranky or snap at each other.

Melisa is *twelve teen* and knows more than her parents ever thought of knowing. But now it is easy for us to let her be, as we know this too shall pass. As long as we are alive and as long as we love each other, everything will be okay.

April 15

Dan would be twenty-three today. It has been thirty-five months since we have seen him. I wonder to myself how he would have changed. I can't visualize him at all. I can't even let my imagination go to what he might have been like now. All I know is he lived, then there is a blank, and he is no more.

The fig tree, the philodendron, and the asparagus fern prosper. As I water them, I remember receiving each one and I remember my reaction to his bringing them home.

"You know I don't have a green thumb. Why do you insist on doing this to me? They'll just die, Honey, and I hate that—it makes me feel bad."

Now every plant he ever brought home thrives as if they had a direct root to Mother Nature.

The weeping fig is a particular miracle. When Danny first brought it home there was what looked like two beige sticks, two feet tall, in a huge pot. I got up one morning and there it was in the middle of the living room. When he got up I said, "What on earth is that?"

"Oh Mom, it's the prettiest tree. It's got deep green pointy leaves and it bends, really graceful, like a willow. You should see it."

"Deep green leaves, huh? Where? Dan, the thing is dead. Look," I broke off a tiny tip and it was hollow and dry, "there's no life here."

"Just keep it for a while and try for me, will you, Mom?"

"Dang it, Danny. Oh, all right. All right."

Three weeks later he was gone.

The sticks stood in dirt in the living room unattended for weeks and weeks. Finally, good neighbor Joe suggested I get rid of it. He cut one of the two little trunks and showed me, it was as dead as could be. "There's really nothing left here, Mary. Do you want me to take it out for you?"

"I should let you but I just don't want to throw it away yet. I know it's probably ridiculous but, I don't know, maybe I'll tie ribbons on it or something, maybe use it for a flag pole." I smiled and he patted my back, "Sure," he said, "Why not."

Now, almost three years later, the one remaining stick is five feet high and its many branches are covered and bending under the weight of hundreds of deep green pointy leaves. And it is really graceful, like a willow.

May 7

The two-by-three chest, filled with notes and trinkets, the remnants of a life, is pulling at me. Once it was a tool chest belonging to my dad. When I was about thirteen and very romantic, I begged for it. Dad helped me scrape it and sand it. I painted and polished, lined it with satin, and decorated it with love birds. I turned it into the perfect, and perfectly ironic, hope chest. But, is it finally time to face it?

197

No! Not yet. The panic I felt in connection with sorting through the tangible bits of his life is now gone but I'm still not ready to go in there. We were sad for so long and now are more resigned—I want to be stronger before I go into those dark places again.

Throughout this journal I have used references to the ocean, from drowning to surfacing, from being tossed in the tempest of the sea to beginning to swim for my life. Now I feel as if I have washed up on shore, barely alive, beaten and battered but stronger, wiser, better—a survivor.

May 8

I have such strange feelings today. Laughter and tears, and like oil and water, they don't mix, so I am off balance. Ah. It is Mother's Day.

Late last night I lay dry eyed in bed, thankful for our son and daughter, thankful for the present, turning the pages of the past. Maybe Mother's Day will ever be one of the hard ones.

Into my drowsy mind comes a line my brother once said, "Of course God answers all prayers. It's just that sometimes he says no."

...It's another May

We are now in our third year. George and I grew up within sight and scent, almost sound of the sea. It is no wonder I use metaphors of the briny deep. Here's another— life, it seems to me, is very like the tide, rising full with the flow of happiness or ebbing sadly away.

Then between that ebb and flow there is an in-between place, special moments known to mariners as slack tide, when the waters are still, at peace with the forces that push and pull them. I don't know if that is reassuring or scary that the tide always turns. Guess it depends whether you're on a rising or a falling tide.

I have pulled the pieces of myself together at last and very rarely, any more, do I split into those three parts. Looking back, I can see how well my family and I were served by that disembodied phenomenon. As out of body as it often felt, especially in the early months, it enabled me to deal, in a semi-normal way, with all the stuff of life while allowing the deep grieving I was actually living with to run its rutted zigzag course. I appeared to the world to be carrying on remarkably well, perhaps making the process easier for all. Now I think I can see the top of the mountain. My journey may be just about over.

I'm looking back, wondering what we've learned, and trying, as I always do, to figure it out, wishing there was a guru at that mountain peak with all the answers to share with me today. My writing always helps clarify things for me, but I wish for more absolutes. I mentioned the guru idea to George yesterday. He grinned and, ever patient with my whims and questing, he said, "I'm glad there isn't one. You'd want to go climb that mountain and I'd have to go along to protect you from all the bugs we'd find on the trail." Then serious he said, "I think you actually did climb it. I think you climbed it for all of us. And I think the only guru you found was in yourself. And because you found that, you have led all of us on up the mountain." His tone took my breath away.

So today I'm asking the guru why I felt so much guilt and self-blame. I thought it was because it was me who pushed him out of the house. It was the right decision for the rest of the family, probably for Dan too. It was time for him to grow up. But because of my decision, he never will.

Now I can see that he, who bore the harshest penalty, also bore some of the responsibility. He chose his behavior and I responded in the only way I could see at the time. But all the rationale in the world paled before this fact—Danny died.

I hated Death so badly. I hated it! I would have destroyed it if I could. I would have beat it bloody with a rage I did not know I was capable of feeling. But I could not grasp it to beat it, so I mentally beat my husband for making a small attempt at a joke, and I beat Dave for playing his music too loud, and I beat Melisa because she forgot to make her bed some mornings, and I beat and beat and beat myself for every real and imagined mistake and sin, not only that I had made as a mother but every mistake and sin that was ever made in this world. Now I am beginning to give myself a little credit for making it this far, for helping my family make it this far. Just as it was before when all we could see were our mistakes and we were blind to our good family qualities, so it has been as I look back at all the mistakes I've made in handling this grieving stuff. It has taken till now to see I believe I did a lot right for my family too.

I don't know when I began to really think about George's and my differences in grieving. The differences shouted at us immediately but all that shouting did was make us more deaf to each other. George expecting me to get on with it, me furious that he could seemingly pick up the

199

pieces so easily. Maybe it was when we went by ourselves to the San Juan's and had a large block of time to talk. On the first day we agreed to just wait, wait for the dust to settle.

The hurricane had come through, now the water would recede, the mud would dry and the bulldozer could scrape a level spot again. Trees would be replanted and the world would be rebuilt. But first we must…just…wait. No blames, no demands, no movement, just wait. We set some ground rules. He needed to talk at his own pace with no pressure from me. I needed to be held, just held, with no pressure from him. He needed to ask me to be quiet, with no guilt. I needed to be able to say no, without guilt.

After twenty-one years of marriage, in the quiet and in the holding, I began to understand that sex, for George, was as basic a need as tears were for me. I didn't get it at all but I knew the core of my husband. I knew his loving heart. I knew how deeply he internalized troubles. I knew he had to be feeling some of the same terrible anguish I felt.

I had to give him every benefit of the doubt. We must not ever give up on each other. And George? He had to learn a tough lesson too. He had to learn patience.

He, as a pretty typical guy, was used to seeing a problem, picking up whatever tool was called for, and fixing it right away. This time he had to face himself as the problem and he didn't know what tool to use to repair himself or his family.

We learned. Patience, patience, patience. Try to walk in my shoes my love and I will try to walk in yours.

Early on we promised there would be no finger pointing or blame. Then we promised each other we would not become one of the more than ninety percent of couples who are in deep trouble after their child's death. We promised not do that to each other. Let us understand that our best is not good enough now. We have to do better than our best just to hold this marriage and family intact, to save our love.

And so we learned once again a lesson of love. Love isn't just a dozen red roses on an anniversary, sweet with perfume. It is also the thorns that don't just poke or scratch but can rip flesh to tatters. Smelling the fragrance of the flowers is the easy part, binding the wounds from the thorns is where the real test of love comes in—not impossible…but almost…almost.

Melisa has asked twice to go see the place where her brother died and I tell her we will go someday. I don't know if David has ever been and I don't ask. I don't consciously avoid going there but it's one of those things we just don't seem to get around to. I know we should. She must need it. Usually if I have been someplace once I seem to be able to unerringly find it again, but I'm not sure about this place and there never seems to be the right moment to mention it to George.

The man who owned the house has long since torn it down and built three or four new houses on the property. George and I have been back only once since we haunted it in the early days seeking other haunting. I can still see the blackened shell of the original house super imposed on the new ones.

Just being at the property where the house once stood has exhausted us and I believe we are saying goodbye to this area now. We most likely will not be back.

As we drive home I ask, "Honey? If you had to come up with one feeling that stood out over all the others, what would it be?"

"Do you mean since he died?" George's voice ends in a wince.

I nod and shift my body a fraction in my seat to bring myself closer to him. Constrained by my seat belt the closeness is more implied than actual, but I know he feels the added intimacy because his hand reaches to cover mine where it rests on the seat between us.

"One feeling" he says, "beyond the constant emptiness, the missing of my son? Beyond the fear I always carry now for the rest of you? Beyond that unbelievable pain? Anger I guess. At myself for being so helpless. I wasn't there for him. And I didn't know how to fix it for you. I tried to read the Bible you know. They always say it's a comfort but it didn't seem to make any sense to me. I thought there would be something helpful there. I was wrong and that made me mad too. And I was so angry at the fire department for taking so long to get there. And I was really mad at the guy who owned the place. I wish he had had the guts to at least send a card. It happened in his house, he could have at least said he was sorry it happened. That doesn't admit guilt, does it? Who knows why it happened. But saying sorry, well, that's just being human isn't it? To say you're sorry when something awful happens?" He sighs, "And I was a little mad at Danny and feeling guilty about that. I felt like he forced our hand by ignoring our rules so we felt we had to make him move. But I kept wondering, if only we had been a little more patient. And how can I be mad at him when he paid, god, he paid. I was just furious at the reality."

"You've been blaming yourself?" I ask in surprise. "I was the one who made him move. I've blamed myself from the moment I first heard. And you were blaming yourself? You have no blame."

"Neither of us has any blame. If you remember we both agreed it wasn't good for Dave and Melisa to see him come and go as he pleased. We made the decision. Just because you spoke the words doesn't mean I didn't agree. Right?"

I breathe for the first time in years. "Right," I say and pull my hand out from under his. As he's been talking, unknowingly he has grasped my fingers tighter and tighter until they are almost crushed. "But you're fine now, right? No more bitterness?" I ask and flex my fingers.

"Sorry," he says, nodding at my hand and it's his turn to smile. "I think I'm much better but not fine yet. Is fine a goal? Haven't I heard you say 'fine' is your favorite four letter word that starts with an F?" He pauses then starts slowly, "You know, I think your story of the chestnuts helped."

"Oh. I'm glad."

I close my eyes, lean my head back and remember chestnuts. It was a beautiful day about a year ago when Melisa came home from school with her lunch sack filled to the brown serrated top with lime green horse chestnuts.

"Look what I've got! Can we make a necklace? No, Licorice! Don't sniff them, you'll poke yourself." She held her curious dog back with one arm as she dumped the husks on the kitchen floor. Their sharp spines penetrated each other's soft skin and they clumped together in an interlocked pile. Each was the size of a golf ball and looked like a weapon from the Middle Ages.

I smiled remembering how, as a kid, my brother and his friends would have fights, throwing those tiny, painful weapons at each other. When the boys had roared through and moved on, we girls would gather the now open shells and make jewelry for ourselves with those beautiful rosewood and mahogany colored nuts.

"Don't touch your mouth until you wash," I warn, "Or you'll be sorry. Nothing is quite as bitter. After you change we'll make a necklace."

"Bracelets too?"

"Sure, bracelets too."

"And for Shanny?"

"Sure."

As she and Licorice ran toward her room she chattered to him about her day and I thought how good it was that she had this best friend.

Bounding into the kitchen the two of them crashed into my reverie and we headed to the basement to collect the hammer, a nail, and a hunk of old board.

Out in the backyard, we found that the ripest of the nuts had already started to crack out of the shell. Being cautious, we peeled them all the way out and Melisa shined each already polished nut on her shirt. With the hammer, we pounded the nail through the nuts as I held them on the board. A quick puff of air through the hole we bored and it was ready to string. Twenty minutes work produced a necklace for both Melisa and Shenan.

Melisa took off up the hill to share with her friend and I was left with a mess of sharp shells to contemplate. I picked up one of the still enclosed nuts and rested it on my palm. Just balancing it there, it poked a rude dent in my flesh as its miniscule weight began to make an impression. There must be some toxic substance in the covering that releases when the nut is picked. They aren't pleasant to hold.

I curled my fingers over the spines and held it a little bit tighter, testing the hurt, and then I squeezed harder and harder until a couple spikes pierced my skin. I had to shake my open palm to make this deceptive instrument of torture drop off. I sucked the blood that rose to the surface and spit out a mixture of bitter resin and blood. But the pain was insistent. I went in to wash off the burning residue and make a cup of coffee. While I sipped my coffee, the girls came back and were now making *jewelry* for all their friends. I kept rubbing the sore spots on my hand and thinking about the lesson I was just given by a chestnut.

Holding onto bitterness or working to keep anger alive is very much like my holding that spike covered nut. No one looking at me with my closed fist would have any idea why I was frowning or even guess that I was in pain. The only person that was hurting was me. As long as I held tight to this painful little item I could not feel better. And that is how it is with anger and bitterness.

I think, now, about George and how he is still angry and how it worries me. I know he just wants the man at the rental house to feel as badly as he feels, and who knows, maybe he does. But that guy doesn't feel George's pain. George absorbs each and every day the barbs and slivers and is getting more and more tense and cranky as time passes. But those chestnuts taught me that hate can only hurt you—no one but you. This was a major epiphany for me. Holding hate does them no harm. Holding hate does you no good. You might as well let it go.

"Besides, it's bitter as bile," I whisper, there in the car beside my husband.

"What did you say, Honey? I thought you had fallen asleep."

I open my eyes to the brightness and we are still on the freeway. "No, I wasn't asleep. I was just remembering the chestnut story. I'm glad it helped you. I learned too. Funny, those darned things still hurt when I think about it. Under that pretty colored husk with its horrible spikes is one of the most beautiful nuts imaginable. Inedible, almost untouchable, but a priceless learning experience. There's got to be a great metaphor in there somewhere."

"Well", my husband says as he pats my hand, "let me know when you find it."

December

Forty-four Months

And now it is our fourth Christmas without Dan.

This one is so much less painful. Much has changed. Now when we decorate the tree Melisa does most of the work. She is thirteen and lovely and hums as she hangs her ornaments and Dan's, leaving Dave's for him to hang when he stops by later. Occasionally her sweet alto voice brushes over me and makes me smile. I don't say anything for fear of embarrassing her to silence.

Lying under the tree, fully alert to his mistress's every mood, is Licorice, now grown to 115 pounds of love and protection. An important member of the family of whom a friend says, "If reincarnation is an option, I want to come back as one of your family's dogs."

George and I can smile as we see the old ornaments, more

precious for their age, peeking from the branches. There is love in my mending heart.

Later, when the house is silent, I will tuck a little package with a red rose-shaped ribbon on a high, deep branch. It is my old present from Santa Claus and it goes on the tree every year. Then I will hook a tiny white dove and a little boy angel dressed in a blue gown and sporting a tipped halo, on the tree. George and Melisa will be long asleep and Licorice will be by my feet as I spend an hour with my memories. I will whisper Merry Christmas to Bobbie, the friend who stopped by one day with these two little ornaments saying, "These are for your son." I will whisper Merry Christmas to all those who make my life worth living and to all those I loved who have passed on. And of course, to Danny. And I will remember another Christmas and the dark sad night when a secret Santa brought a little light to our hearts. I won't pretend that everything is just fine. I don't think it will ever be *just fine* again but I know everything is okay, and okay is fine enough.

Of all the beautiful words written and spoken, rhymed and sung to give comfort and strength and hope, to give some degree of understanding to the unacceptable, these are the ones that count, as complex as breathing, as simple as breath, just, *Love one another*. I know now that every place where love has been shown us, a patch was fused to our hearts.

April 15

Forty-seven months

George picks great cotton candy gobs of lilacs. Their perfume fills every corner of the house. He knows I love them. Today is Dan's birthday and though the blossoms blur with my wet eyes, I can see clearly they are glowing. They are soft purple. The colors are back.

May

Tonight I ask myself, not guilt-ridden or torturing, but gently, why did it take me so long to understand that we honor his memory by going on with our lives

For a long time I thought if I went on without him, I denied my love. I now know that is not true. But—grief is a process and it takes its own time. Nine months to gestate a baby, a year till that baby walks, twelve years of schooling—life is a process, and so is accepting death. Patience is required.

I might be a slow learner but at last I recognize one present his death has brought me. His gift was in teaching me the priceless value of life. If I refuse to go forward with happiness and peace, I am refuting that gift. I have chosen not to reject it, D'Mark. *"I thank you, my son. I honor your life. I will live and savor this gift. For you and for me."*

Early September

Fifty-two months

Bundled in parkas, we lay on chaise lounges sucking ice out of the frozen air. We are on the open deck of the ferry *Columbia,* chewing up green miles of water, spitting out white foam. This is our dream, to go to Alaska. I am eager, George is hesitant. I love new places, he prefers the familiar. Our trip is in honor of our twenty-fifth anniversary.

A young woman threads her way through the bedrolls and pup tents that have sprung up on the open deck like mushrooms after a rain. Her rust colored hiking boots take root next to my chair. I glance the short way up toward her face, past her blue jeans and the blue backpack that counterbalances her from thighs to neck. She has a sweet little face on which is perched an outrageously oversized pair of prescription glasses. I return her smile and she speaks. "I've been watching you for a while. Gosh, you sure look happy."

I feel my smile spread. I feel my heart give a tiny clinch. I feel a stinging tear that was probably just caused by the wind and as I reach to touch the silver medallion at my throat I nod and tell her the truth, "I am."

You will often hear, "I treasure life even more now," but what does that actually mean?

I'm sure it must mean something different for everyone.
But for myself, first let me tell you
what it DOES NOT mean.
It does not mean I am always happy.
It does not mean I never get annoyed or angry,
or tired or cranky or unreasonable, sad and worried or angst filled.
It does not mean when I am hungry and hot and need to use the ladies
room and it has been a long day and the traffic on the parking lot called

Interstate 5 is an endless line of red taillights, my gas gauge is heading
toward the E, my exit is approaching and no one cares but me,
that I am filled with the milk of human kindness.
No, it does not mean that.
But what it does mean for me is
that as I stood in my morning shower I was grateful for the night's sleep
from which I had awakened, and grateful that I HAD awakened.
Grateful for the warm water coursing on my body
and the sensuous slide of soap across my skin.
Present and pleased with the light fragrance of my shampoo
and the wafting of the coffee scent that
called me to the kitchen.
It means, for me, that as I grab my cup from the cupboard
I notice the colors, my favorite emerald and cobalt, and I smile.
It means that my daughter will probably call to say good morning as she
drives down the hill to the freeway and we will both know we are
blessed.
It means Dave and his family are healthy, that my friends may call or I
can phone them and they will be there for me. And it means George.
It means that when I AM hot, tired, the gauge on empty, Interstate 5 is a
parking lot again and all I want to do is go home,
I am able to remember that all these people around me have a car and
gas and a job to go to and all THEY want is to go home too.
And I can know that "this too shall pass" and I bless us all.
I guess what I am trying to say is that in losing my son, I lost
the ability to take anything for granted.
I lost the need to compare or condemn others or be judgmental.
It means I now know that all of life offers little gifts, all the live long day.
I now recognize them.
With a pleasure that is sometimes humble, sometimes exalted,
noisily joyful or quiet as a baby's slumber,
sometimes with a smile and sometimes with a tear,
I now recognize each of those little gifts of life

> *I accept each of them*
> *And I rejoice.*
>
> *~ Mary M. Fern*

May

Another anniversary…it has been five years.

The words pulsing through my head want to choke me as I speak to my boy in my deepest heart, *"Oh Danny, I know you would be so proud of us. Remember that family circle that I had torn into ragged fifths? That circle that I felt I couldn't put back together as it had been before? Well, I was right, I couldn't—I couldn't make it be the same wholeness again…but…When I took your piece of the circle and tore it into quarters and adhered one quarter to Dave's piece, one quarter to Melisa's, one quarter to your dad's piece and one to my own, I was able to form those ragged pieces into a circle once again. Not a diminished circle, Honey but a full, whole, complete circle.*

When at last, each of us shared the pain and each of us shared the responsibility for treasuring each other and our place in the family, when each of us allowed the others to have their own feelings in their own way, a miracle occurred. We honored you. We honored your past. We honored your place in the family. And together we began working toward a future. Honey, my D'Mark, look what happened.

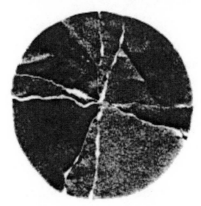

A RAGGED CIRCLE IS A CIRCLE STILL

I know it isn't perfect, but when is any family perfect? Now that we each hold a part of you in us to remain a part of each of us forever, the circle is complete. Scarred but complete. We will always miss you. We will always love you, but we are at peace with you and with ourselves. We are a family, Honey. And Danny, you never left us at all ".

They say time heals all wounds. I don't think that is true.
Time does nothing but flow by like a river.
It is what you do with that flowing river of time that can heal wounds.
If you sit on the bank nothing will happen.
Swim upstream and you fight time and battle the currant to exhaustion.
Let the water do what it will with you and be bashed and eddied about.
But learn how to swim and you conquer that swift flowing river of time,
and you can only learn to swim by jumping in.
This thought is not original with me—
still, I am proud to have learned how to swim.

~ Mary M. Fern

Late September

This morning I open at random an inspirational book I couldn't pass up because it has on its cover the silver bird soaring through the golden skies that is so symbolic to me. The book is one of those *Thoughts for the Day* types I picked up in a used book store while searching for any size bandage to stem the hemorrhage of my heart. Now it opens to say, "To everything there is a season and a time to every purpose under Heaven." Ecclesiastes 3:1.

I am stunned.

We requested only two readings at Dan's memorial. This is one of them.

When I catch my breath, I am driven to read today's thought. It says, "Trials and troubles may seem to overwhelm you. Do you not see that you cannot be destroyed? From now a new life is opening out before you. Trust and go forward unafraid."

In my heart I whisper my love to my son. There can be no more temporizing. *"The time is now Danny. What can I do? I'm going forward. After five years, three months and twenty days, I'm going forward. And one last time I'll sing to you, your goodnight song"*

"Oh, Danny boy the pipes, the pipes are calling
From glen to glen and down the mountainside
The summers gone and all the roses falling
It's you, it's you must go and I'll abide
But come ye back when summer's in the meadow
Or when the valley's hushed and white with snow
And I'll be here in the sunshine or in shadow
Oh Danny boy, Oh Danny boy
I love you so"

~ Frederick Weatherly

Epilogue

As We Are Today

"Do not be afraid of death.
Be afraid of the unlived life."

~ Natalie Babbitt, Tuck Everlasting

You could assume that after a loved one dies, the family would immediately realize how little time we have on this earth and be eager to act upon that realization. You might also assume that a realization like that would lead in short order to all the survivors grabbing glorious life to ride it for fun, like a Harley Davidson motorcycle, excited and exuberant.

Some, I suppose, do.

We did not.

Our grief took a long time.

Our mourning even longer.

All these years later, there is still a trickle of mourning in the stream of our lives. We got back into living the way a baby tries a new food, staring suspiciously at it first, and then touching it with one finger before sticking that finger into our mouths. Eventually we each tasted life again, and then bit, chewed, swallowed, and liked it. We did not love it, but liked it once again. We were happy.

And I resigned myself to that. I was so grateful to have finally found a bit of happiness at last. I really never expected joy. Joy was forever behind us, but after the hell that was also behind us, well, happy was plenty good enough.

We were, once again, aware and active participants in life as the years passed.

Licorice became a fierce protector of Melisa and her family. Underneath his satiny coat, drooling, and tail thumping, he was the best

211

dog ever.

And our hearts were happy.

We watched Dave return successfully to school and excel. He lived on his own for a while then moved in with one of his friends, Jack, who had been so instrumental in helping him deal with his grief. We watched genuine laughter and fun return to our son. He graduated from the University of Washington and fulfilled his lifelong dream of becoming a high school math teacher and football coach.

And our hearts were happy.

We watched Melisa become a beautiful, self-assured, young woman, through driving lessons, proms and first jobs. And there was one moment, at her junior high graduation, where I watched as she, lovely in a tea length, café au lait colored satin dress, danced in her father's arms, and my heart was very happy. And the years passed.

Joe and Darlene, the neighbors, one on each side of our house, who had helped hold me onto the planet in my time of need, both died of cancer. It was very hard. I was privileged to be with each of them in turn as they passed, helping to give back some of the love they had showered on me. That love forms a silver circle in my memory that links us through all time.

Our little boat, the *Nameless II*, has taken us many more nautical miles through the waters of our state and once again we found the beauty because we carried it with us.

Three of the new friends who so bravely refused to leave me, when staying was hard and leaving was easy, have become so dear to me they are the sisters of my heart.

George is almost his easy, peaceful self again, though his face carries some lines of sadness. He is content with his job, his home, and his children, and very content with me.

I, too, am content. I quit the job that I didn't like and began learning the craft of writing that calls my heart. I took extensive training and became a grief facilitator in a local hospital's hospice program and in giving back, I receive so much.

And our hearts were happy.

I spend four intense hours in advanced bereavement training, and as we break for lunch, the sun cuts through the rain-clouded sky. I choose to take a brisk walk to clear my head. As I gulp in the fresh, washed air, I happen to look down at the rivulets in the gutter and the puddles on the street and this poem writes itself in my muddled head. I grab my checkbook, tear out a page, and leaning against a dripping tree, write:

PERSPECTIVE
Cigarette butt boats riding oil-sheened rivers
reflect rainbow-like in the puddles at my feet.
Puffy white clouds stitched by blue sky
reflect quilt-like in the puddles at my feet.
One moment I see one,
one moment the other.
One moment the dregs of this world,
one moment the heavens.
And though reality is both,
I am free to choose my focus.

~ Mary M. Fern c 1990
I AM free to choose my focus, aren't I?

Then one day Dave came to us with wildly mixed emotions and announced that his application to teach full-time had been accepted…in another state.

Melisa was just beginning the long process of collecting college brochures.

The years had passed.

George and I decided we needed one last, big, indelible memory to share before we closed this chapter of our family's story and started the next.

So, off to the paradise of Hawaii we went. It was our first time there. We gasped with delight at the colorful fish as we snorkeled,

213

laughed as we tried to turn over on air mats in unbelievable, warm-turquoise waves, pointed out strange flowers to one another, each more fragrant than the last. We rubbed on lotion, brushed off sand, and basked in each other's company.

On our last day we splurged on a helicopter flight. Nervous and excited, we donned head phones that piped music that enhanced the awesome spectacle of Kauai from on high.

The kids kept up a running dialogue, teasing each other and making light of the breathtaking beauty. "It's not cool to be too impressed," they said. But about halfway through the flight, as we swept over the needle-like pinnacles of the NaPali Coast, a rainbow stretched like a gift, and even they fell silent. From the front seat George turned back toward us, locking his eyes with mine we looked into each other's souls. He reached back to physically connect. Dave, Melisa, and I spontaneously lurched forward and in the same instant grasped his hand. Each of us was seriously searching each other's faces and in each face we could plainly see an overwhelming peace that could only have been Danny's benediction. We began to smile and our smiles grew and grew. And in this healing place as my eyes filled with tears, my heart began to fill…with joy.

TO OUR EARTHBOUND CHILDREN

This is the kind of poem, my loves, that speaks of a brother
now gone.
Of his loyalty to you and his undying love, his pride at how
you've carried on.
It's such a long time now that he left this place for wherever
a Soul is bound.
And I guess it might seem odd to some folks that our hearts
still keep him around.
But keep him we do, and keep him we will, a part of our
memories forever.
Just as we hold you, and all those we love, with a cord God
will not let us sever.
In passing he led us to treasure our lives with a sweetness

they might not have had.
He loved you so, he would wish for you to grab life, hold
tight and be glad.
Do you still remember his belly laugh, so big, so infectious,
so grand?
No one was more swift to lend a smile, his last dime, or a
helping hand.
And we know he'd be sorry for pain he caused as he went
about his Earthly business.
Still, if there's a Heaven we also know there'll be lessons
about forgiveness.
Now you have lost a brother, my children—and we have lost
a son.
We don't know why he came to us—or why he was so soon
done.
Once upon a time he and I danced transcendent on a full
moon shore
He said the bliss of moments like these were what life on
Earth was for.
"Mom, you and Dad find your heaven on the ocean, your
paradise in the salt of the sea,
Where Melisa will go no one can yet know. Dave and I find
ourselves when we ski."
So:
Today we scatter his ashes, atop his mountain where hawks
dip and dive.
Lift your eyes to the highest peak and beyond—know that
his Spirit's alive.
How do we know his Spirit lives, that it soars like the hawk
high and free?
You have only to touch your soul and your heart and there
find his memory.
Sometimes you'll smile when you think of him. Sometimes

you'll utter a sigh.

But as long as you hold him in memory his life will never die.
My heart is more sorrowful than you'll ever know that he's not here with you on this Earth.
Why is it only when we lose them we see just what a sibling is worth?
Many loved ones have been lost to us now, and it's clear as the leaves on the tree
that often the farther away one goes the closer they seem to be.
Look to your hearts, Earthbound Children of mine, find the truth of what I say.
Family and friends fill us with real love, and love NEVER passes away.
At last we've completed what he would have wished and he is at peace I know.
And twenty red roses spiral silently down to scatter like rubies on the snow.
Love is always.
And so it is.

Mary M. Fern, May 26, 2008

A Conversation with George

A long time later, on a wedding anniversary, George and I were counting memories, like coins, the way folks do on those kinds of occasions. Just a few days ago we had finally hired a pilot with a tiny seaplane and droned up to Steven's Pass to scatter Danny's ashes over Seventh Heaven, his favorite ski run. Our emotions were again fresh.

Now sitting on the balcony of a bed and breakfast overlooking one of the islands of the San Juan's we sip a nice Merlot and reminisce. We've gotten as far as the darkest days of our marriage and I click on my little tape recorder, take a deep breath, and ask, "What do you remember of that time?"

Shaking his head in annoyance at himself he says, "My mind is mostly blank when I look back. I knew I would have this trouble."

I nod, but say, "It's just that if the kids ever want to read this, your voice should be here so they will better understand how it was for us. Your perspective is far different from mine in a lot of ways and it is important."

George goes on, "You know I'm finding I don't remember a lot. Sometimes it seems as if I often checked out."

I nod again. "Besides we just don't live our lives by memory. Life always moves forward and keeps coming at us so fast, but anything you can remember I would truly appreciate. So if you can tell me what you were feeling I'd like that, if you can't…well Honey…that's okay too."

"No. I want to try. You know I've got feelings…but even under normal circumstances, even with you, they're hard to express."

"I know. It seems to be such an ingrained male trait. Maybe it's part of the reason you guys often die before we do. Maybe you just explode your hearts with all the stuff you cram into them and won't let out."

He nods. "For me this is just so personal and I didn't want to pass

217

it on. I don't want anybody to feel…" he shrugs, inarticulate, pauses, then says, "But I think you were right when you talked about Dan and how often he was late because he stopped to help someone along the way, like to help one of the neighbors or to help that old man with a flat tire. I remember his boss telling me they wanted to send him to management school and the customers loved him but the store might have to fire him because he was so often late. And I think you're right that he is trying to tell us this is the last time he can help someone. What you call lessons that he taught us, maybe he needs us to pass them on."

"Wow. Thank you."

"For?"

"Seeing it that way."

We both sit forward in our chairs till we are on the edge of the seats and now collapse back and try to shake the words down. After a moment George begins again.

"It was about ten in the morning and somebody, probably the store manager, said I had to go to the office right away. I asked what was wrong and he didn't know. 'They just said stop whatever you're doing and return to the office.' And all I could think was…what happened? I was caught so off guard I was confused.

"I remember when I walked in my bosses head hung so low over the desk and he took forever to raise it and look at me. He said, 'This is the hardest thing I have ever had to do.' Then he said Dan had died in a house fire. I knew he wouldn't joke but I didn't believe him. It had to be some kind of a mistake. But why would he say it if it wasn't so? Then I remember dropping everything. All I could think was I had to get home to you."

His words start to speed up as he says, "I remember Joe was there. He was sitting at the table. I remember thinking how nice the weather was, how nice the house looked and I had these awful words inside me. I remember saying them but I don't remember what words I said. And when Joe saw the state I was in he couldn't wait to get out that front door."

"Do you remember me backing away from you?" I ask. "I thought you had gone crazy."

He nods sadly as I say, "But you kept reaching out for me. You wouldn't stop."

"Then I made some phone calls. I called the police right?"

"Yes. I tried but I couldn't make my fingers work." We frown as I extend the fingers that failed me and I shake my head as George goes on.

"So I called the police and the coroner and they didn't know anything, they had no record. So now I was really confused. That's when you said isn't it in a different county? I don't know how you thought of that." I shrug and he continues. "Then I made those calls hoping not to confirm it, hoping it was a mistake...but it wasn't a mistake. I remember getting through to somebody and they confirmed it after they asked a lot of questions to find out who I was. Then I ...passed it on to you."

"We were both on the phone. I was on the extension."

"Oh. I didn't remember that."

My arms are crossed and clutched over my chest as I say, "I'll never forget the coroner asking you question after question and finally I just screamed at him, 'Just tell me! Is it our son?' And he said yes and it sounded as if the word strung from here to forever."

"Now I remember. I heard you shout at the man on the phone and I heard him say...yes."

"Did the word seem to last forever to you?"

There comes a slow, slow nod of his head.

"Then Dave came upstairs and you pulled him into our arms and...you told him."

Now I shake my head with disbelief. "Then we left. We just left. I can't imagine leaving that poor kiddo like that, but we did. It was so urgent to get to both our moms before they heard it on the news. Your mom would have heard it first because she always had her ear to the radio. So we needed to get to my mom and she would have an immediate circle of support and she was so strong, but I knew we would have to stay with your mom because she only had us nearby. So it was quick to my mom so we could linger with your mom. And I still don't know how you managed to drive clear out there and then back to town. How did you do that?"

"I don't know. Maybe it was a way to take my mind off that other thing."

"Do you remember going to your mom's?"

"I don't think I do. It was bad, right? I probably erased it." He

219

pauses, then, "I guess I do remember going in but I don't remember giving her the news." He frowns, puzzled at himself, "I was probably trying to block that because I didn't want to deal with it. I didn't want to go deep so I just left it on the surface so I could try to brush it off." Then he asks, "Was it really awful?"

And it's my turn to nod.

"How bad?"

I shake my head. "It doesn't matter anymore, Honey. You don't need to know that now."

"Yes. I think I do."

I take a deep breath. "You wrapped your arms around her as she sat in her big chair. She was screaming and weeping and wailing and trying to fall on the floor. I finally got a tranquilizer in her and we stayed until it took hold and I called her sister and she said she'd come right away. We stayed for a while but I was wild to get home to Dave and Melisa."

The silence stretches long until George inhales and begins, "I read what you said about that little neighbor girl Shenan. I just remember her as one of Melisa's little playmates and I didn't realize what a big factor she was in helping Melisa through that."

"Yes, she was. Just like Jack and Dave S. were for our Dave. But I didn't realize it at the time either. She was just this giggly bubble. You know how tiring they can be, as they bounce around like Tigger so full of nine year-old energy. And then there was her mom, Jean. I don't think I ever adequately thanked her at the time but maybe one can't. She had Melisa over all the time for dinner or whatever, just normalcy. I never looked at it that way until right now. If I remember her story correctly, she had lost her husband in Vietnam when Shenan was an infant. If that is correct she would have known what we were going through. She was another of those angels we were blessed with."

George nods and then begins again, "Did I ever tell you about the morning my dad died?"

"Tell me again." I say.

"I can remember that morning so well. Isn't that funny? I was fifteen. We didn't have 911 back then so my mom had me call the fire department and turn on the front porch light, and I remember standing out in the street in my pajamas, waiting for them and waving them to our

220

house. It was dark and cold. Then a little while later, I got dressed for school and got on the bus. Somebody knew or I volunteered that my dad had died that morning of a heart attack. There was total shock and silence—nobody knew what to say.

"I could have stayed home, but I remember going so I wouldn't have to deal with all my mom's emotions. Now that I think about it, she probably needed me but I wanted to get away from it. She had her sisters and dad's brother there but I can remember running away right from the first day, because I didn't know how to deal with it…so I ran."

"You were fifteen, Honey. A house full of wailing women when you couldn't do anything to help? Of course you ran. Your mom's family was into drama anyway and this occasion…a middle-aged husband suddenly dying in the middle of the night right by her side…well, your mom needed to go a little crazy. Just like you needed to escape."

He takes my words in and I see them go to his heart and his face relaxes. Then he asks, "Did our kids go to school right away?"

"Yes. Melisa chose to go and Dave didn't have much choice because he was in the midst of finals at college. We all just carried on. How did we do it? At least I could work from home and look terrible and cry at times, but you guys had to face the world every day. I can't imagine how much courage that took."

"Going to work didn't take strength. I think it was a way for me to take my mind off something I couldn't fix. And I felt an obligation to the company as ridiculous as that sounds now. I should have taken some time out to just be with you and Dave and Melisa. They would have given me all the time I needed but I was selfish. I just wanted to be away from the pain of it all and you wanted to stay in it."

"No. I didn't want to stay in it. I just knew that for right then, the pain was all we had left of our son and I didn't want to let him go. Someone had to stay with him for a while and I guess I was elected."

"It should have been both of us." He says again as he reaches for my hand. "The kids needed both of us, not just you." There is a long pause and then he breaks the silence. "Did you resent that? Did you resent me?"

"Maybe. I don't remember. It doesn't matter now you know. I think we were pretty caring about each other anyway and became more so, but it took a long scary while before we could figure out how. And I don't know how you did it when your own role models had been so very tarnished. You were a boy once and boys run and men stay. I think they often still don't know what to do or say…but they stay. And not all boys ever do grow up and become men, but you did. We both went into automatic mode I guess, responsibility and obligation."

George begins again. "I can remember when you wanted to go see Danny and we were advised that it probably wouldn't be a good idea and I thought, why not? Then I got these images of why. I remember thinking, oh god, I hope we don't have to do that, I really don't want to remember him like that, but if she's going I'm going with her…so I was relieved when you chose not to go."

"You begged me not to and I honored that."

"Oh. I did?"

"Yes, and I'm still sorry. For me there were two things I wish I had done. We should have scattered that free bird's ashes immediately, he should never have been confined. I'm so glad we finally did that. But I still regret not holding him, my baby. You said, "Oh god, Honey, no!" and your tone was so tortured. I knew if I insisted you would insist on going with me, and I thought if you went with me you would die. I know how dramatic that sounds, but you did sound so incredibly tormented, as if your heart had only a few beats left in it. I wanted so badly to push you down and say, 'Stay there, I don't care, I need to see my son.' I explain in the book how they laid him on my belly all waxy and bloody and I held him because he was my baby. And after his accident on the dirt bike I would not have recognized him for the mud and the blood yet I held him. When he had the flu so badly that we thought we might lose him and he had lost control of himself and was drenched in vomit and all that bodily flu awfulness…I held him. Moms hold their children. Remember that news story on TV, the woman who held the body of her decapitated daughter and talked to her…because moms hold their babies. And God or nature or something puts that head back on that body so you are holding your child. I don't think men get that. I know doctors don't, police don't—it's forever, 'Get back, get back, don't look.' But we don't see that mutilated body, we see our child. And I think authorities are more worried about how they can control the situation because most men are at such a loss when a woman cries or screams. They call it hysteria, right? And it rocks their world. If we just lost control like guys do and punched something or bellowed in anger, they could approve of that, right? That's why…Well anyway—I think not going saved you."

The pause lasts for many beats of our hearts until he whispers from a very deep place, "Probably."

Again we are silent for a long time before George clears his throat and says, "I can remember going to the house." His voice lowers. "I didn't want to go there."

"Did I make you go?"

"You were going. I was going with you."

My throat and voice go thick and now it is my turn to whisper. "I love you so much."

"I love you too."

He begins again, "I remember the owner's brother being there…or somebody, another couple…"

"It was the owner's sister, her husband, their daughter, her husband, and their baby boy."

Now there is a little anger in his tone as he says, "And we were supposed to stay out, behind that yellow tape because there was an investigation going on and I thought we better not go under this tape— and then I thought, how ridiculous is that, we're here and I'm going under no matter who comes along to stop us. Then I was kind of glad. We got to see the layout and to find the album so we had some memories that we could recover. I remember you just wanting to stand there and look and I had seen all I needed to see and I just wanted to go. And Jeff's description, the fire department had been called…telling us…it took them so long to get there…so long. Describing how he and Mark were calling up to Dan at his window that he had to get out. And they saw the window covering move, I think it was a sheet or blanket or something because he didn't have curtains on the window yet, but it got sucked out and they thought he was pushing it out and he was going to come out…but he didn't and that blanket or whatever fell to the ground…" he shudders to a halt.

My heart is hammering as I say, "Jeff said they thought they saw him at the window and they thought he said something but didn't know what and I've been haunted all this time if they saw him or not and what he might have said."

Our words are tumbling over one another as George says, "I remember standing outside the house looking up at that window…that window's space…that empty space was still there."

"And I knelt below the window and you were trying to get me up because the ground was all covered in glass and I was clutching his bathrobe…so maybe he had used that for a curtain, I don't know, but I was on my knees and you kept saying, 'That's glass Honey, get up.'"

His voice has dropped so low I discover I must replay the tape again and again to pick up his words.

"I saw his red Rainier coat hanging in the closet all scorched. And I looked at the electrical panel and saw how that wall was scorched all around with the darkest black going straight up from the panel."

"How did we get out of the house?" I asked. "I can't remember. I just know you kept speculating on how it happened and I didn't care, only that it had."

"That's right. I just had to know how—you just wanted to know why."

"Boy, that sure speaks a lot to gender differences, doesn't it? Your mind went to attorneys, fire departments, detective stuff and mine went to emotion and caretaking. I didn't care about details. He was gone and nothing else mattered except Dave and Melisa. I guess we both ran away in a way. Only I couldn't run as far or be as removed. I had to stay for the kids."

And in the shade of big trees on a beautiful day as we sit on this tiny balcony, our eyes meet with understanding and so much compassion the rest of the world disappears.

I find my place in the manuscript and begin reading again. I am at the place where we have gone to Dan's roommate's family home and I read this line, "I just need to tell Jeff's mom how glad I am that her son is alive."

George stops me. "I'll never know how you did that."

"What?"

"How you could think to be like that in the middle of all this."

"Be like what?"

"So kind."

"Kind? Thanks but it wasn't kindness. And it wasn't really thinking. It was just that I couldn't stand the idea of anyone else's death. It didn't seem good or kind. I just hated death. I didn't even want a flower to die. I wanted everything to live forever."

"But you thought about other people. You did that. I just followed along."

His compliment feels itchy, misplaced, and I don't know what to say so I ask another question.

"Was Jeff's dad there? Do you remember the yard strewn with all the wet remnants?" I ask.

His head nods, slow and sad before he answers, "I think the dad was there but didn't say anything. She didn't say much either. They were so stunned to see us. We would have been, don't you think?"

"I know. When I thought about it later I put myself in her position...what could you say? You face these parents and your child is alive and theirs is not...what would you say? And all I had wanted to do was to tell them 'I love your boy and I'm glad he is alive.'"

George is shaking his head as he says, "It's interesting isn't it? Now that we can look back at it, we experienced so much with the same thoughts and feelings and so much with such differences, as if we were fused, living in each other's heads at one moment and can't even recognize each other the next."

For long moments we are silent again, each deep within ourselves before I say, "I know so many times you wanted to hold me and I just turned away. I still did not understand what a release of emotions sex is for a guy. At least that's what we're told now. Most women are so much the opposite. If it's true that it relieves you, for us it just adds big time to our emotions and I was so overloaded I didn't have room to add any more." I breathe deep, and then begin again, "I don't know how you tolerated being pushed away. I must have hurt you badly."

"I don't remember being pushed away. I can remember you felt uncomfortable with sex and, ah, I hope I honored that by not pushing."

"You did. But I think that's what breaks so many couples up. It seems men often turn to...and women turn away. Not always, but too often. And men—maybe they think, "Okay, if I can't turn to you, I'll turn to somebody else" And women they might say, 'I don't care'... and Honey, you didn't do that."

"This is something I do remember." He starts again, "I don't know where it came from but the question of infidelity came up and I can remember thinking, god, I could never do that to her after what she's been through. But...did I tell you...can I tell you...there was a girl.

There was a girl, a woman, who worked at one of my accounts and she was kind of putting the make on me. She was about thirty or thirty-five and had never been married. The rumor was that she was born to very strict parents and through her teenage years she rebelled against them with sex and so she went after whoever was coming through her life at the time. She wanted to take me out for a drink after work."

"Did she know about the situation or anything?"

"She knew. But that one day…after she invited me out…when I was leaving there that day I can remember thinking, you know, there's a real temptation here but, you would never, ever, after what we'd been through, be able to take one more disappointment in your life and…ah…so I didn't pursue it. In fact I didn't look forward to going to that store for a long time afterward for fear of running into her."

Tension leaves his face as I start to weep and say, "That is so you. And how you behaved is so great. This horribly difficult thing we are doing here today…well, part of the purpose is to say that a couple can get through this with patience and respect for each other and it isn't the death that splits a marriage…it is many things and infidelity would be the final straw. You were right you know, I was already tenuous about my husband because he's the father of this child and my grief-crazed mind said if we hadn't been intimate to begin with there would not be this child to be grieving for, so I was stretched too far. But what you said needs to be said, needs to be shouted from rooftops. It is one of the reasons we are still married. You were so honorable. I was pretty hard to love. I only had enough at times to give the kids and try to do right by them—sometimes I just didn't have much left for you. That's also why I treasure so deeply the friends who hung out and hung in when I didn't want any friends. I was so afraid to love…it hurt so much to lose. But you stayed and some of them stayed…and we survived."

He surprises me again as he changes the subject and asks, "Do you still have the poem about scattering the ashes? You said it all in that poem and I want to read it again."

I nod my thanks and say, "At home."

The wine bottle clinks against the glass and George gestures with it toward me. I shake my head and smile at this incredible man and we breathe easy until I break the stillness saying, "Are you ready for another question? Do you remember when you almost came to blows with your rival salesman when a bunch of you had gathered at the grocery store to clean and reposition your products? They say there's always anger in grief and nothing that I know of personally demonstrates that more clearly than that episode. I know you internalize a lot of emotion but you are always so steady on the surface. This story reveals what sometimes simmers beneath."

He smiles a rueful smile, "I do remember that. He was a supervisor and always pretty much of a jerk. So whenever he got the store's nod to reset the beer cooler it was always tense—stress ran high as we all vied for the largest space for our product. I didn't know it at the time, but learned later that he was into cocaine. In that store I was by far the biggest seller and you're supposed to do a set up by percentage of sales. He had one good seller and one off brand, but he was in charge that day and he kept reading from his schematic in this singsong rhythm, almost a chant, annoying everyone, as if we were a chain gang or something. He was just crucifying me because I was the strongest competitor. We had all done this dozens of times before and were usually pretty friendly but the way he kept looking at me, mocking me, trying I guess, to intimidate me, well even his salesmen were getting embarrassed.

"So I ended up last and he gave me this little section for the best selling beer in the northwest. My other salesman was angry and so was I even though I knew the store would have me change it back the next day. Then somehow I went past being annoyed or angry and right into fury. I just wanted to take him out. Of course neither of us was in normal emotions, him high on cocaine and me just so low. I can still visualize him but, isn't that funny, I can't remember his name. Anyway I went to swing at him and the other guys stopped me and some of them hustled him out of there. I was just quivering inside. It was an awful experience. And that's the story of that guy."

"I remember when you came home that night and you said, 'You've told me I've changed and others have told me I've changed and I haven't changed!' But your jaw was clenched around the words and your temple was throbbing and I knew that other guy was pretty lucky not to have been seriously hurt. You were so full of anger with nowhere to put it and I was so full of guilt with nowhere to lie that down."

"How did we do it?" He asks once more.

"You said before it wasn't easy...and it wasn't. But that night you shocked me. I've only seen you mad once, no, twice, and even at that, never furious. Yet here you were, hours after the incident still shaking

227

and saying, 'What's the matter with all those people who say I've changed?' And I'm thinking, oh for heaven sake Sweetheart, go look in the mirror."

Again we draw shaky breaths and rest a moment before he begins again. "I remember talking to our neighbor, the fireman, Mr. L."

"Um-hm. That was days later though."

"Days? Time didn't mean much did it? I remember asking him if he thought Dan died of smoke inhalation and what does that actually mean? And he said when you are overcome with smoke it is believed you know nothing from that point on so it would have been painless. So when they found him at the base of the window it looked as if he had gotten that far and been overcome. Jeff could have seen him but…"

"That was what you wanted to believe?" I ask. "Me too."

Now George asks me, "Do you recall seeing that boy with cerebral palsy in the wheelchair waving to us as we drove by when we left the house? I remember thinking he's here like he is and living his life and at least he has a life while our son used to have a life."

I guess I am silent for what must be a long stretch because George is looking at me with a puzzled expression as he says, "Honey?"

I pull out my words trusting him with them. "I remember…oh, this is hard…ah…I remember thinking as we drove up to that boy…here we are on this clear sky day with spring flowers everywhere and I am still panting with horrible emotions and I can only gasp for air because my head is so full of smoke from the house, my heart is crushed and here is this handicapped young man smiling and waving to us and I raised my hand and somehow formed a smile and I waved…and I was thinking Dan might rather be gone than be horribly scarred or tremendously incapacitated. I don't know if that is true or not but he was twenty, you know, and that's the age where your first thought might be, god that wouldn't be a life, I wouldn't want to even be here like that but that's at twenty.

"Lots of people have terrible things happen to them early in life and grow spiritually and acknowledge that is your life and they do good things with it. But at that time he was…well, looks were so important, he was so vain about his hair and so incredibly shy inside—no, shy isn't the right word, what would be? Maybe just so insecure. An introvert who was wanting to be and trying so hard to be an extrovert. Maybe that's part of the reason for that huge group of friends, all of them stumbling a

228

little and full of bravado to cover their insecurities. None real strong yet though some of them I'm sure have grown to be, and he would have, too. I remember that young man and thinking, I wish Dan were here, but I don't know if he would wish that if he were terribly burned…I…I think he had such good stuff in him that he would have been okay about it one day. Just not today…but I don't know." My words have raced and once again I must sit back to catch my breath. And George leans forward to catch my hand.

After a while I ask, "What do you remember of the memorial?"

"Nothing. Nothing."

"Really? I watched you put your arms around a lot of those big old kids. So many of them had been on your little league teams over the years."

Again he shakes his head slowly. "I know we lived it but…"

"I know," I say. "I understand. If I hadn't have gone to bed every night with pencil and paper to recapture the day and make sense of it, I believe all this would be lost. But in my mind's eye I still see you comforting broken young men that day. I see it. I thought that day would never end. It was the longest day of my life. But you were pretty amazing.

"Now I recall. Of course…that long day and night, of course…"

He goes on, "You tell about watching me sleep and getting up to write letters to all the kids hoping to comfort them and I just can't imagine…well, yes I can…you were thinking about somebody else again."

I start to laugh and shake my head saying, "You keep commenting how I think of others but don't you get it, Honey? Right now, right here…you aren't thinking of yourself are you? You're thinking about me. Comforting me. So…ditto, ditto on you, Honey."

He gives me a little smile before he says, "But it annoys me that I know only a little of that stuff until I read it, then I remember all but…I don't know, it's like driving into a town where I spent time once but haven't retained the street names or anything."

"I keep telling you, Honey, I couldn't say it out loud either. I was unable to speak to anyone but you. It was truly unspeakable. And you needed me to be silent…so I journaled. And you went off to work."

"How long was I off?"

"Not long enough. Not nearly long enough. Part of Tuesday and the rest of that week. The memorial was Saturday and Monday you went back to work."

"I should have taken more time. Like I said before, I should have stayed to be there for you and the kids."

"Woulda, coulda, shoulda," I say. "We had an expression at hospice when I was working there that said, 'Don't should on yourself.' And I think it's time to stop, don't you?"

We're both getting a little cold by now so we pour a last bit of wine and pull a blanket off the bed to wrap around ourselves. George shrugs it around his shoulders and sits down again with a look on his face that makes me laugh out loud.

"The old man? Is that what you're thinking?" I ask.

"Yep." The answer comes in a grump. I laugh again and make him stand up so I can put part of the blanket on the chair seat as a wind block then when he sits I use the rest as a cover over him.

"Thanks, but how can I finish my wine if I'm all swaddled?"

"Not to worry Honey, I'll feed it to you," I tease while he grumps again.

"Has Melisa told you what she plans to do with us when we do get really old?" I ask.

"Um-hum. She told me she's going to roll us out onto her front porch and let the birds land on us and do what birds do and when her friends come over for a dinner party and admire her great statue she will say, "Oh no, that's just my mom and dad, but don't worry, they like it out there."

As we share a smile at our daughter's crazy sense of humor, hoping it really is a joke, I say, "I heard a line recently that I liked, it went, 'Some days you're the statue, some days you're the bird.'"

He laughs with me then gets serious again and says, "There's so much in your pages we haven't talked about for years. I know how hard you tried to get me to talk and I didn't want to and I'm sorry."

I nod, acknowledging all the water under the bridge and say, "You have to remember though, that any journal is the perception of the one doing the journaling. But it is, I believe, very accurate. At that time I could hardly put a sentence together so I sure wasn't doing any creative writing. But there's more than that. You know you've been surprised by some of my insights over the years. I don't know how, but sometimes I just know things. I know much more than I would ever tell. My intuitions have always been clear and when I listen to them they are usually accurate. I feel people's thoughts and I hear people speak when their mouths are closed and I'm not putting words in their mouths. I hear them…and sometimes their emotions are so overwhelming they seem to spill out and saturate the very air around them and I am washed with their soundless voice and unexpressed feelings…I…I just know sometimes."

The blanket slips and as he reaches to touch my hand again, he nods and says, "I know. I've seen you do that many times. But for me I guess I just locked all the emotional stuff in a corner of my mind."

"Um-hum. That's exactly what I think you did. And everything else that was emotional slid off like rain on a waxed car."

I wait a second and then say, "I want to change directions for a moment here, okay? Do you remember me telling you about one of the young women I met at the writer's conference last week? Andi? I told you she lost her husband last year and has written about it."

He nods.

"Well she asked me to read a bit of her book privately and tell her what I thought. Offering your book to a stranger's eyes takes an incredible amount of trust and a huge leap of faith. Anyway I found passage after of passage where she and I had expressed the same exact things but in such a different way. I was reminded of the counseling groups I facilitated. Each of those people had the same bruises from the same pitfalls. This grief business is such a universal thing. And helping open eyes to these terrible truths is important.

One woman at the conference had just had her book published and it was so poetic, the words were a melody like a ballet. It was a beautiful tribute to her husband, but it seemed to me to be more involved with words of the head than the raw feelings of a crushed heart. My words aren't pretty—mine are down and dirty, no holds barred, like rock and roll or break dancing. It's the gritty street and it's hard and it's real. But Andi's is a waltz, beautifully written and achingly real. Somewhere between a ballet and a break dance.

"Reading along I came to the passage where she speaks of

disassociating. She is sitting at the hospital and they have just told her that her young husband has died and they are wondering what they can do for her and who they can call. She speaks of sitting and watching her own body 'over there' scrunched up in a chair while she is getting the news. She speaks of trying to phone a neighbor but being unable to hold her hand still enough to use the phone. Just like me. Over and over I read these little things that I knew were not unique to us. This is a commonality of human beings that never gets really talked about. Whoever has the courage to read this story will have a window on this experience unlike any they might get elsewhere.

"You and I had each other even as we stumbled along. She was alone. And the words she uses are haunting. But it's not just the words that she uses—it's what she manages to convey. She couldn't get in the car because the keys in her hand would not open the door. Someone reads this and thinks, what do you mean you can't open the door? Sure you're shaking—sure you're in shock, but really...? But it isn't about being shaky and shocked. It's about not being able to make that key go in that keyhole. And it isn't about keys or keyholes or phones or any other everyday normal thing. It is about the world being so upside-down that normal has instantly become bizarre and bizarre is somehow becoming normal."

George nods again, "I do remember what that was like. It's just doing what you have to do I guess."

I shake my head. "Maybe. But I think it's more than that."

"Maybe it's this," George says. "I can remember going through emotional states in our lives where God or something seemed to come in to help us over a hurdle. Something would give me a hand one time and the next time it would be you getting the strength to overcome when I wasn't worth anything. It kind of went back and forth. When we needed spiritual help it was there. Not all the time. But sometimes, and it made me think someone is up there helping us."

"I know. I felt it too." I agree. "But sometimes I think it's just the very deepest best in ourselves that we are somehow able to pull out. Not some god out there but something in here." I tap my chest. "It's inside us. And sometimes all we can do is lean on one another. And even the willingness to lean comes from within. And sometimes life isn't one step forward and one step back—it's more like, gather all your strength and just stand. We get mad at ourselves because we're not moving forward, but if just standing upright is all you can do, then standing upright is enough."

"Maybe...Maybe. Still it was eerie at times. You know how people sometimes ask, "Do you believe in God?" George chuckles. "I know I should say yes. I don't want to say no...so I guess so—but I don't know who or why, and then when I had this experience I thought, okay I believe in God. I felt a presence when I needed to help you through a hard time. And then you were consoling me so much of the rest of the time. Remember I tried to read the Bible?"

I nod.

"But it didn't make any sense at all. Even when you tried to help me, it wasn't understandable, so there wasn't any comfort there for me." There was such a long pause before he added softly the words that have become his theme, "So it wasn't easy."

"No it wasn't and the dismal divorce statistics prove that. Plus, for every divorce there are probably a hundred marriages that go on...lifeless and sad. Funny isn't it? Everyone and everything dies and somehow we just never really take that in. Until that one death—the one that changes your life. I guess young death in particular just stinks. Remember that old line from the hippies in the '60s during Vietnam? The protesters tried to get the public to think by holding up placards that said, 'Somewhere someone is sewing handles on body bags.' I remember thinking about the millions of young people who have died in wars and wondering if somewhere there's a proud parent with a beautifully folded triangle of our flag displayed in their home—and no matter how proud they are, I wonder if in a very deep place in their heart they whisper, 'Was this worth it?'"

"Did you ask yourself that?"

I throw the question back at him. "Did you?"

"Maybe. I think I asked more like...what was it all about?"

He makes me smile and I say, "Ah yes, the little questions. What is the meaning of life? Is it better to have loved and lost...?"

He interrupts. "And what do you answer to that?"

I'm a long time in answering before I say, "That's one of the toughest ones of all and it took me a long, long time, but now I do know this for sure: I would not have wanted to miss meeting...miss...knowing, our Dan."

233

"Well, I think that's the book you wrote. Not the one that says go exercise and let the endorphins dull the pain or just keep busy and time will fix everything. You wrote the truth of how hard it was, how it's a drag through the mud, but it can be done. We did it, didn't we?"

I nod. "Thank you. Really. Thank you for that. It was through mud that tried to suck the life out of all of us, or maybe more like quicksand. That is what it is. First you die yourself, then you grieve, then you mourn, then you're just sad about a life that was cut off too soon."

"It was way too soon." George agrees. "But I think it is better to have loved because"... George leans back and pauses again, "because I'm glad I didn't miss knowing him either."

"You know, I said it before and I'm so glad you agree about what we've learned," I say. "I keep thinking he is trying to tell us to pass it on. And now with the story you have shared with me this is, at last, done. Maybe that's why it has taken so long. I needed to realize that your words would have a power that was necessary to complete this mission."

"Will you ask the kids about their memories too?" he asks.

"I don't think so. I hope with all my heart that this might shed some light for them on the journey we all traveled together and that they will always speak of Dan to us. I know his death has colored their lives in such profound ways just as it has ours. But until Bob and Ellen died, I couldn't really address how a sibling would feel. Losing my brother and sister, even though I've seen so much death now and they each lived a full life, it laid such a weight on my chest that at times I found I could barely breathe. Even now I am stunned with sorrow when I think of how Dave and Melisa must have felt, at their young ages and lack of any experience with tragedy. Our poor kids. But somehow they too survived to be good people. They're neither reckless nor afraid to live and love."

He nods and we're quiet.

Outside, the day is shifting slowly to dusk. In another few minutes we'll need a light. Inside, the atmosphere shifts subtlety too. I am again conscious of my breathing and I feel myself smile as George exhales long and says, "What do you think? Are we done?"

"Just one more, okay? Jackie asked me a question when we were up at her house in Point Robert's last month and I want to ask it of you."

Jackie is my cousin, my priceless friend from earliest memory. Our moms were beautifully bonded sisters and we've been heart sisters since I was three days old.

"She asked...how did she put it? Tell her, if we could, so she might understand, how do our hearts react now, when we think of him? Is there ever acceptance? Is there ever closure?"

George blinks, and then says, "Leave it to Jackie to ask a question at the center of everything. You first. What did you tell her?"

"I told her I hadn't examined myself with that question for a long time. That for years I asked myself what he would be like if he were still here and for years I brought myself up short at the futility of the question. Each time I wondered, I ran heart-first into the rock wall of END. He was...he isn't anymore...what can one do with that?

"For me there's no acceptance, it's more a resignation. And closure? Get me my soapbox. Closure is about America's fear of death. It's about the fear of the pain of loss. It's about the hope that if ever— God forbid—you must have to face such a loss, you will be able to quickly shut all those emotions off and not have to grieve or mourn. I looked up the definition of closure in my giant old Webster, it said: 'Conclude, End, Shut off.' Well, I remember everybody who has passed through my life and passed on. So closure? Not a chance...Danny goes on."

"But isn't that just an expression?"

"No. Not for me. But I had to go to the dictionary and look up all those relevant 'stages of grief' words. You know, I just couldn't and still can't use acceptance and closure. Webster says acceptance is agreeing to what is offered with a consenting mind, and that has never been how I've felt. Then I looked up 'resignation' and it says 'submitting to fate, unresisting acquiescence,' and that fits my feelings more closely. I am resigned. And the way we use 'closure' when we're talking about death is pretty recent. People used to be able to acceptably feel their sorrow— society allowed it and honored it. Now people hear 'closure' over and over and begin to believe you can shut off grief, shut down sorrow. You know, forget absorbing the death—just get on with celebrating the life. The trouble with that is, it makes you think there is something wrong with you if you grieve or mourn for 'too long.' I think it is fallout from this instant, hurry-up society we all live in now. Think about it for a minute. When was the last time you thought about your mom or mine? So if you can still think about whoever has died it hasn't shut off or concluded has it?"

"I guess not." George paused, and then went on, "So how do you think of Danny now?"

"I'm supposed to be asking you the questions."

"I know but I need to hear you."

"First, I thought of him a billion, billion times a day. Then a million, then a hundred, then ten…and now? Now, once in a while. I believe I carry so much of who and what he was, his good qualities, with me all the time, that they are now part of who I am. But even with that said, I still see him when I catch a glimpse of that perfect shade of red he loved, or happen to glance at a tall, lean young man. I hear a big, rich laugh on the street somewhere or a few notes from an old rock-and-roll song. My nose meets the fragrance of a rose as I walk up a sidewalk or I catch the whiff of a remembered shampoo, or I touch the edge of my lip where he kissed me and I remember…I remember. Not every day, not even every week, but often. On family kinds of days and Mother's Day and his birthday or any birthday and, oh…oh Christmas. And when the moon's full or the snow falls. Sometimes I laugh or sigh, sometimes I get a little weepy—and that's okay. And once in a great while, he comes back home to me. Like when I'm struggling over and over with a too-tight jar lid or stretching to a high place for a book just out of reach. And I hear myself plead aloud, 'Dan, where are you when I need you?' And suddenly, magically the lid spins itself open, the book moves a millimeter toward my grasping fingers…and I hear…'I'll get it for you, Mom.' And I feel his love and I smile."

I take the last of my wine down before I say, "Now you. How does your heart react when you think of him now?"

I wait, watching him gather his thoughts. At last he begins. "When I think of him now, it is usually sadly. Not with a heavy heart, but just sad for all the experiences he's missed over the years. All the family stuff when he should have been there." He pauses for a couple of heartbeats, and then, "I don't think of him very often and it makes me sad as I hear myself say that. I'm still reminded when I see his picture, of course, and I like it when one of the kids mentions him, and I can remember all of them at home a long time ago, and that's good. Is that acceptance or closure? I don't know. I know it's not a pain any longer. I know my heart carries him all the time, but it's not a burden weight anymore." George shakes his head as his eyes fill with tears and, with his voice low, says, "Do you know the saddest thing? It's how final it is. Anything I didn't say then…now it's too late."

He shrugs out of the blanket and pulls me to him and tired now, a peaceful silence grows between us. We clutch the blanket around us. Our eyes are red, our noses are red, our strange anniversary has drawn down to sunset, and as we hug and put sadness and old memories away for now, we stand, breathing as one, wrapped strong in the circle of each other's arms.

...and we both know, we'll never say goodbye.

About Mary M. Fern

Author, poet, life advisor, friend, proud mom and grandma. Lover of dangling earrings, wild colors, and Rock 'n Roll. Mary has always been the "go to" person when you needed someone to listen with and speak from the heart. Years of volunteer counseling in a Hospice Bereavement setting at a large Seattle hospital plus continuing education, hands-on life experience, and a natural compassion have earned her a rare wisdom.

Northwest natives, she and George, the love of her life since they were kids, live in a small town outside Seattle where he keeps the garden a peaceful park and she is at work on her next book.

CPSIA information can be obtained at www.ICGtesting.com
Printed in the USA
BVOW08s1351281013

334816BV00001B/1/P